Stepping Out from Ashtead

1944 - 1964

An entertaining look back on twenty years work and play as a boy became a young man in Surrey and far beyond.

By

Brian F Simmons

ISBN – 13 : 978-1979661539
ISBN – 19 : 1979661537

Author's Note

This book first saw the light of day two years ago under the title Born in 44. It was my first attempt at self-publishing and not surprisingly was something of a learning process. Whilst essentially the same story, since then I have taken on board a lot of very welcome feedback regarding both content and presentation in creating Stepping Out from Ashtead.

The title, I believe, now reflects more accurately what the book is actually about as well as hopefully appealing more directly to readers from that part of the country although I do believe that it will resonate strongly with anyone who lived through the same post-war years.

As a memoir it is a true account of the first twenty years of my life during which time I had a lot of laughs, learnt a so much very quickly and got up to quite a few silly stunts – some at other people's expense.

There are also recollections of events that for reasons that will be obvious may show individuals in a less than perfect light or possibly cause embarrassment to those that are still living and I believe quite a few are.

Therefore, where appropriate and in order to spare their blushes and possibly to avoid them coming after me with a big stick, I have changed names and other personal details.

Where language is used or attitudes expressed which today would be regarded as inappropriate, please bear in mind that this was the norm for the period being described and is not intended to give any offence.

STEPPING OUT FROM ASHTEAD

This book is dedicated to Frank and Eileen Simmons my beloved and now sadly departed parents without whom none of this would have been possible.
Thank you both.

All photographs reproduced in this memoir have been sourced from my own records or other non-attributable sources with the exception of those supplied from the Francis Frith Collection, Paul Messerschmidt and The Leatherhead and District Local History Society

TABLE OF CONTENTS

Introduction

I had often said "I don't remember much at all about my childhood."

And then I thought, "That's crazy. I know memory goes to pot as you get older but it's usually the short term stuff that is hard to retain."

The result of this chat with myself was the initiation of a personal challenge to see what I could remember and the result has been for me at least quite amazing.

I used the "mind map" approach by just thinking of different periods of my life and writing down words as they came to me. By then focussing on each word in turn I found that there was almost an avalanche effect when that word triggered the memory of something else and another and so on.

Once started I found that it was almost unstoppable and the result was pages of notes that I didn't have a clue what to do with and then I got to wondering if it just might be worth the effort of trying to turn it all into a sort of memoir.

So with grateful thanks to tutor Jane baker of the Guildford WEA writing group, this is the result.

This part of my story describes the first twenty years in which I grew up on a council estate in Ashtead, Surrey where I got up to all manner of hilarious and sometimes dangerous escapades. Following a fairly undistinguished academic career; I became a research chemist; ran away to sea and sailed round the world then joined and left the Metropolitan Police and all before I was old enough to vote.

This story was not written for profit but mostly just for the exercise and the interest and amusement of family and friends.

If you have bought it then I thank you. If not – enjoy it anyway.

Brian Simmons

CHAPTER 1 – Hello World I'm here

The voice said *"Good Morning Sir"* and I almost fell off the window sill.

Clinging desperately to the bedroom window frame with one hand and clutching the business end of a very old lavatory brush in the other I looked down. The policeman stood below shining a torch up at me. It was about four in the morning with just a hint of dawn light in the sky.

.

"Well what have we here then?" he said, and even at this point I could see the hint of a smirk around the corners of his mouth so he clearly realised he hadn't chanced on villainous Burglar Bill in action.

"I can explain everything." I blathered, desperately thinking how I might talk my way out of yet another scrape of my own making as he *said "Well young man I suggest you come down and try."*

What I certainly didn't tell him was that it was all down to raging teenage hormones and I was just returning from a night of passion but in my lust-fuelled haste had forgotten my key.

I came up with some tosh about never having been out in the middle of the night and being such a lovely moonlit night had decided to go for a bike ride but managed to lock myself out.

Amazingly he bought it but still insisted we knock my parents up just to confirm I actually lived there.

The truth is much more interesting but this little escapade was actually some fifteen years after the point when my story begins.

oOo

The 15th July 1944 was a good night for Bomber Command by any standards. D-day was a month past and the bombing offensive against Germany's industrial base was in full swing.

Of the 748 bombers and their shepherding fighters committed that night all but five returned. Tragic indeed for those lost and their families, but in military terms, a successful night.

In the Orkney Islands to the far north of the UK, Lance Bombardier Frank Simmons looked out over the glass smooth waters of Scapa Flow. As early light crept into the sky and Sunday the 16th dawned at the end of an uneventful night on the anti-aircraft battery he longed to be home.

The war was only supposed to last months and it was now more than four years since he'd been called up to 'do his duty' for King and country. They'd seemed long years too. Although being older than many conscripts and perhaps therefore spared the front line, he almost wished he could have seen some real action, if for no other reason than to make the time pass more quickly. He knew he was lucky though and whilst there had been a few hairy moments and many laughs he hoped that this time they were right and, as was now being said, the war would soon be over.

Frank smiled as he recalled some of the events. Like the night their game of cards in the hut had been interrupted by the abrupt shouted challenge of the sentry on guard. "*Halt! Who goes there?* And a moment or two later the shout "*Halt or I fire!*" followed by the staccato burst of gun fire. They'd all tipped out and mounted a search of course but without success or at least until morning light when someone found the dead donkey. That had taken some getting over and it had cost a lot of cigarettes to persuade the farmer not to make his well-justified complaint official.

There was also the day when one of the lads who was seeing the farmer's daughter had invited her to eat at the camp and she'd gone home and told her old man the soldiers on the battery were feasting on chicken. That had started a proper rumpus with the farmer coming up to the camp and accusing the boys of stealing his birds.

They'd told him it was a load of rubbish and what sort of farmer's daughter was she if she couldn't tell chicken from rabbit. It was his chicken of course but without proof and just a hint of doubt he'd no choice but to let the matter drop.

Around the same time that Frank was mulling over his war and several hundred miles further south, it had been a far from quiet night for a 30 year old Irish nurse.

Ellen Simmons had been in labour since the previous evening and around half past seven, much to her relief she gave birth to a healthy baby boy. I had arrived but it was to be two or three days before word reached my father and several weeks more before we would meet each other.

I was duly brought home from hospital to the Victorian semi my parents were renting in Ashtead, a small village near Epsom in Surrey. Gladstone Road was a T shaped cul-de-sac but only the upright of the T was fully surfaced so where you turned right and downhill to their house at the far end, the road was just rough stone and full of pot-holes and as Mum told me later " *the very devil for pushing a pram*". I think I even have some vague memory of being bounced around in my little push-chair on that surface

Dad's sister, my Auntie Dorrie, lived in the same street with my uncle, Frank Williams an upholsterer; my cousin Joan, and Nana. They were at No.1, first on the left as you came into the road and up a steep flight of five or six stone steps.

There was a tiny sloping front garden where, quite artistically, Frank had created a little pond out of an old china sink and built a small rockery planted with snowdrops and violets.

A side passage led to a 'front' door that opened to the foot of a steep, dark staircase with doors to left and right. On the right was the parlour where we only ever went at Christmas or, as I discovered later, when someone died and friends arrived to pay their last respects and then afterwards to eat their post-funereal sandwiches.

The left-hand door opened into the dining room, which was also the main living room and contained a small three-piece suite in reddish-brown leatherette. The sofa and chairs were pulled up close in front of an arched cast-iron open fireplace and a wear-worn oak dining table and four chairs were pushed back against the far wall

Brown was clearly the colour of the period. For all the time I knew their house, the upper half of the walls was covered with a sort of buff paper with what I think were bamboo leaves whilst below a dado rail a sort of textured paper had been painted a dark reddish brown gloss.

A door led off this back room into a very basic kitchen with a large china sink and one cold water tap. Hot water when needed was heated in a huge black kettle that sat on an equally black gas cooker. Beyond the kitchen was a scullery area and dark coal cellar. There was no inside toilet so a trip to the loo necessitated a short walk across the back yard passing the old mangle and galvanised tin bath hanging against the wall to arrive at an original 'thunderbox' toilet.

A wad of neatly torn newspaper threaded onto a loop of string was suspended from a nail on the back of the door.

Further up the garden there was a vegetable patch on the left with a row of bean sticks that never came down from one year to the next. Then came a bed for onions, and the potato patch and at the far end a tiny area where despite its limitations Uncle Frank grew the most wonderful dahlias.

On the other side of the path a very ramshackle shed provided Frank's upholstery workshop and I can remember as a very small boy sitting in there watching him work.

He used to give me a handful of brass-capped furniture studs to hold and pass to him one at a time as he worked his way around the edges of a newly upholstered chair or other item. Without me to hand them to him he simply shoved a handful of them in his mouth and cleverly managed to produce them one at a time the right way round so he could use them straight away.

I can only assume that the proximity of these relatives meant my mother had plenty of support in her early days of motherhood and although I lack conscious memory of those early months I'm told I was a happy and contented baby.

My mother Ellen, or Eileen as she was always known, was born in November 1912 She was the last but one of eight children in a staunchly Catholic family that farmed a small holding near Dungannon in Northern Ireland. It was not a particularly auspicious time to arrive on the planet given that the 1st World War was in the offing and the rapidly developing tension in Ulster.

Life in the farming community had always been difficult. Apart from facing the daily challenges of endemic poverty and unpredictable harvests; the political and religious divisions prevalent at the time were threatening to destroy whatever normality did exist.

Small wonder then that as the siblings grew up they endeavoured to escape the rigors of rural life as soon as possible, especially as it was understood that the farm would eventually pass to the eldest son; my uncle Charlie.

Three of the brothers headed south to Eire, as it was then known. Alphy, studying pharmacy and eventually becoming the successful owner of a chemist shops in Dublin's Talbot Street whilst Malachy became a carpenter.

Grandmother Brigid with sons Malachy, Brian and Jimmy

I know little about my uncle Jimmy other than at some point he kept a guesthouse called "The Wicklow Hills" in the seaside resort of Bray just south of Dublin. I remember we went to stay there once on a family holiday.

I do however have cause to be grateful to him as he failed to make a will. Intestacy rules decreed the dispersion of the estate among the siblings and as my mother had by that time also died; my sister and I came in for a small inheritance.

Reconnecting with my Irish relatives in the course of writing this memoir I made the startling discovery that my Uncle Jimmy had at some stage fathered a child. As this was out of wedlock and in the strongly Catholic south, the baby daughter was immediately given up for adoption.

She was baptised Gail and no-one of my generation would have been any the wiser had she herself not decided to research her background and made contact with some of her cousins and mine in Dublin.

The sad irony was that Jimmy was still alive at the time Gail first got in touch with my cousins Monica and Maura. Given Gail's history they were initially a little hesitant about shouting the news of her discovery from the rooftops.
Unfortunately Jimmy died suddenly before he heard of her reconnection with family and although he knew of her existence they never met and the first and only time Gail saw her father was in his coffin.

My namesake and youngest of the siblings, Uncle Brian, had also studied pharmacy but in the 1950's he gave it all up to enter the priesthood, which brought him to St John's Seminary at Wonersh, not far from our own home in Surrey. Eventually however, he concluded that he didn't have a vocation and returned to Ireland where he too opened a chemist shop. This was in Arklow on the coast south of Dublin.

Brian also undertook further studies to become a dispensing optician thereby adding a useful second string to his occupational bow.

I mention the doings of these uncles because their commitment and success was a major influence on my mother who saw in them perfect role models for her son, as she often reminded me over the years when I was less than diligent about my studies.

Although if the truth be told in Jimmy's case it was probably his drinking that saw him out so perhaps not such a fine example.

Mum had this thing about the 'professions'. "*Professional people,*" she would tell me, "*are worthy of respect*". She classed doctors and lawyers and similar occupations as 'professional' and because it suited her, chemists, opticians and probably guest house owners too. Broadly speaking anyone who had been 'properly educated', especially if they'd made a few bob. However, I never heard her explain exactly what a 'proper education' might be.

The uncles weren't alone in their break for freedom from life on the farm. Mum's two sisters took distinctly different routes, one heading for holy orders as a nun with the Sisters of Nazareth and another for the nursing profession. In both cases these decisions got them away from the farm and out of Ireland altogether to England.

My mother also left Ulster in the 30's and came to Epsom to train as a psychiatric nurse where she met my father some years later. I never met my Irish grandparents and know very little about them; how they fared during the war or the subsequent difficult years in the north of Ireland.

Apart that is, from a piece of 'top secret' family mythology that was only openly spoken about after the death of my uncle Charlie. Apparently he had once been involved in helping to 'spring' an activist from Derry jail.

I've no idea about the political persuasions of my Irish forebears but being catholic I can only assume they would have been republican. I'm afraid it's a long time since I regarded myself as Catholic apart from by upbringing but maybe more of that later.

There is a distinctly ironic element to this religious history. Mum, whose maiden name was Hurson, always claimed she was descended from French nobility, which I have since discovered is likely to be at least partly true.

Grandfather James Hurson

Research suggests that forebears of the Irish Hursons were probably Huguenot mercenaries – so not exactly nobility but Protestants from France fighting for William of Orange at the Battle of the Boyne in 1690. There is apparently a lot of idiomatic and vernacular language in the Tyrone area that supports this theory and there is also a village in Northern France called Huson or something similar.

This would suggest that French Protestant fighters who remained would have had to change their faith to Catholic in order to marry into local families. I can't help wondering how that information would have played with the devoutly catholic Hursons of Tyrone if it had been explained to them a couple hundred years down the line. I think Mum would certainly have found it hard to swallow. "*Descended from Protestants! I don't believe it.*"

My mother's early life is something of a closed book and was not a subject I really remember her speaking much about. She was, as I've said, brought up on a farm in Northern Ireland and from the little she ever said it was a pretty impoverished existence dominated by the Catholic Church on the one hand and efforts to make ends meet on the other.

Dominated indeed by the Catholic Church. One thing above others does stick in my memory and that was the way, as Mum described it; the faith was literally beaten into them as small children.

Apparently she used to wear bone or plastic combs in her hair as a child and she bitterly recalled how they would cut into her scalp until it bled when the teachers cuffed her around the head if she was less than word perfect in the recitation of her catechism.

This was brought sharply back to me by Frank McCourt's jaundiced comment in his book Angela's Ashes:
"*Worse than an ordinary miserable childhood is the miserable Irish childhood and worse yet is the miserable Irish Catholic childhood.*"

One way or another though it seems the system worked because she was a devout believer right up to the day of her death. It certainly appeared to give her some comfort although it was never something she could talk about easily. Certainly she was unwilling, or dare I say unable, to discuss points of faith and in that sense it was to my mind a blind faith born more of indoctrination than any level of real understanding. This was to become in future years a major source of difficulty between her and my sister.

There was one significant event in my mother's early years that seriously affected her throughout her life. When she was about two years old she suffered a very bad burn that resulted in severe scarring both physical and to some extent psychological.

We were always told that she "*fell in the fire*" although it never was explained exactly what this meant. Whether it was a bonfire or a fire in the house was never made clear. The scarring however was unsightly and affected the whole of her right arm from wrist to shoulder.

Apparently the injury went untreated – certainly in any comparable way to today. It seems that the only person offering any sensible treatment was an old lady living nearby who made my mother carry around a basket of stones in an attempt to limit the effect of the tendon contraction caused by the burn. Mum never was able to fully straighten her arm and was always very conscious of the ugly scar that precluded her from ever wearing short sleeves.

If she was self-conscious about her scarred arm she was also extremely conscious of her legs which she hated. For all the time I remember Mum she had a thing about her weight but a particular issue was the shape of her legs which the Hurson genes had decreed would have a rather sausage-like shape below the knee rather than the slender calf and well-turned ankle that fashion deemed desirable.

Whilst not tall at five feet two inches, the young Ellen Hurson was a proportionate and very attractive young woman with dark brown hair and a fresh clear complexion she nurtured and was lucky enough to keep most of her life. So it was little wonder that when my dad and his chums went to hospital dances he noticed her and began their courtship.

However, back to the Hurson legs. Although not especially noticeable to my mind, the wedding photos when she was 30 do show the shape clearly enough and sadly as the years passed and a bit of weight went on she became more and more self-conscious of them. Mum wasn't alone with this issue though as her elder sister B.A. had the same legs only worse and was even more depressed by them.

(Just so you know but it doesn't matter anyway – B.A. stood for Brigid Anne who was usually known as Auntie Molly. Confused? – I was for years and never did know why).

I would guess it was in the early 60's that Molly made the decision to try to get something done about the legs and went in for a session of cosmetic surgery with horrible consequences. Clearly such techniques were nowhere near as advanced then as they are today.

As far as we could tell the process involved little more than opening up Molly's legs down each side below the knee and removing tissue in an attempt to reduce the bulk which was successful as far as it went. However it totally failed to create the shapely calves she so desired. Instead she was left with a pair of thin straight 'sticks' below the knee and protruding below her hemline above which her more than ample thighs and backside simply drew attention to the contrast.

There's a lot to be said for the philosophies of "If it ain't broke don't fix it." or "Be careful what you wish for."
Dad's early life was by contrast, pretty much an open book. And as he was always more than happy to tell and re-tell us kids about his younger life I have as a result 'dined out' on his stories on more than a few occasions.

My paternal grandfather was David Simmons who died aged 73 only six years before I arrived. He and Nana had been employed as a housekeeper and coachman by a wealthy local doctor, Carl von Bergen who later became well known in the area for his commitment and enthusiasm leading to the existence of the Leatherhead Hospital.

He must have been a man of some means because according to the 1911 census when he was only 35 he was already able to run a substantial household including domestic staff. His son Lieutenant Mark Von Bergen was killed in 1942 when serving with the Royal Navy.

With the arrival of the first cars David Simmons became the family chauffeur and as his employer prospered the family moved to progressively more impressive houses. I can remember my father pointing out to me at least three properties in Leatherhead where he had lived at different times – albeit, in a 'below stairs' capacity.

One such house was a farm cottage at Thorncroft Manor off the Dorking Road at Leatherhead in an area of low-lying land near the river Mole. In winter months the river was prone to flood and it seems that the family were quite accustomed to finding their furniture afloat in the morning if they'd omitted to put it up on blocks before going to bed. No public enquiries in those days with demands that "something must be done". "*Rivers flood – Get used to it*" – Imagine the response to that these days!

The family also lived in a house called Priors Ford on Gimcrack Hill that was later owned by Donald Campbell before his death at Coniston Water in 1967. Apparently Campbell used to park the iconic record-breaking Bluebird car in the driveway next to his mini which must have looked really strange. The house has since been converted to apartments and renamed Campbell Court in his memory.

Doing a little "memory lane" wander around the area whilst researching this information I actually found Thorncroft House and opposite were the former stables with rooms above and I wondered if I had actually found my father's childhood home.

It is certainly very likely because a short distance beyond the house the track crossed the railway and I remember Dad telling us kids how he and his boyhood friends used to call it 'Puffer Bridge'. He made us laugh when he described how as small boys they would stand on the bridge to pee on the steam engines as they passed under in an attempt to "*get it down the funnel*"

If my grandfather's history is all hearsay and official records my grandmother or 'Nana' as we knew her was a very different matter. She was very much alive during my childhood. She featured significantly in our lives and we had the pleasure of her company until she died quite suddenly but peacefully on my sixteenth birthday.

Originally from Tongham in Surrey, Nan had been in service since she was 14 and as far as I can make out she and Grandad probably continued in those roles until sometime in the thirties when he retired or possibly until he died in '39

She was everyone's idea of 'Nana'. Short, determined, strong, usually cheerful and always busy. She had a full head of silver-grey hair right up to her death and I can easily conjure up the mental image of her in a washed-out blue floral housecoat working away at the big old clothes wringer or mangle that stood in her yard. It's strange how some images are so strongly etched in memory. The old mangle is an example. Faded blue-green paint was peeling from the cast iron frame and the large wooden rollers had gone white and hairy with the effect of years of soapy water.

Despite her diminutive build, we used to laugh that Nana had arms like 'Popeye' and she could wind the big iron wheel with ease. However by the time the above picture was taken she was a bit frailer but still had about seven years to live.

The second youngest of seven children, my father had a basic education at Poplar Road School in Leatherhead after which he started work at the International Stores. This long established grocery and provisions company had shops on almost every major high street in the southeast but was taken over by B.A.T. in the 70's and with the disappearance of personal service grocery shops they morphed firstly into the Gateway Supermarket chain and more recently into Somerfields.

Dad is the smiley lad in the third row

That of course was long after Dad used to ride a delivery bike around the district. They were still quite a common sight in the late fifties. I can recall from my own youth the heavy old bikes with a large wicker basket on the front and the triangular plate set into the frame sign-written with the name of the local grocer, baker or butcher.

You'd see them propped up against a gate post while the red-faced delivery boy ran puffing into the house with the weekend joint wrapped simply in white paper with the odd blood stain seeping through.
No plastic trays or shrink-wrapped Clingfilm in those days and re-cycling was what the delivery boy did on his way back to the shop.

In the 1930's Dad discovered motor bikes, in fact he had one of the first chain driven machines in the district; a Royal Enfield. This meant he could travel a bit further afield for work and he joined Stevenson and Rush in Guildford which required an early start for the twelve mile journey to be at work for 7 o'clock.
Such early starts meant that he was still half-asleep as he drove hunched up against the frosty air through the dark and misty early mornings. Shivering with cold and goggles all misted he later told me he wondered how he managed to stay on the road.

One day, he'd run into a thick fog and been reduced almost to walking pace when he felt something brush his leg, and then another and another but the strange thing was he couldn't see anything. He was really spooked by this and he stopped. Something else brushed by him and he reached out touching a strange damp softness.

As his hand made contact he was immediately almost deafened by a loud Baaa! And then they all started bleating at once.

He was surrounded by sheep, which, because of their colour, the darkness, the misted goggles and the thickness of the fog were almost totally invisible.

On another occasion, also only half awake, he came round a bend to be confronted by an elephant in the middle of the road. Jamming on the brakes, he skidded and came off, sliding sideways with his bike towards the animal, finally coming to a stop almost at its feet. Apparently the elephant had also stopped and just stood looking down at him when he heard a voice say "*Blimey! You alright mate?*"

Thinking for a bizarre moment that he almost run into the world's only talking elephant he suddenly say the man seated high above him almost hidden by the animal's head. It turned out that the circus was heading from

Guildford to Epsom and as there was no truck large enough to carry it, the poor old elephant had to set out early and walk.

There is one other motorbike tale that I heard Dad relate a few times that brings tears to my eyes in more ways than one.

It seems that not a lot changes over the years, at least not in the way daft young men like to show off when there are girls around.

Dad and two or three of his friends used to take their girl friends out on their bikes and naturally on a nice summers evening they often headed out into the country, and Headley Heath was one of their favourite spots.

One reason for this (apart from the attraction of a roll in the heather), was that beside the road there was a ditch that with the passage of time and countless feet tramping over it had become rounded into more of a gentle undulation than a deep gully.
The fellows used to ride their bikes into the hollow and up the other side just to give the girls a bit of a thrill and on this evening speedy Frank Simmons led the way.

What he didn't know was that someone had been along and done a bit of work that included digging the ditch out nice and square.

He wasn't expecting it and didn't see it until too late. Fortunately, although he wasn't going that fast it was more than fast enough.

As he rode into the ditch the front wheel hit the opposite bank and the bike stopped dead but Dad and his girl friend did not. The girl went more or less over Dad's head and landed in a heap, fortunately uninjured. Dad's fate however was slightly different and distinctly more painful.

The petrol tank on those early bikes had a filler cap on top secured by a large butterfly or wing nut. As the bike stopped dead and my father continued onward he slid forward from the saddle and along the tank with his most vulnerable parts on a collision course with the filler cap and an all too predictable result.

In the same way that hernias and haemorrhoids are often seen as amusing for everyone except the person suffering the complaint, my father now found that near-castration by petrol filler cap fell into the same category.
He was rolling on the ground clutching his severely crunched (but fortunately still present) wedding tackle, the girl friend was standing over

him not knowing what to say or do and all his best friends could do was stagger about laughing.

The story probably explains why when he came to teach me to drive many years later his favourite mantra was "*Expect the unexpected son and you'll be alright*"

...oooOooo...

When it came to writing about my parents it was quite a shock to realise how little I knew them as people. They were just Mum and Dad who were just there doing Mum and Dad stuff but what they actually thought about anything I don't really have a clue. I found this an awesome and almost shameful realisation.

That said, in those days life was very different and thinking back on it children and parents existed in a kind of parallel world situation. They did their parental thing and we did kids' stuff and the overlap was mostly in making sure that both these worlds trundled on without too many problems.

Today, by contrast I feel pretty sure that my own children know what I stand for, the kind of things I believe in and what interests me. This because from quite a young age such things have been discussed around meal tables and my children's opinions listened to and given due credit.

I guess that what I take from my parents are their values of honesty and integrity and a strong belief in a work ethic. Mum passed on a strong sense of religious faith with the attendant issues around sin, guilt and forgiveness all of which I took on board in my early life but have since substituted for what I choose to think of as a sense of spirituality.
From Dad came not religion but practical ability and an immensely strong sense of duty which I have tried (not always successfully) to live by.

Dad in the centre with some friends – early 1930's

Chapter 2 - Bramley Way

After the war ended my father found himself in Germany for a short period on what the army called 'mopping-up' operations. Here apparently he did eventually see a little bit of action dealing with what we'd today call 'dissidents' I guess, which were a few isolated pockets of German military that didn't want to accept, or maybe hadn't been told the war was over.

Anyway, sometime around the middle of 1946 he must have been demobbed because my mother became pregnant again and my sister Angela was born in the April of '47.

Now although it is generally accepted that on average the earliest retained childhood memories start around three and a half, I must be a bit above average because I certainly remember going with my Dad in the taxi to the hospital in Epsom to bring her home. I can also remember when Angela was still very small that we all went to Ireland so that we kids could be taken around all the Irish relatives. My main recollection is the great amount of cooing over Angela and the words "wee ba" being used continuously (ba being the short for bairn I suppose).

Sometime towards the end of '47 or early in '48 my parents got the tenancy of a new council house on an estate being built in another part of Ashtead and we moved from Gladstone Road to Bramley Way.

Mum's little prayer was "*Us four and no more for ever more. Amen*"

Like many of the immediately post-war estates it was well laid out and unlike many modern low-cost or social housing developments, the properties were spacious and well-built. With quite large gardens front and back they were set well back from the road behind wide grass verges.

There were no garages as very few tenants had cars. Garage blocks and parking areas were created after a while just a short walk from the house. In later years however it was possible to get council permission to drop the kerbs and enable the construction of a 'run-in' to provide off street parking.

Inside our brand new 'no-nonsense' red brick semi we had large sitting and dining rooms with a square open arch between the two, which in the early years had a heavy curtain that we could draw across to keep the heat in the sitting room.

From the dining room at the back a French door opened out into the garden and a small concrete terrace for sitting out. We later graduated to a set of Marley doors between the two rooms. They were all the rage at the time and I see you can still get them today. I find that amazing but I guess it goes to show what a good design they were. Not fancy but functional.

A small kitchen provided just enough space for basic functions and little else. In front of the window that looked out to the back garden there was a deep china sink with a wooden draining board to the right that over time and with much scrubbing became bleached white and bristly much like the rollers in Nana's old mangle. On the other side Dad constructed an L shaped Formica working surface that turned the corner to meet the gas cooker.

There was a built-in unit that provided storage for anything from sweeping brooms to kitchen utensils, food storage and crockery. It included a set of drawers with our cutlery in the top, dusters and polish in the second, shoe cleaning stuff in the third and a miscellany of 'possibly useful' stuff in the bottom.

Through the centre of the unit was a serving hatch to the dining room where we always ate. Firstly, because family meals were the norm in those days and anyway there was no space for us all to eat in the kitchen and secondly, because the era of TV meals on trays in the lounge had not yet arrived. I remember how Mum would deposit a handful of cutlery on the hatch with a shout to no one in particular, "*Could someone lay the table.*" If there were no response the follow-up to me or my sister would be a more strident "*Would you get yourself in here and give me a hand.*
"

Wash days, usually Mondays as I recall, were something of an event and took up quite a lot of time in the early days. Mum used to stand at the kitchen sink hand washing small or delicate items but when it came to large things like sheets and towels reinforcements were called for in the shape of the 'copper'. This was a large galvanised boiler that usually lived tucked away under the work top beside the sink.

Cylindrical in shape and two feet or more in diameter it stood about four feet high on short legs and underneath was a circular gas burner. Known as the 'copper' because earlier ones would indeed have been made of that metal; the thing had first to be filled with water, initially by transferring buckets of water filled at the kitchen sink and then later via a length of hose on the tap. Once filled it was connected via a flexible rubber tube to a gas tap beside the cooker. The burner was then ignited by inserting a light through a hole in the casing

It was impossible to just use a match as the burner was too far inside for the match to reach and as tapers weren't within our vocabulary let alone possession Mum usually resorted to a rolled up piece of newspaper lit from one of the gas rings on the cooker and then thrust into the hole.

This was fine if the paper didn't go out en-route as it sometimes did and then the temptation was to go back to the cooker to relight it without turning off the gas to the boiler. You know the expression "more haste – less speed". All the while you were trying to light the 'torch' and then shield it while moving back to the boiler the air around the burner was filling with gas so that when the flame was eventually introduced it would go off with a dramatic whoof and a sheet of flame all around. It really was a miracle she didn't blow us all up.

Once lit it then had to get up to temperature which was more or less boiling I guess and then soap and the laundry items were dumped in and stirred around with the 'copper stick' as it was known. This was just a length of broom handle but like the mangle rollers and the draining board with the passage of time and the effect of hot water, this too had become bleached white and distinctly hairy. Only in jest it's true but Mum used to threaten us with the 'copper stick' and chase us around the house with it if we misbehaved.

I'll never forget the joy with which the old boiler was kicked out and the excitement and fascination that greeted the arrival of the new Hoover washing machine. Pretty primitive by today's standards; this at least had its own integral electric heater and an impellor in the side that rotated to agitate the wash.

You had to be careful though because if you accidentally knocked the ON switch before the impellor was fully submerged you were guaranteed to shower the whole room with water. By the time we got ours, the wringer was also electric so the misery of hand-wringing things like sheets came to an end along with generations of back yard mangles.

The only other appliance in the kitchen in the early days was the little Ideal solid fuel boiler in the corner for heating the water. A fridge came later but not for some years so bottles of milk had to sit in a bucket of water to stay reasonably cool and they still went off in a couple of day. What on earth do they do to milk now so it keeps for ten days? Makes you wonder.

Upstairs there was a bathroom, separate toilet and two good-sized double bedrooms as well as the small single room over the hall that was always mine. There was a sloping bit in the floor of my room where the stair case came up but once again clever old Dad built-in a really neat little desk and cupboard that I could use by sitting on the end of my bed. It served me well for homework, chemistry sets, jigsaw puzzles and stamp collecting through all my years until I finally left home at age twenty three.

A back door from the kitchen led to a side path and a brick outbuilding that housed two coal sheds and an outside toilet. It also contained Dad's little workshop where all our bikes also lived and which we had to climb over in order to reach anything.

There was sort of concrete slab roof that bridged across from the house to the 'sheds' as we called them and provided a certain amount of weather protection for the trip to the coal shed or loo. Later on Dad extended it into a form of 'conservatory' by putting in end walls and doors and a glass roof.

It worked very well and provided an early form of utility room or what Nan would have called 'the scullery' and was especially useful for the washing machine when it arrived as it wouldn't fit into the kitchen. Mum also got into house plants that flourished on a series of shelves Dad put up, turning it into a council house version of the 'hanging gardens'.

From a very young age I remember being fascinated by Dad's workshop and would stand for hours watching him as he mended our shoes or simply made up the odd item that might be needed indoors. He was very clever that way. And naturally as I watched I absorbed it all like a sponge in the way that kids do and as a consequence have always enjoyed and been fairly good at DIY.

I loved to sort through and 'tidy up' his boxes of nuts and bolts, screws and nails and so on and the highlight was the day I discovered a couple of live bullets.

He shouldn't have had them of course but they were just a couple of 9mm rounds that he had somehow managed to bring home when he was demobbed.
"*Did you catch a German in the war?* I'd ask and he'd say, "*I expect so son – can't remember exactly but they're certainly Jerry's,"*

I thought the bullets were just so exciting and whenever I could I used to sneak out to the shed to look at them. It was a fascination that lasted for ages then one day he found me out there playing with them and decided to hand them in to the police before I worked out a way to set them off. I think he just said he'd found them.

The garden at Bramley Way was quite large. Immediately behind the house there was a concrete paved area that served as a small terrace for sitting out and then an area of lawn with a short slope that we used to roll down as small kids. A path led to the far end of the garden where Dad had built a garden shed and a chicken house with an outside run.

We usually kept up to six or eight hens for eggs but woe betide any one of them that got lazy and went 'off-lay'. That was a passport to a quick trip behind the shed with Dad to emerge dangling by its feet and flapping around in its death throes. I must have been a funny kid because I really loved to watch him pluck and draw their innards and even have a go myself.

When he cut the feet off a bird Dad used to make us squeal by pulling the tendons to make the claws move and then he'd chase us around the garden with it, a trick I quickly picked-up on and played on my sister and her friends.

When we were very small there was a large sand pit at the far end of the garden where we'd play for hours on end.

Later when we grew out of that Dad built what we called the 'monkey bars'. This was a climbing frame of vertical and horizontal steel tubes at different levels that he'd constructed for us and it used to provide hours of healthy fun and exercise climbing and swinging about on them.

Dad was a good gardener and as I recall he created quite a productive vegetable plot including a small greenhouse where he produced tomatoes and bedding plants. He also planted a couple of apple trees and a Victoria plum that over time did very well. There was also a thornless hybrid variety of blackberry that climbed along the fence and produced fruit in abundance so blackberry and apple pie was never in short supply.

I don't remember seeing Mum in the garden so much apart from when she was hanging out washing on the line that ran the length of the garden path.

However if Dad was in the garden we'd often hear her call out, "*Cup of tea Frank?*", and then Mum would appear with a couple of cups of tea and they'd sit on a bench seat he'd fitted along the side of the greenhouse and chat while they shared the moment. Come to think of it; in the summer she was also quite inclined to take a rest in one of those old-fashioned striped canvas deck chairs.

(It's a very strange experience forcing one's self back to recall those times not often remembered and even stranger coming to the realisation that your relationship with parents was different to what you had always believed. I say this now because I am aware how often I am talking about Dad and how much of an influence he was on me at the time. This is curious because if I had been asked which of my parents I was closer too I would have said my Mother and that was true. It was always Mum who'd be there for a cuddle even when I was much older and I guess that because I stuck with the faith for most of my younger life there was a religious affinity that I didn't share with Dad.

However with the benefit of hindsight and a more mature outlook it is clear that Dad was a far greater influence than I ever realised. Both as a role model for moral characteristics such as duty, responsibility and the work ethic as well as a teacher of things practical without which I'd have had serious difficulty over the years.)

There was a row of tall elm trees at the end of the garden that we kids used to climb quite fearlessly, all dead now sadly from the awful Dutch Elm infection. We had constructed a crude platform across a couple of branches that we used to clamber up onto and defend our 'tree house' against all invaders.

In the early years the land behind our houses was just fields and some allotments where we used to play safely for hours on end. As with most youngsters of the period, making 'camps' in which to hide and play was quite a big thing and the allotment provided a perfect spot.

A wide ditch, dry for much of the time, provided the space and by damming it in two places we created end walls. We then roofed it over with branches on which we laid an old tarpaulin followed by sods of turf so that we created a waterproof (more or less) hideout large enough for three or four of us at a pinch. In order to guard against being flooded out we laid several scavenged drain pipes through the centre under a beaten mud floor. I remember one year we even managed to create a little fireplace and chimney and our 'secret' home away from home was complete.

This little hideaway was where we first got into playing 'doctors and nurses'. However, that interesting little role play didn't last long after one of the girls went home with a scratch or graze around her 'privates' and she blurted out to her mother how we'd all been examining each other in a hole in the ground. Why is it 'grown-ups' always want to put a stop to the best games?

There was also another area of unbuilt land between our houses and the main A24 road where we used to build camps and hideouts for our various games and where every year we used to build the Guy Fawkes bonfire which was a tremendous community event.

Talking of fires brings me back to the domestic heating arrangements at Bramley Way. Early on there was an open fire in the front room but in later years this was replaced with a closed solid fuel stove in a sort of mustard coloured enamel finish.

Normal practice, when either lighting it from scratch or resurrecting almost dead embers in the morning, was to leave the door just open an inch or so to increase the draft. Similarly if the fire was a bit sluggish Dad would say "*I'll just roar it up a bit.*" and in a couple of minutes the stove would be literally roaring.

I don't remember Dad ever forgetting it but if Mum or either of us kids tried the same technique we'd occasionally be diverted by something and forget about the fire.

We lost count of the number of times this happened and the panic that ensued when someone discovered that the stove was now almost unapproachably hot or the chimney was on fire or both.

However, after a few similar episodes we learnt not to panic and that control could be regained by simply shutting the door down, easier said than done as it felt a bit like approaching an open blast furnace. This would change the frightening roar to a somewhat eerie moan that lasted for several minutes and eventually died away.

I'll never forget that smell of hot soot that could persist for days as a reminder to be more attentive in future and the gradual discolouration of the enamel from mustard to a russet brown that was a permanent testimony to the number of times we'd let our attention wander.

The boiler in the kitchen could also be a bit contrary and presented similar challenges in the fire safety department. However there was less risk of this being overlooked, as Mum was more likely to be on hand to keep an eye on it. On the occasions when it did get forgotten we were reminded in a different but equally sonorous manner by the sound of the water boiling in the pipes and hot tank immediately over our heads.

Life on the estate for us kids was wonderful, especially in the early years when houses were still being built. There was none of the morbid fear that seems to haunt society today of murderers and paedophiles around every corner. We were simply allowed "out to play" and that meant more or less anywhere.

There was a distinct sense of community although at that age I wasn't aware of it as such. There were always builders about, in fact for us little ones a favourite pastime was playing in a heap of building sand until we were the bright orange colour of little gingerbread men.

Of course the builders kept an eye on us, "rubbing better" the odd graze, sorting out squabbles and taking the inconsolable home to their respective Mums. I can remember sitting on a bench in a wooden hut with a bunch of bricklayers and drinking sweet tea from a large chipped blue tin mug.

There was however the occasional downside to allowing a bunch of builders to baby-sit the kids as illustrated by one legendary event that has become part of our family history.

This was the day when I apparently appeared indoors earlier than usual and Mum said

"*You're in early. Where are your friends*?"

"*Oh, they've all gone home.*" I said

"*Why's that?*" said Mum

To which I replied, aged about four, "*No fucking bricks*"

No one remembers what my mother said next.

Chapter 3 - School Begins

As I've said, life on the estate for us pre-school youngsters was really quite idyllic. Being among the first residents of these newly built houses meant that many of the tenants were of an age, - i.e. relatively young parents with young children. As a consequence, there quickly developed a sizeable network of playmates as well as numerous 'aunties and uncles' and that's not including the builders.

As well as being able to enjoy our games and adventures in and around the on-going building, there were fields, woods, common land and the allotments where we played safely for hours on end and all the while were never more than a couple of hundred yards from our homes.

Inevitably the time came when those totally carefree days had to come to an end and arrangements were made for me to go to school.

Because Mum was Catholic and Dad wasn't, the church required that she promise to bring us up in the faith. Consequently my sister Angela and I had been put down to attend St Peter's Catholic Primary school at Leatherhead rather than the local C of E primary where most of my friends were going to go and I remember that as a cause of great distress at the time

Leatherhead was some two or three miles away and entailed a bus journey for which the fare was a 'penny halfpenny'. Obviously at first we were not just sent off alone and a group of parents arranged between them a sort of roster whereby one adult would accompany the small group of catholic kids off the estate on the morning journey and then someone else would meet and fetch us home in the afternoons.

The morning journey was potentially more risky as it entailed crossing the main road at both ends of the trip. However in those 'no nonsense' days we were expected to learn quickly how to stand on our own feet and make the journey by ourselves.

It's true that unlike today, there were conductors on the buses who soon got to know us kids and where we lived. So apart from keeping us in order they also became yet another group of 'pseudo' uncles and aunts that helped to ensure our safe passage to and from school.

The boy in the top right corner – James Harding - became the CEO of a major company and many years later when I was doing some private chauffeuring I found myself working for him briefly before he sadly died. Strange how the wheels of life turn.

St Peter's occupied an austere looking detached villa in Victorian Gothic style with grey stone walls, steeply pointed gables and intricately carved fascia boards painted a sort of magnolia colour.

It was situated in Garlands Road, a pleasant residential road on the outskirts of the town and sandwiched between the catholic church of the same name and Well's builder's yard that ran along beside and behind the playground that had obviously once been the rear garden of the house.

Inside, walls had been knocked through and the house had been arranged to accommodate three classrooms with a staff room in the former kitchen while a toilet block had been built in the playground. At lunch times the ground floor room had to be quickly re-arranged to serve as a dining room in time for the arrival of the grey Surrey County Council dinner van.

A variety of insulated aluminium pots and trays from the van would be set out and in the early days the teachers would serve the meals as we filed past.

It really was a bit Dickensian and I can't imagine the response had anyone had done an 'Oliver' and had the temerity to ask for more. Mind you, that would have been a bit unlikely as in general the meals were not that appetising. Who can forget the gristly meat of those early school dinners, the thick lumpy gravy and solid semolina?

There were just a few exceptions that I recall were almost universally popular. These were the crisply overdone roast potatoes that would ooze fat when jabbed with a fork, chocolate sponge pudding with chocolate sauce and the baked jam roly-poly with custard. It's amazing we survived knowing what we do now about diet and nutrition but in those days we used to run any fat off rather than sitting for hours with a video game.

Teaching staff comprised two nuns and two lay teachers. The headmistress, Mother Catherine was a severe-looking elderly nun who I guess must have been approaching retirement because she was soon replaced by Mother Mary Anna.

She was a younger but only slightly more kindly looking woman who unfortunately had a brown mole to one side of her mouth that sprouted several stiff dark coloured whiskers. These moved as she spoke in a strangely mesmerising manner that made it difficult to look her in the eye because you were so busy watching the whiskers.

The second nun, Mother Theresa was a much younger and gentle woman who took the reception class which was just as well if the new arrivals were not to be put off school for life by their first meeting with the head mistress.

Classes two and three were taught by the lay teachers Mrs McKay and Miss Dyke. Miss Dyke was the typical 'school marm' with her substantial build, severely bobbed hair, rimless spectacles, tweed suits and sensible shoes.

Although she could be more than strict enough when required, I was to discover as time went on that she would make a more positive impression on me and my attitude at the school than anyone else.

However, those early school days were not a happy time for me. Apart from the fact that I had been separated from my usual playmates by being sent to St Peters, I was desperately shy and found it very hard to make friends at first.

Apparently our neighbour, Lew Armstrong who worked in the builders' yard next to the school, told my parents how he used to see me standing alone in the playground looking so miserable he could almost have wept for me.

Well apparently I wasn't going to put up with it and by the middle of the second week I'd had enough and decided to come home.

I don't remember the whole episode but I can recall getting to the bus stop and boarding the first bus that arrived. That turned out to be a bit of luck in itself as several different routes used that stop and I could easily have been on the wrong bus.

Obviously I had no money as we were still at the stage of being taken to and from school but I remember the conductor kept asking me if I had a pass and clearly I had no idea what he was talking about so I just kept saying *"A what?"*

However we quickly covered the couple of miles from Leatherhead back to Ashtead and, pass or no pass, the conductor saw me off the bus at the top of the road and a few minutes later I was back indoors where all hell broke loose.

Mum was furious and took me straight back to the school where I remember I was treated a good deal more kindly than I had been at home.

Mother Theresa put me into the care of a slightly older girl called Susan who was really nice to me and made sure that I was included in games and generally kept me company. The trouble was she was too 'mumsy' and the next thing I knew was that I'd become the butt of the boys' jokes for being looked after by one of the girls. Life can be hard even at five years of age.

I must have been very unsettled in those early months because there was an embarrassing period of bed-wetting and an even more terrible incident on the way home from school one day. We were travelling unaccompanied by now and I was walking to the bus when I had some sort of stomach upset and dirtied myself. The bus stop was just outside a private driveway with large wooden gates and I remember hiding behind the gates and using dead leaves in an effort to clean myself up.

I got on the bus when it arrived but it wasn't long before the other kids realised from the smell that something had happened and gave me a pretty wide berth. So I sat in glorious isolation and after each stop when someone came and sat near me within a few moments they got up and moved away.
I must say that on this occasion Mum was a bit more sympathetic.

I guess she had hoped that dirty nappy days were behind her and I'll never forget the look on her face as she held me out at arm's length and stood me in the bath to be washed down. Not a pleasant experience for either of us. I'm just glad there wasn't a hosepipe handy or she would probably have turned it on me.

However once the grotty part was over I was wrapped up in a blanket and treated to a comforting cuddle. She was good at that. Eventually I settled very well at St Peters and enjoyed six happy years there.

As there were initially only three classes, each teacher was looking after two year groups which must have been quite challenging for them. I think it was in my second or third year that some land on the other side of the church was developed to provide a building with three more class rooms, a proper dining and games hall and a much larger playground.

The three junior classes moved to the new building while the three senior classes remained in the old house and class 6, Miss Dyke's or the Top Class as it was known, occupied the large upstairs room and was literally the top class to which of course we all aspired.

After the first year that was mostly play-based, lessons at St Peter's majored very traditionally on the three R's plus geography, history, PE and perhaps most significantly RI or Religious Instruction.

Being a Catholic school, RI was a priority and was taught in two ways. Religious doctrine was regarded as extremely important and involved learning The Catechism by rote.
"Who made me?"
"God made me"
"Why did God make me?"
"God made me to know Him, love Him and serve Him in this world and be happy with Him forever in the next."

It's funny how easily those Catechism responses come back. Some things you never forget. You might stop believing but you don't forget. And so began the bribery of *"pain and sacrifice today in return for salvation and reward tomorrow"* that as far as I can see is the cornerstone of most religion, although I didn't at the time.

What I enjoyed more however were the Bible Stories that really brought religion to life for me and I found I could identify with the person of Jesus and where he was coming from far more than with the two other invisible members of the Trinity.

It wasn't that I didn't believe, in fact I bought the whole deal and was the most devout little chap you could imagine and stayed that way for years. There was a period when I used to get up early every morning and bike up to the church to serve mass, after which the altar boys were given breakfast in the presbytery by Miss Weston the priest's housekeeper.

The Leatherhead parish priest was Father Smoker who was often to be seen in and around the school. He was a kindly man, probably in his sixties and he had a huge and cuddly Chow dog that followed him around everywhere and especially liked coming to the school where it was greatly fussed by the kids.

Father Smoker used to come into our RI classes from time to time and ask us questions about what we understood of different aspects we were learning. I guess it was part of his role to monitor how the faith was being imparted to all us little Catholics.

I don't know what the Church teaches now as I no longer practice the faith but at the time they used to refer to reaching the age of 'the use of reason' – in other words knowing right from wrong. This was reckoned to be about the age of seven and so it was around this time that we were introduced to the idea of going to Confession.

I remember that we were all given a Confession Book which was a little guide in fairly basic language setting out the process of Confession and included some prayers to be said.

The first step for us young penitents was to pray for the grace to make a good confession because of course with God's help anything is possible. Even if you've been the most evil little sod He will listen and help you do better.

The next step as I remember was that to make a good (and presumably meaningful) confession required an examination of conscience. This was basically trying to remember your sins for which we were taught to use the Ten Commandments as a check list.

Once the mental list was complete the next box to tick was to say an Act of Contrition. This was a prayer that we had in our books expressing sorrow for offending God and resolving not to sin again.

The final stage was the 'biggie'. This was where you went into a little cubicle with the priest on the other side of a mesh or curtain and kicked off with the script that we'd had to learn by heart.

"Bless me Father for I have sinned. This is my first confession" (or however long it was since you were last there)

The priest would then ask you what you wanted to confess and by way of a penance would direct that you should go away and say certain prayers such as two Our Fathers, three Hail Marys or whatever.

Today it might seem strange to put this on kids at such a young age but back then the whole of the previous two years had been against a background of religious instruction including the concept of sin, contrition and so on. At least it did instil some basic moral standards as well as a sense of humility both of which do seem in rather short supply nowadays.

When we were aged about eight or nine we made our first Holy Communion which was, and probably still is, a really big event in the life of a young Catholic. By this time we were well and truly indoctrinated in the faith and the fact (infallible of course because the Church said so) that the little white wafer the priest would place on our trembling tongues was not bread at all. It really was Jesus in disguise.

Well, that's not what they actually said. It was, they said, and I quote

"By the miracle of transubstantiation, the living body, blood, soul and divinity of our Lord and Saviour Jesus Christ under the appearances of bread and wine and given up for us in the sacrifice of Calvary"

Never mind the concept but in terms of vocabulary alone this would be quite a challenge for an eight year old today.

There was also a strict method involved in receiving Communion which included allowing the Sacred Host (wafer) to more or less melt on the tongue. And so, they warned us, God help any-one who chewed Him up which would be disrespectful to the body of Christ. Or even worse, was tempted to take Him out of their mouth for a closer look and risk dropping Him on the floor.

Now you'd think that with all this we'd have been a bunch of nervous wrecks but not a bit of it. We took it all on board and repeated it back on demand which I guess says something for the education system of the time although I'm not quite sure what.

First Communion day

All in all, the years at St Peter's were really very pleasant and in their different ways the teachers were quite inspirational.

I remember that reading was a huge priority, a fact for which I have always been very grateful. Reading was taught from first principles in real 'Janet and John' style that meant no-one I knew left primary school with any reading problems. In addition the teachers used to read stories to us on a regular basis.

It was usually a period on Friday afternoons before we were all trooped off to the church for the Benediction service and we looked forward to it in almost the same way that a child today might look forward to a weekly TV episode. The whole system imbued in me a love of books and reading that I've never lost. It also introduced us from the earliest years to some of our greatest literature including Gulliver's Travels, Treasure Island and Robinson Crusoe. All good inspirational stuff, but The Famous Five and Swallows and Amazons were adventurous and great fun too.

One thing that St Peter's did lack at first was any form of playing field and the playgrounds were quite small which limited the amount of sport we could play on the premises.

We played mixed rounders in the playground and the boys could play five-a-side football after a fashion while the girls were introduced to netball. But the hard tarmac surface was very unforgiving and there were frequent bumps and grazes although fortunately nothing more serious.

In those days kids were encouraged to shrug off such minor injuries and if not, a hug from the teacher and a quick "rub it better" soon sorted things out. Sadly, such 'loco parentis' behaviour might be frowned on today but was just normal at that time.

I was never much good at sport, not being that out-going or competitive and as a consequence was usually one of the last to be left standing in line when captains were asked to pick out their teams. The problem was that as a result I came to believe that I really was useless whereas with a little encouragement and tuition I probably could have been better.

About half a mile from the school there was a low lying field known locally as 'The Dip' and the headmistress managed to arrange for us to go there on Wednesday afternoons for sport. It was wasteland really but somehow she had organised with the local council to get it mowed, marked out and some goal posts installed so it was a tremendous improvement over the tarmac playgrounds and we could even play two games of football at a time. Sadly the The Dip has since disappeared under the M25

If I was mediocre at football my cricketing career never got off the starting blocks.

In an attempt to improve our hand / eye coordination someone had got hold of a catch trainer. This was a device like a giant 'trug' basket of wooden slats on a metal frame. The idea was to throw the cricket ball into the frame from which it would rebound at high velocity in unpredictable directions to be caught by the team standing around it.

I never stood a chance. The ball came out of the frame like a rocket and before I could get my hands up, hit me smack on the nose knocking me out cold. I finished up in hospital with concussion and a broken nose so is it any wonder that I have been nervous of cricket balls ever since?

Obviously those days were not all about lessons or sports days. Once we were old enough to go to school by ourselves, I along with two or three mates, used to go by bike and so once mobile and free of adult supervision we were all over the place and up to just about anything. Not malicious you understand, just a bit mischievous.

There was one memorable occasion shortly before Guy Fawkes Day. The shop was to blame of course for selling us fireworks but we had bought some bangers and also a rocket from the sweet shop by The Plough roundabout at Leatherhead.

Not content with dropping the odd banger we wanted to set the rocket off and looked around until we found an old bottle from which to launch it. My mate Tony was the one who always had matches, but unfortunately just as he lit the rocket and the fuse started to fizz the bottle fell partly over so it was at about 45 degrees. Suddenly the rocket went off and soared away, not vertically as we had intended but in a graceful arc towards the other side of the roundabout where to our horror a policeman on a bike was just appearing around the corner. Seeing the rocket streaking towards him he promptly fell off in a heap on the kerb.

We didn't wait to see any more although he had clearly seen us. We were on our bikes and away as fast as we could go which thank goodness was a great deal faster than he could pedal. The problem was that he had seen our school uniforms and two days later the whole school was assembled in the playground while the policeman attempted to identify the offenders, which happily he was unable to do.

Fortunately there was no question of sanctions being imposed on everyone if the culprits didn't own up so we just kept mum and I'm ashamed to say that this is the first time after more than 50 years that I've owned up to what was a very stupid stunt. Not, I'm afraid, that it served to put me off a few other daft escapades over the years.

Another one I recall was not so much connected with my school as with my group of mates at home some of whom were also at St Peter's.

There was a family along the road from us called Penny. They were what Dad would call a bit 'rough and ready'.

I think Mr Penny was some sort of itinerant dealer and he had this old lorry that he used to park in the road just around the corner from his house.

He was often on our case because as kids we used to play tag around the street and would often end up chasing each other around his lorry, which infuriated him no end.

On of my older friends, Adrian who lived at the top of our road seemed to know a bit about vehicles and came up with the idea that we should stuff the exhaust pipe on old Penny's lorry with something that would apparently stop it from starting. It was me that came up with the potato and volunteered to do the deed while Mr Penny was indoors having his dinner one day.

While three of my mates kept a look out I scrambled under the truck and rammed this huge spud hard onto the end of the exhaust pipe and we all dived behind a hedge about fifty yards away to watch events unfold. After a while old man Penny came out, hopped up into the truck and tried to start the engine which turned over and over with a deal of spluttering but wouldn't start. This produced a huge tirade of swearing and off he stomped indoors calling out to his son, "*Reg. Come and give us a hand. The bloody lorry won't start.*"

Meanwhile, behind the hedge we could scarcely contain ourselves.

He re-appeared a couple of minutes later with his son Reg and together they had another go.

The engine churned and churned ever more slowly as the battery gradually lost power. What we had no idea about but were shortly to discover was that as the engine turned over without starting it was pumping unburnt petrol vapour into the exhaust system and silencer.

Then Reg had the bonnet up and peered nonplussed at the engine for a few minutes while the old man wandered up and down swearing and complaining. Then Reg shouted "*I'll try it again from here Dad*" and pressed the starter from under the bonnet.

On this occasion the engine must have sparked because there was an almighty bang from the exhaust as the unburnt fuel backfired.
Reg jumped about a foot in the air while my enormous spud flew off the exhaust pipe right into the backside of old man Penny who was standing beside it.

Well, the air was blue as it dawned on him that he'd been sabotaged. I honestly have no idea how we managed to contain ourselves but I'm really glad we did as I'm sure he'd have killed us if he'd seen us and realised we were responsible.

I think perhaps our life on the Bramley Way estate created a slightly false sense of security for us youngsters and maybe our parents too. I certainly remember that from a fairly young age I was often out and about on the estate and beyond on my bike both with friends and by myself.

Photo Courtesy of the Leatherhead and District Local History Society

One of my favourite places was the large village pond opposite the common at Lower Ashtead where we used to fish for minnows or 'tiddlers' as we called them. Early on this took the form of dipping about around the edges with a net so our 'catches' also included sticklebacks, tadpoles, froglets and even newts of which I seem to remember there were several varieties in those days. They're quite rare and protected now of course.

Thanks to Paul Messerschmidt for this great snowy scene

I couldn't resist including this shot of the iced-up pond as I recall the times I ended up with wet feet after tentatively testing the ice around the edge.

From time to time I remember seeing more experienced anglers who were able to cast out into the middle and pull out some larger fish. I really fancied this and pestered Mum and Dad for a rod which they got for me and Dad showed me how to set it up and even took me along to the river Mole at Leatherhead which I enjoyed although with no great success.

I don't remember ever being told that I shouldn't venture any further afield by myself although I do remember being told that if I ever met anyone who frightened me or was worried about anything I should find a policemen. One day I had cause to bear this advice in mind.

By this time I was probably about eleven or twelve and had gone on my bike by myself to the river at Leatherhead and was fishing not far from the old fire station when a man started talking to me. He seemed a bit scruffy, almost like the tramps we used to see walking the Epsom Road as we waited for the school bus.

He was kindly though and seemed to know a bit about fishing because he showed me the depth to set my weights and float for that stretch of the river.

One of my fishing spots at Leatherhead behind Ronson's

He talked about all sort of things but eventually the conversation included questions about my family and life at home.

He then said *"I expect you've got a nice bathroom haven't you?"* I can remember thinking he could do with a wash himself but at the same time it began to occur that this was an odd thing to say and a bit more personal a question than I should be answering so I said nothing.

Then he said *"Do you wash yourself or does Mummy come and wash your little willie or perhaps it's not so little?* He grinned.
I said *"I've got to go home now."* and immediately began to collect my stuff together.
"I'm sorry." he said. *"I didn't mean to be nosey."*
"It's alright but my dad is waiting for me in the town." I lied and ran off along the path. Just under the railway bridge I came to the fire station where a couple of firemen were smoking outside. Maybe it was the uniforms, I don't know, but I thought I should tell someone what had happened so I told them that a scruffy man had just been asking me about my willie.

"Oh did he indeed?" said one of them *"We'll go and have a chat with him. You go off home sonny."* And together they set off quickly the way I'd just come. I never did know the outcome but often wondered how it went. Probably better not to know. Perhaps they threw him in the river.

My final year at St Peter's was with the redoubtable Miss Dyke who despite her somewhat stern appearance was really lovely and a brilliant teacher. Apart from RI and the three R's it was the subjects of history and geography that she really brought to life for me. I will always remember the big wall maps that she used to use for competitions. Sometimes the teams would be 'boys v girls' or sometimes between the red, blue, green or yellow school houses to which we all belonged.

Members of each team would be brought out one by one to answer her questions or point out countries or features like rivers and mountains on the map. It was a wonderful way to learn with the information sinking in almost as if by magic. It was certainly competitive and we were no worse off for that fact contrary to the view of some modern educationalists who seem to believe that issues like winning, losing and failing give kids neuroses.

She also put a history time-line up all around the picture rail of the classroom on which she marked notable dates with picture of the various saints, monarchs, knights and rebels preaching, marching or plundering their way around the walls. The thing was in front of our eyes every minute of the day and once again it was almost impossible not to learn.

Although quite rightly corporal punishment in schools is today very much a thing of the past, that was far from the case at St Peter's, a fact that is the more shocking given the children were aged from just 5 to 11 years.

There was no cane at St Peters but there was "The Strap". This was a two-inch wide strip that had been cut diagonally from a rubber floor tile and so was about fourteen inches in length, and when deemed necessary; punishment was administered across the outstretched palm. However as the strap was so flexible it tended to whip over and sting the back of the hand too leaving an arrow shaped weal.

Now I wouldn't want to give the impression that our teachers were sadistic but they certainly did not shy away from the use of physical punishments that also included hard slaps on the forearm (a favourite of Miss Dyke) and the use of a plimsoll around the calves of the leg. On one occasion I was actually given a stroke of the strap for making spelling mistakes, which was undoubtedly over the top but certainly made me work harder at learning my spelling.

There was one other memorable occasion when several of us got the strap. We had been spotted exchanging notes across the line between the boys and the girls' part of the playground and when asked what we were doing had said '*Nothing Miss*'. Despite repeated questioning we'd stuck to our story and in the end were punished not for passing notes to the girls but for lying.

It would seem that I had developed a bit of an eye for the girls at quite a young age. It would lead me astray and into the odd scrape over the coming years.

The top class with Miss Dyke. I am front right aged ten or eleven.

Chapter 4 – Home Life 1

After the war ended, Dad would ideally have liked to return to the grocery trade in which he'd been trained but that was apparently not possible at that time. Too many returnees I guess for the number of jobs on offer.

He found work as an assistant in a long established family-run department store called Moulds. Situated in Leatherhead High Street, it was an imposing sort of place with double glass doors set well back from the street and flanked by large curved glass windows displaying everything from three piece suites to sharpening stones.

Moulds is the arched window on the left

Above the doors on the first floor there was a large arched window where the toy department was located on eye level with passengers on the top deck of passing buses. I remember as a small kid going to the shop to see Dad at work and sitting on a rocking horse in the window looking down into the street as I rocked to and fro. It was pure heaven, or it was, until one day I rocked so hard that I made myself ill and threw up all over the place.

To a small child Moulds was a wonderland. Naturally the toy department was always a great attraction but I remember finding the hardware and ironmongery areas just as interesting. I would wander about staring in fascination at the tools and implements, cutlery and saucepans, sandpaper and sticky tape - strange sort of kid really. The worrying thing is, I can still do the same today. Now how sad is that?

However, the single most fascinating, and I thought just so modern thing about Moulds was the cash transfer system. Told you I was odd.

Most people my age will recall how some shops had a centralised cashier's office connected to various sales departments by a sort of overhead wire system that was used to shoot little shuttles containing money to the cash office which were then returned with change and the receipt.

Moulds had an updated version of this that operated on a twin pneumatic tube system. The cash was popped into a small cylindrical cartridge that was inserted via a sort of spring-loaded gate into the suction side of the system at the point of sale. From here it whizzed around the ceiling clattering like a miniature Bakerloo line to arrive at the cashier from whence it returned in a couple of minutes via the other tube crashing out of the valve into a metal basket.

To me at the time, it was pure science fiction but they were actually quite common and remained in use until the 1960's. After that I guess they perhaps started to trust shop assistants enough to let them use the tills.

Isn't the Internet wonderful?
Thinking about this old cash system I idly entered "old cash transfer system" into Google where incredibly I found chapter and verse on their history. I also found out somewhat to my dismay that my Dad's shop (as I came to think of it) was not in any sense in the forefront because they had apparently been in use since 1880 – in America of course. I also discovered that they are being re-introduced in situations like high volume retail and casinos as a means of removing cash from point of receipt and thereby reducing the likelihood of robbery.

If you are interested, look up the "cash railway website" – it's pure nostalgia and heartening to discover that there are a lot of other sad old geezers out there with a fascination for odd and archaic machinery who probably also wander around the DIY stores looking at drill bits and sandpaper.

The love affair with this old shop started before I went to school because Mum would sometimes take us kids into Leatherhead and leave us with Dad while she went shopping.

However, after I started at St Peter's, I sometimes used to walk into town after school and come home with Dad, perched on the crossbar of his bike.

Actually it was more than a bike – it was a 'Cyclemaster'. This was an inventive kind of motor-assisted push bike that had a special rear wheel with a small two stroke petrol engine built into it. It was quite a toy really and whilst it took a lot of the drudge out of pedalling uphill, if you opened it up a bit going downhill it could really fly.

Made me crow with delight at the time but thinking back on it now the bike still only had normal cycle brakes so it was probably quite a risky thing to be doing.

Perhaps it was because my uncle Frank was an upholsterer that I also used to enjoy wandering into the upholstery workshop at Moulds. It occupied a corrugated iron shed behind the main shop; in fact it was perched on the edge of an old quarry into which most of the High Street waste seemed to get deposited. The workshop was freezing in winter and the three or four men that worked there used to keep a little pot-bellied cast iron stove burning in the centre of the room. I found my way down there whenever I got the chance.
"*Hello son*" one of them would say "*Put the kettle on will you*"

The big aluminium kettle boiled up quickly on a single gas ring connected by a length of perished pink rubber tube to the gas tap in the wall. A complete health and safety nightmare in today's terms but it worked fine.

I would make the tea in a blue china teapot with a spout so chipped it used to pour at an angle of 45 degrees. Then the teapot had to brew.
This meant at least ten minutes simmering on the little stove until it was strong enough to take the skin off your teeth.

"*Just the job son.*" they'd say and I'd sit there snuggled down into a pile of fabric off-cuts, once again drinking tea with the big boys. The only difference from my experience with the builders was that these chaps didn't swear or at least not in my hearing.

Another reason that I liked to visit Leatherhead was because my Auntie Mag had a shop there and I was always guaranteed a welcome that invariably included a sticky bun or some similar magnet to a young child.

Opposite The Dukes Head pub in the High Street, the shop was millinery and haberdashery store that seemed old fashioned even then. I remember the pale blue fading and rather flaky paint of the shop front with its window containing a somewhat sparse display of ladies hats on stands.

The name "***Salon Thurloe***" *was* in darker blue script over the window. To one side the recessed door opened with a loud clang from the bell that always startled me even after years of visiting and once inside I remember that it seemed like a step back in time.

Not brightly lit, the shop had a vaguely musty smell laced with a hint of Mag's 'Lily of the Valley' perfume. A long glass counter contained wooden trays in tiers with a range of goods including buttons, pins, packets of needles and reels of cotton in a range of colours more varied than you can imagine.

Shelves and more glass cases around the walls contained fabrics and linings, rolls of lace and a hundred different styles of binding and trims while beside the counter a metal rotary stand displayed cards of buttons in more styles, shape and colour than you'd believe could exist.

If Mag was in the shop or if after a moment or two she emerged from the back room, the greeting was always the same, "*Hello darling. How's my favourite boy today? Got a kiss for your auntie?*"

Then I'd be enveloped in a big hug which was nice enough although I wasn't so keen on the kissing bit that always left a lipstick smudge on my face, nor on the perfume that was a bit overwhelming that close up. Overall though I liked going to the shop because the welcome was genuine and Mag was very kindly and always interested in what I was doing.

Behind the counter a faded blue velvet curtain covered an opening that led through to the back where Mag had her little workroom as she called it. Not that she did much work there as far as I could see but it was very comfortable in a pleasantly tatty sort of way. There were two old armchairs placed either side of a round cast iron stove beside which a tall scuttle of coke stood ready to top up the fire when necessary.

To one side of the back door a china sink and draining board and a very ancient gas stove provided a little kitchenette area where Mag made tea and from where she always managed to find one of those cakes.

The room was never bright as the only daytime illumination came from a small high-level window and a half-glazed door with opaque security glass but somehow the room seemed cosier for its dimness. The door led out to a tiny back yard with a couple of rusting galvanised dustbins and to the alley or service road that ran along behind the shops.

There was little spare space as most of the walls and floor area was taken up with stock that just seemed to have been plonked down on the next available spot and there it remained. God alone knows how she found anything but I don't think I ever remember her having a problem with it.

Mag's husband, my uncle Ted also had a shop in the High Street. Wayside Cleaners was a tiny lock-up premises a few doors up the street on the opposite side to Salon Thurloe. Whenever I visited Mag and she made the tea she would say *"Pop over the road Brian and tell your uncle the tea's made."*

Ted usually ran the shop by himself although I think he had a girl who came in sometimes to give him a hand although I think he also gave her his hand if you know what I mean. He had a bit of an eye for the girls. Still, he was always very nice to me too and when summoned for tea he used to hang a sign on the door asking customers to come and find him at Salon Thurloe. Then he'd take my hand and we'd wander back across the High Street for tea and buns in auntie's shop.

Dad had two brothers. Ted was the youngest, Dad next and then uncle Reg. Like my father they were all mild mannered chaps. Of the two uncles, I knew Reg better as we visited him more often, probably because Dad and he had more in common. Reg worked as an electrical engineer for Buchanan and Curwen that had at a workshop in Leatherhead. Like Dad, he was very practical and seemed able to make or fix more or less anything needed around the house.

When I was bit older I used to go on my bike and visit him in the workshop for tea and a chat. Researching this I was pleased to see that the company is still in Fairfield Road and has grown over the years. In addition to sophisticated modern electrical installations they now offer a range of security systems too

My father was the tallest of the three and Ted the shortest but by far the most dapper. Dad and Reg had both been in the army and had the bearing to go with it and when occasion demanded could cut the mustard with the best in terms of appearance, but Ted was different.

He was smart almost to a fault and I never recall seeing him otherwise. Even behind the shop counter without a jacket he'd wear a smart tie and those elasticated metal armbands to keep his shirtsleeves at just the correct length – no more, no less.

When he was out and about he was the epitome of good style right down to the kid leather gloves, hat and cane – quite a dandy in fact.

Sadly, of the three brothers, Ted died quite young from a stroke. Hypertension runs in my father's side of the family and took them all out eventually. A fact I constantly try to bear in mind with regard to my own diet and lifestyle although in Ted's case the gin undoubtedly played its part.

Talking about Leatherhead I am reminded of the times we used to go there to the pictures or the 'flicks' as we probably said then.

Opened in 1939 and in the Art Deco style, The Crescent Cinema boasted a 1200 seat auditorium and was a regular destination of ours in our early and middle teenage years. Sadly with the increasing popularity and availability of television during the sixties the cinema which was owned by a local family had to close and morphed into the Thorndike Theatre after the actress Dame Sybil Thorndike.

It provided a much needed new venue for local and visiting thespians as the old repertory theatre in the High Street was in need of significant modernisation but there was little enthusiasm for such an investment following the murder there in 1968.

However The Crescent was still a popular cinema in the early sixties and after a trip there we had to catch a bus just round the corner in High Street right outside a record shop that always posted the latest 'hit parade' of pop music or Rock and Roll as it was at the time. So while waiting for the bus we would avidly read and discuss the relative merits of this or that particular single which by that time were on the new 45 rpm vinyl format as opposed to the earlier brittle old black shellac 78's.

I do recall a very funny incident one day whilst waiting for the bus. A young couple riding a Triumph Tiger Cub motor cycle had to stop at the traffic lights right in front of us and the girl who was quite tall put her feet to the ground as they waited for the lights to change.

Now the Tiger Cubs, for anyone who doesn't remember them, were very small machines. The girl was probably looking in Wakefield's shop window but certainly not at the lights. So when a few moments later the lights went green, the guy in front let in the clutch and zoomed away, she was left standing astride in the middle of the road as though she'd lost her horse.

Leatherhead High Street

Like many of these things it probably doesn't sound so funny in the telling after the event. But you had to see it really and we thought it was just so funny we were helpless and fortunately so did the girl.

Probably a couple of years before we were going to the Crescent in Leatherhead we also used to go to Saturday Morning Pictures at The Odeon (Odious as we called it) in Epsom.
Apart from the predictable Mickey Mouse and Tom and Jerry cartoons there were two series that I loved. One was The Invisible Man and I was just so intrigued how they did it and created this suited figure with no head but with a hat perched on empty space and this void in the shirt collar where the neck should be.

The other one was King of the Rocket Men who was a slightly later (1949) super-hero contemporary of Superman who first kicked off in American comics in the 1930's.

However unlike Superman, Rocket Man couldn't just zoom at a moment's notice because he needed to put on his rocket suit which was kind of leather jacket, metal helmet and this back pack with a couple of jet or rocket tubes. All Superman had to do was nip round the corner and strip off to reveal his true and powerful persona.

Rocket Man was more believable to me as I've always had a bit of a scientific or technical inclination. So the fact that he needed mechanical assistance to fly worked better for me even if the rockets were a bit like 'Blue Peter yoghurt pot' creations.

King of the Rocket Men – c. 1955

Chapter 5 – Homelife 2

Overall the Bramley Way community worked very well. I think this was largely because it was pretty well balanced in terms of age. Certainly there were quite a lot of young families like ours with youngsters of a similar age all growing up and naturally meeting the same challenges together which meant that there was plenty of support and understanding when difficulties arose.

There were also a number of bungalows on the estate allocated to more elderly tenants who sometimes seemed to adopt younger families and were able to offer advice and support to the inexperienced. Sometimes this was as a shoulder to cry on or as mediation at times of dissent and frequently as 'stand-in' uncles and aunts to provide a welcome babysitting service.

I guess that another factor contributing to the generally good nature of the community was that everyone was pleased to be alive having survived the war. Also a great many of the men had fairly recently come from a service environment where discipline and self-discipline had been strong elements of their lives.

Our immediate neighbours were a delight and as I said, having all moved in around the same time, getting to know each other was pretty well unavoidable.

On one side there were Vi and Eddie Thorpe and their two sons Tony and Terry. I can't recall for certain what Eddie's job was but I have a vague recollection it might have been to do with the Post Office telephones. Tall and dark haired, Eddie was a lovely man; calm and gentle but very capable, a bit like Dad I suppose.
Vi was short dark and Welsh with a lively personality and like most wives of the period with young families didn't go out to work. She and Mum got on

well together and would often spend a few minutes chatting over the fence. But unlike the northern stereotype, were never in and out of each other's houses for a 'cup of sugar' or whatever apart from the relatively rare occasion where we might be invited in for a cup of tea.

An exception to this norm was the Christmas parties that Mum and Dad used to throw when the house was filled with our relatives and our immediate neighbours. It was very different with us kids of course as we were always 'going to tea' with our friends although 'sleepovers' didn't exist as they do these days.

Of their two sons, Terry was the elder by a good bit so I didn't have much to do with him. He was interesting though because he was fascinated by all manner of animals – *creepy-crawly things* Mum used to call them and with some justification because he had quite a collection of snakes, lizards, slow-worms, newts, frogs and so on. Either to foster his son's interest or perhaps to keep them out of the house Eddie had built an enclosure in the back garden that comprised a brick wall about three feet high surrounding an area of perhaps fifteen by eight feet. Inside the wall a water filled moat surrounded a central mound on which Terry had constructed a complete habitat of gravel and grass covered earth with old logs and buried drain pipes as tunnels for the creatures to nest in. There were a variety of small trees and dead branches and the 'land' rose up to a sort of summit in the middle, in every way a microcosm of a true habitat but made secure (well relatively) by the moat and the smooth rendered inside of the wall.

I remember Terry also built an aviary at the end of the garden where he would put injured birds he rescued and nursed back to health. He also had a baby squirrel that became so tame he could let it out for a while into the elms at the end of the garden and it would always come back. I have reason to remember the thing because one day it jumped onto my shoulder. Terry shouted *"Don't move Brian"* but I still took fright and startled the thing into biting my ear right through so I'm not a great lover of squirrels, well at least not too close up and personal.

The Thorpe's other son Tony was my age and we became close friends for most of the years I lived in Ashtead, at least until I moved to London some years later. He and I together with Ray Harris who lived next door on the other side became something of a trio, usually to be found together and quite often up to some mischief or other.

Ray's parents were really nice too. His Dad, Peter, worked at the Goblin factory on the boundary of Ashtead and Leatherhead where they made the once well-known Goblin vacuum cleaners and the other product whose reputation still endures as something of an icon of the period – The Goblin Teasmaid.

I never knew precisely what Peter Harris did at work but he had quite a lucrative hobby as a clock and watch repairer and became well known as such in the area. He had a small work bench in the corner of their living room that fascinated me because of the miniature nature of the tools. Tiny little screwdrivers and drills and even a little lathe on which he could actually make the tiny wheels and bearings to go inside clocks and wrist watches. He was very skilled indeed.

Try as I might I just cannot recall his wife's name but he always called her 'Tink' – obviously a pet name. She was a martyr to asthma and would often be laid out by the illness wheezing and gasping for breath.

Like Tony, Ray had an elder sibling, a sister called Sylvia who was tall, blonde and extremely attractive and made something of a name for herself locally when she landed a job as an air stewardess.

This was seen in those days as the most glamorous and exotic of employment as so few people had any first-hand experience of air travel at least not in Bramley Way. I think she worked for BOAC that later became BA but I imagine the reality of the trans-Atlantic runs could have been a bit grim in those early pre-jet days given that the east-west flight time was up to eighteen hours and due to head winds required two refuelling stops at Shannon and Gander.

However there were the inevitable families that for one reason or another were a bit different. For example, there was the Brennan household where there always seemed to be some sort of trouble mostly due to Mrs Brennan's drinking. This often gave rise to the noisy rows that sometimes used to spill over into the garden or street. These would have poor old Mr Brennan desperately trying to reason with his wife and get her to come inside quietly.

"*Iris my darling would you keep your voice down, you're disturbing the neighbours.*"
This rarely worked and more often than not he would eventually have to call on his son for help.

"*Dennis can you come and give us hand with your mother, she's poorly again*"

Then between them they would bundle her indoors where they apparently used to lock her in the airing cupboard until she went to sleep and eventually sobered up.

Dennis was alright really but his appearance and manner really used to irritate Dad. At the time Dennis was in his teens and doing his Teddy Boy thing and Dad used to watch him with his long greasy hair, drape jacket and drainpipe trousers as he slouched along past our house.

"*Look at the state of that kid.*" He'd grumble.
"*Needs to get in the army and do a bit of square bashing. That'd soon sort him out.*"

Well it wasn't long before Dad's dream and Dennis' worst nightmare came true when he was called up for National Service. Dad was proved right too because after his initial training Dennis was transformed. He was smart, upright and as far as Dad was concerned a great result. I've no idea what Dennis thought about it though.

The Slade family were a rather strange lot. Well it was mostly the son Derek who had a bit of an odd look about him and couldn't speak properly.

Today I'm sure the political correctness police would require us to say he had learning difficulties whereas in those days we kids all called him Dopey Derek and threw sticks at him so it was hardly surprising if he didn't fit in. Even Dad who rarely had a bad word to say about anyone thought he was "*a sandwich short of a picnic*" and said he'd be trouble one day.

In the event Dad was proved right once again because years later when I returned to the area as a police officer I had to arrest him. He was basically a bit simple and used to get fixated on people; usually girls who he'd follow around and try to kiss. He actually meant no harm but in the end we had to charge him with common assault and get him 'bound over' which of course he didn't understand so it was just another problem for his parents.

It's curious how in estate situations families that my parents used to call "a bad lot" or "a bit rough" seemed to group together and indeed still do, hence the sort of ghetto situation that arises where "bad" seems to beget "worse".

This happened to some extent on our estate as time went on and there was one road in particular that had such a reputation, and where, if there was any trouble going, it was more or less guaranteed to occur. However it was only in later years that I had any real understanding of this and was always puzzled why Mum in particular wasn't keen on my friend Tony Archer who lived in the road in question.

There was one other factor that contributed to an element of both division and unity on the estate and that was religion. Half a dozen or so families at our end of the street were Catholic and there existed this connection and a certain air of smugness that distinguished the families and set them slightly apart from others.

The Catholic church of St Michael was a short distance off the estate and easily within walking distance, not that there was any choice in those early days as cars were few and far between. The usual Sunday morning routine then would be for us to be thoroughly scrubbed up and usually head off around 8.30 for the walk to the church and 9 o'clock Mass.

Within a few steps we would fall in step with one or two other families and march off the estate looking sanctimonious. It was Sunday after all.

Dad not being a Catholic was not a part of this charade. However, he was marvellously patient and supportive. It was him as much as Mum that got us up and dressed and generally organised then remained at home to do the chores. These included riddling out and re-lighting the boiler, hoovering the carpets and best of all having a wonderful Sunday fry-up ready for us on our return.

Later on when after we ascended to the dizzy heights of car ownership Dad used to take us to church and back in the car. As they were still something of a rarity on the estate we felt ever so posh and my sister and I used to sit in the back practising the 'royal wave' whilst looking seriously straight ahead.

Overall, my life as a young child growing up on the Bramley Way estate was pretty marvellous really; cosseted within a loving home, happy in school, with plenty of friends and places to play. But, as they say, nothing lasts forever,

My final year at St Peters was really geared up to preparation for the Eleven Plus examination that in those days marked the first major educational milestone in our young lives and in which success or failure determined the standard of secondary education we would receive.

It was certainly a big thing in our house. I've said how Mum had this thing about getting a 'proper education', and how to some extent her attitude seemed to be informed by the need to keep up with my Irish uncles.

Don't get me wrong. It's obviously right for parents to want the best for their kids. However there was a certain amount of educational snobbery involved in Mum's case and I think that her desire for us to do well was perhaps as much about her and how she would appear to others as it was about us.

The choice, particularly for us Catholics was relatively stark. If you passed the exam, no problem. You got to go to Wimbledon College and be taught by the Jesuit Fathers or to The John Fisher School at Purley.

Both of these were fee paying private grammar schools and were seen by Mum and her Catholic friends as the 'be and end all' of secondary education in the area and of equal importance, passing the Eleven Plus meant you could go there without paying.

On the other hand if you failed the exam, well to be honest, in our house it just wasn't an option that was discussed.

This was because it meant that you finished up at the local secondary modern with, as Mum saw it, all the 'rubbish " *that were never going to do any good.*"

Now, after all this build up, you're probably ahead of me. Yes, I failed the bloody thing. I was actually not very well on the day being in the aftermath of a dose of 'flu which didn't help. Whatever the reason, being off colour, not studying hard enough or simply not being bright enough, the result in-doors was terrible. It was as though the world had come to an end.

Dad wasn't so fazed by the situation but Mum was really disappointed and there were hours of discussion over what should be done. In the event, and I'm eternally grateful to them both for this, they decided that they would pay for me to go, not to the Jesuits, but to St Peter's at Guildford. This was certainly not in the same league as Wimbledon College or The John Fisher School but it was a private Catholic grammar school that had a good reputation, even if a bit second division.

Of course their reasoning wasn't shared with me at the time but I later learnt how they had come to their decision to foot the bill to get me a better education and it made me feel humble and very grateful.

On numerous occasions whilst Dad was working at Moulds they had tried to get a mortgage to enable them to buy their own house.

Even before they moved to Bramley Way they had the offer of buying the old house in Gladstone Road for £400 but they couldn't afford that at the time. Not that Dad minded living in a council house but this was another of the things that used to exercise Mum's mind and was for her almost certainly bound up with social status issues in the same way that education was.

Time after time the answer had apparently always been the same,
"*Sorry Mr Simmons. You're not earning enough.*"

After several years Dad had managed to leave Moulds and get back into the grocery business with Baldwin's a small shop in Ashtead village. Here after quite a short time, due to his extensive pre-war experience in the trade, when the manager moved on Dad took over his job.

Obviously this improved his financial position so once again he applied for a mortgage only to be told on this occasion. "*We're sorry Mr Simmons. You're earning enough but you are now too old.*"

They were in a trap. Dad was earning good money. Mum was earning too as she had gone back to part time nursing but the building society wouldn't take her income into account. So there were no particular money problems but they still could not buy a home of their own. It was thanks to this situation that when I failed the eleven-plus they were able to pay for me to have the education that I probably didn't deserve.

Now, I wouldn't want you to run away with the idea that life was all church, school and angst about the eleven-plus because of course it wasn't. There was a whole other life running in parallel that was about growing up; making friends and sometimes falling out; gangs and scout troops, family holidays, youth clubs, crushes and heartbreak, the need for pocket money and how to earn it and the whole range of childhood and adolescent experience that makes of us the people we are.

These also included the substantial catalogue of scrapes and stunts we got into and somehow survived that I'm sad to say a great many of today's youngsters never experience in the risk-averse society we seem to have created. Not that I think kids should be neglected or put at serious risk. However I do believe an element of risk and risk management is desirable both in the raising of children and in general.

Risk and learning to live with it is important if life is to have any buzz to it and if we are to produce offspring who will have a go at things rather than turn away from a challenge.

The only thing I've omitted from the above list is day to day family life. Sadly, in some households this can provide all the challenge a youngster needs simply to survive unscathed, but which, I'm happy to say in my own case was idyllic.

That's not to say there were never any domestic crises. I'm sure there must have been but they were certainly not communicated to us kids. Sure, Mum and Dad got cross with us on occasions and neither was above administering the odd clout. Whilst unacceptable these days it didn't seem to do us much harm although one could argue as to whether it did any good or not.

"*Wait till your father gets home.*" was the classic phrase guaranteed to send my sister and I scurrying to our respective rooms where we kept our heads down until the implied threat had passed.

The milestones marking those early years are too numerous to fully recount although several are worth a mention.

One of the strongest memories for me was the arrival of television in our house. I'm not sure exactly which year it was but it was certainly early in the 1950's.

I remember us sitting around this little Bush TV set with its over large wooden cabinet and tiny opalescent grey nine inch screen watching the Coronation in 1953. Perhaps it was the need to be part of that event that prompted my parents to take the TV plunge. I recall we had a few of the neighbours in to watch the ceremony too so that would have ticked some 'one-up' boxes for Mum.

Other TV memories include the fact that early sets had to warm up. Having switched the thing on we'd sit staring at the screen until wonder of wonders the picture, or quite often the test card, would emerge, spreading from the centre of the screen in the same way that it would disappear into the little white dot as the set was turned off.

Early children's programmes included puppets Andy Pandy, Muffin the Mule and of course Bill and Ben the Flowerpot men whilst adult audiences were introduced to the forerunners of the modern soaps in the shape of The Grove Family and The Appleyards. Take Your Pick with an over-the-top Michael Miles was the first TV quiz having transferred to the small screen from radio Luxemburg in 1955.

The early police dramas soon followed in the mid to late 50s with Pc George Dixon patrolling Dock Green. Then came "No Hiding Place" featuring Raymond Francis as Inspector Tom Lockhart and the old Wolesley police car sweeping out of (or was it into) New Scotland Yard.

And who can forget the 'Interludes'?. Programming schedules in those days were less slick than today and back then TV advertising didn't exist to fill any gaps. So to keep them amused audiences were treated to a variety of short and supposedly restful interlude films. These included the Potter's Wheel, The Windmill, The kitten playing with the ball of wool and my personal favourite "London to Brighton in 4 minutes". Hardly restful, that one!

Writing this I find myself wondering what on earth my grandparents or even my parents would have made of the enormous modern flat screen TVs; mega-watts of surround sound, recording systems and now even 3D television in our living rooms – whoops, I mean 'home cinemas'. I reckon that the Brighton run in 3D would be quite something.

Going back to the Coronation, I was about nine then and I do recall it being a very significant event, not just for the country but also in our street and accompanied by a lot of community activity.

We had this huge street party in Bramley Way with red, white and blue bunting draped along the hedges whilst trestle tables and chairs were set up along the road with everyone contributing bowls of salad, sandwiches, cakes and miscellaneous party food. There were races for the kids and parents and I remember Mum and Dad running the 'egg and spoon' race and me doing the sack race.

There was also a fancy dress competition for the kids and also for the best-decorated bike, dolls pram or trolley.

Dad really went to town on this. On my bike he set up a loop of wire above the handlebars into which he fixed a hardboard plaque and another triangular one in the frame. These were painted pale blue and the wire and frame he wrapped with red, white and blue crepe paper while on the panels he stencilled God Save the Queen and E II R. Angela's pram received a similar treatment but I can't actually remember now how we fared in the competition.

How simple and delightfully naïve it all sounds now when we look around at the complex world in which we live today. I must say though how nice it is even in these cynical times, to see people turn out in droves for some national celebration or anniversary. I guess everyone loves a party.

Probably the next highlight in our family life was the arrival of a 1949 Ford Prefect also, I would guess, around 1953/4. It was one of those we now refer to as the "sit up and beg" Fords, with a 900cc side-valve engine, and a long, somewhat imprecise lever to operate the three gears compared to the 5 or 6 we have these days and a long black bonnet. Black because they almost all were. I can still remember the registration was KPF925. Surprising how these things stick.

It's only now looking back that I realise quite how well off we were compared to some of the neighbours for whom the then luxuries of TV and a family car did not materialise for some years if ever.

Predictably the car dramatically changed family life for us. No more the walks around Ashtead Park on a Sunday afternoon or the railway journey to Littlehampton for an annual holiday in a rented shack on the beach, and no more walking to church. We were really on the up! The world was now our oyster and Sunday afternoon runs to Climping came within reach provided that 'Lizzie', as Dad had christened the car, would make it up Bury Hill without boiling over.

In addition to the required tool kit, spare wheel, jack and tartan travel rugs the boot also contained the little spirit stove. This we shielded from the wind in a Jacobs biscuit tin and Mum would use it to brew up the tea in the Climping car park (free in those days) or in lay-bys and field entrances en-route if the fancy for a cuppa should take us. Remarkable the joy we derived as a family from these little weekend or holiday expeditions and the wonderful bonding effect the experiences had for me at least.

And it wasn't just the south coast that came more easily within reach. Family holidays now included trips down to the west country with nights camping out on Exmoor (well, sleeping in the car to be more precise) and perilous descents of the infamous hills at Porlock and Lynmouth where we wondered whether poor old Lizzie would make it back up again.

Lizzie – the 1949 Ford Prefect

Chapter 6 -The Second St Peter's

If my start at St Peter's in Leatherhead had been troubled, Merrow was quite the opposite and I loved it from the outset. Around the end of July 1955 before term started in the September, we had been invited to an open day during the summer holidays when all the new boys and their families were shown around the school and introduced to the masters.

The fact that it was a beautiful day obviously helped but we were treated like royalty and conducted around the school by a senior prefect, smart in his white shirt, red tie, and red blazer with the crossed keys badge of St Peter on the breast pocket. I was so impressed by the uniform.

"*I'm sure you'll like it here Brian*" he said and turning to my parents, "*Please follow me.*"

To be fair, I imagine that we were only taken to the showpiece areas that included the main house, the chapel and the science building and the refectory where tea and cakes were laid on,

For me, apart from the impressive Victorian grandeur of the old house, the high point was the science block. It was divided into three laboratories where, to my young eye, the long mahogany workbenches seemed to stretch into the far distance. Sinks with brass taps and curved spouts, Bunsen burners and tripods, glass jars of coloured chemicals and all manner of mysterious and exciting apparatus had me instantly hooked. Strange thing really, I didn't know a test tube from a spatula but I was in heaven. It felt like a sort of homecoming.

The chemistry lab was the domain of father John McSheehy, a giant of a man who I got on with immediately. "*Hello young man.*" he said with a smile and a voice that was gentler than his size suggested. "*Are you interested in chemistry?*" "*Oh yes.*" I said without a clue what chemistry actually was.

Father Mac was also Master of Discipline. Yes the cane was alive and well at Merrow and given Father Mac's bulk I'm glad that one way or another over the following years I managed to avoid him having to swing it in my direction. Not that I was such a goody-two-shoes. I was just lucky.

The physics master was Father Peter Boulding who I also took to and who, although I had no reason to believe it then, would continue to be my friend long after my time at St Peters.

And so it was that in September 1955 I settled into my five-year stint at St Peter's Private Grammar School for boys in Guildford. They were to be mainly happy if relatively undistinguished years

The school was situated at Merrow on the outskirts of Guildford so travelling to school from Ashtead involved a 12-mile journey on the 408 bus and I remember it cost 11½d (just under 5p) for the 45-minute trip.

It was one of the green double-deckers run by London Country and we always tried to go upstairs if there was space. You could see so much more from up there and it could get a quite exciting if the driver was behind schedule and had to put his foot down a bit because the top deck used to sway alarmingly especially around the bends at Clandon. I recall we were quite disappointed when the road was straightened and the bends lost their thrill.

Founded in 1947 the school had been developed around a Victorian mansion set in extensive grounds although the majority of the estate had been cleared to create playing fields. However in front of the main house there was (and still is) a stand of magnificently tall American Redwoods whose spongy bark used to fascinate us in the way you could punch it hard without injury.

The Headmaster was Father Wake and a number of the teachers were priests while the remainder were lay teachers – male of course. Apart from the kitchen staff and a couple of cleaners, the only female on site was Matron.

She was a strong but quite kindly woman of significant proportions with alarming red hair who stood no nonsense from anyone up to and including the headmaster. If you were really poorly or seriously hurt she was as kind and gentle as Mother Teresa but malingerers got very short shrift.

The brick built refectory and kitchen adjoined the main house, beside which the large tarmac play area extended across to one of the sports fields.

A number of supposedly temporary buildings were occupied by the gymnasium, a chapel, science block and three classroom blocks whilst the old coach house was utilised as changing room, showers and toilets on the ground floor with the sixth form common room above. Another temporary building provided an assembly hall and also doubled as a music room.

The 'temporary' buildings were still in use when my own kids went there more than thirty years later in the 1980's. They were timber framed and clad externally with white painted corrugated iron sheets and inside with a soft fibre insulation board painted in magnolia.

The roofs were open to the rafters and although lined, the corrugated asbestos sheets outside reverberated so loudly in heavy rain that it was almost impossible to hear anything.

Fairly ineffectual heating was provided by gas heaters that used to hang from the roof and had to be turned on and off by using a hooked stick to pull on a chain. I remember how their first use in the autumn terms always gave rise to a characteristic burning smell as six months of dust and dead insects quickly went up in smoke.

The chapel which was of the same construction had endured extremely well but the classrooms were showing their age. Eight years of fairly rough treatment by teenage boys had left their mark in the way of general wear and tear but the soft board lining had fared the worst. Years of wall charts and attack by innumerable drawing pins plus the odd bit of deliberate vandalism had caused the panels to disintegrate in places into irregularly shaped holes revealing the internal construction timbers. As a result when parents evenings came around ever-larger wall charts had to be found and yet more pins were used in an attempt to conceal the state of affairs.

There were also a couple of tennis courts in the grounds and a former gardener's store had been put to good use as the Tuck Shop. This used to open for twenty minutes every day after lunch and here we filled our pockets with four-a-penny Blackjacks, Sherbet Lemons, Flying Saucers, Refreshers, Fruit Gums and such like.

Beside the Tuck Shop could be seen the remains of the original enclosed kitchen garden, and nearby, against an old red brick wall, a fine if somewhat run down example of a Victorian lean-to greenhouse was pressed into service as the art-room.

Along the other walls, even more dilapidated and overgrown, timber and brick stores housed a miscellany of ancient garden paraphernalia, broken pots, tools, cloches and most interestingly to my young eyes an old green Morris van.

Not surprisingly, I began my time at St Peter's in the First Form and our form master, Father Stewart (I believe), was a pleasant enough man but presumably unremarkable as I can only just put a face to him with the help of an old photograph and if I'm honest couldn't swear to his name.

Unlike primary school where class teachers seemed able to teach most subjects except music and PE, in this new environment form masters only took us for religious instruction and whatever other subjects happened to be their speciality. Consequently we had to get used to a procession of different teachers coming to the classrooms depending on what the next subject was on the timetable.

Every month a different class member was nominated as Form Captain who was supposedly responsible for keeping some sort of order in the absence of masters and there was also a door monitor whose job it was to be at the door and shout "*Class!*" to call us to our feet on the arrival of the next teacher.

Naturally some of these masters made more impression than others and for a variety of reasons. Some were notably bad teachers either by virtue of the fact that they could bore for England, had an inadequate grasp of their subjects or simply lacked the charisma or presence to inspire or exert any control. And believe me twenty or so twelve year olds need some control. One who had no problem whatever in the control department was a Father John Price.

A Glaswegian Scot, he was hard and if the mood took him could be a bully. He taught French and Latin and had this notorious penchant for tweaking the ears of miscreants, lobbing the blackboard rubber at the inattentive with unnerving accuracy and twisting the short hairs on the back of your neck in an attempt to remind you how some verb should be conjugated. I can't imagine why he thought that might aid memory.

He was also an absolute stickler for discipline and was feared by us all in the junior forms. Interestingly though, when I was in the fifth form we had him as our form master and he was totally different in that relationship. He certainly still had the same reputation among the lower forms so clearly nothing had changed there.

So perhaps he just related better to older boys or dare I say he thought that if he took the same tack with a bunch of older and physically more mature boys he just might not get away with it. Who knows, but he was certainly very different and we became very fond of him, in what for many was to be our last year.

Another master who I will always remember was Henry McCann. He was short, very round and sort of bowled rather than walked along. As he always wore his mortar-board hat and academic gown that hid his legs he appeared to be on wheels. He had a plump ruddy face with wispy hair and gold-rimmed spectacles and looking back on it, was a bit too 'touchy ¬ feely', which, with his somewhat lascivious smile that would raise alarm bells nowadays.

Henry McCann was however a very gifted teacher. He taught us English, Latin, French and Music and was extremely clever in the way he managed to interest a bunch of teenage boys in what on the face of it for many are dreary subjects. Basically he bribed us. It was the carrot and stick approach without the stick, and the carrot was that if we worked he would read to us on Friday.

He had the most wonderful ability to read aloud and to totally hold in thrall a group of youngsters who in any other circumstances would have had their minds on chatting, looking out of the windows, anywhere but on the English or Latin under discussion.

So from Monday to Thursday we would give him what he asked so that on Friday afternoons he would read. He always came and sat in the middle of the class and we all gathered around. He held us totally spellbound with the doings of Holmes and Watson as they sought to overcome the dastardly Moriarty or Fu- Manchu; and we quaked as he gave us Poe's Pit and the Pendulum or Dickens' Tale of Two Cities punctuated with the sickening thud of the guillotine.

Music was Henry's main love though and here too he had a trick or two up his sleeve. Singing classes were not exactly high in the popularity listings for us boys but once again the carrot approach worked. I can remember standing around the piano in the music room at St Peters while he played to us. He was unbelievably good and could sit there without a sheet of music and simply play.

My two favourites were Tchaikovsky's Piano Concerto No1 and the Chopin Polonaise in A and I have no doubt that it was Henry McCann who first awakened my appreciation of good music and that at the age of about 14. We were so blown away and infected by the music that when it came to Strawberry Fair and the other Olde English songs we just sang our little hearts out for him.

My class with Father Ryan. I am rear right

Another master was 'Old Hairy" or to be more polite Father Albert Ryan; a lovely, larger than life man who earned his nickname from the hairs that sprouted in profusion from his eyebrows, nose and ears. As his name suggests he was Irish with a loud booming voice and strong accent that carried from one class into another on the not infrequent occasions that he was inclined to raise his voice.

He had a small lightweight motorbike, something like a BSA Bantam or Francis Barnett 125 that he used to ride across the playground and which, with his bulk perched on top, cut a pretty humorous appearance.

There was the lovely occasion when by way of a joke a few of us pinched his bike and being so light we were able to hoist it up and put it on the overhead beams in our classroom. Albert soon realised that the bike's disappearance was a prank played by some of the kids but we could hardly

contain ourselves as he stomped about the classroom complaining about it whilst the bike was just a couple of feet above his head.
After the class we got it down and quickly returned it and he never was any the wiser.

I mentioned Father Boulding the physics master earlier. He also had a nickname, well two in fact. One was 'penguin', due to his curious gait.
As he walked he used to swing his arms quite widely which resulted in a sort of waddling or penguin like appearance. He was also known and PeeWee from his initials P.W.

There was one hilarious incident that superbly confirmed the 'penguin' nickname. One day during a free period a couple of boys had been having a crafty cigarette in the classroom when someone spotted a master coming in our direction. Instantly stubbing out the fags they flicked them into one of the aforementioned holes in the softboard wall of the building and thought no more about it.

During the next period someone noticed that there was smoke coming out of the wall, which after a very short time increased to quite a significant amount. The master in charge got in a complete panic and ran out of the class shouting "*Fire Fire*" in response to which Peter Boulding came charging out of the science block with a fire extinguisher.

Following the instructions, he inverted the extinguisher to activate it not realising that he had the spout facing towards himself instead of at the fire.
The extinguisher went off spraying him with foam so that with his black clerical suit and a white front the penguin effect was complete.

By about the age of fourteen, in common with quite a few others I'd started to experiment with cigarettes and in order to buy them we had worked out a way of saving our bus fares by hitch-hiking home from school.

These days I'm sure this would give rise to a great deal of eyebrow raising because of the supposed risks etc. but I used to do it a couple of days a week on average although it was always in company with at least one friend.

Surprisingly we rarely had a problem getting lifts and quite often we'd manage to get a ride almost door to door. But if the lift were only part of the way then we'd just wait for the next bus and be thankful to have saved a few pence from the fare.

I was one of a little clique of three or four who usually went around together and this included the journeys to and from school. On the days we decided to 'hitch' we took a short cut from the school along an alley-way and it was here that we used to stop and do the 'smoking thing'.

One or two others knew about this and I guess wanted to be part of this risky and therefore slightly exciting activity but we were not very keen to extending 'membership' of our little gang to others.
One boy, Michael Watson had become very persistent about wanting to try the smoking and was becoming a bit of a pain so we decided to try to put him off.

Nicky Hunt, whose mother kept horses had an idea and he made up some cigarettes from dried horse manure and a couple of days later on the way home when Watson was again trying to edge his way into the illicit smoking group we struck. "*Ok*" said Nicky. "*Try one of these, they're Turkish*". Watson lit up and took a puff and started to choke.
"*Christ*" he said, "*They're horrible. Taste like shit.*" We were falling about by now.
"*That right.*" said Nicky. "*Exactly right. They're horse shit.*"

Poor old Watson went a few shades of green before he finally threw up but he didn't bother our little group again. Kids can be so cruel.

I think I was in the fourth or fifth form that we got up to another hilarious stunt (hilarious that is in an immature teenage boy sort of way).

There used to be a coffee and burger bar near Tunsgate in Guildford called Boxers that we liked to visit sometimes after school. I was in there one day with a couple of mates who's actual names I cannot now recall except that one was about a year older than me and we all thought he was really cool because he used to smoke Philip Morris cigarettes that no-one else had ever heard of. Because of this his nickname was 'Smoker'.

We were drinking coffee at this table when 'Smoker' said "*Watch this.*"

On the table there was a bowl of sugar and a small jug of ketchup, so he excavated a little hollow in the sugar into which he tipped a liberal dollop of ketchup and then buried it in sugar. "Come on." He said. "*Let's move.*"
And we moved to another table to sit back and see what happened.

After a few minutes a chap came in with his girlfriend and sat down at the table and ordered two coffees. We were beside ourselves with anticipation as he was being really flash with this girl and making as though he was so sophisticated and knew how to treat her and so on.

The coffees arrived and he asked her if she wanted sugar. She said she did and then he dipped the spoon into the sugar bowl and before he realised what was happening had ladled a gloopy spoonful of sugar and red ketchup into her coffee. By now we were hysterical but before he could put two and two together we were out of the door and away, but of course the story doesn't end there.

A few days later at assembly it was announced that a complaint had been received from Boxers about the behaviour of some St Peter's boys and a brief description of the incident was given which caused huge hilarity all around.

The sting was that unless the culprits owned up by lunch time the whole school would be given detention for a week so after assembly we presented ourselves at the headmasters office all prepared to take the consequences. However before two of us knew what was happening 'Smoker' had said it was all his idea and took complete responsibility. (Those were the days when honour meant something even in school.)

We were then dismissed and told that we would be advised of any punishment in due course.

Presumably there was then some discussion between the school and the café owner because Smoker was told that his punishment was to go to the restaurant, admit responsibility, apologise and offer to pay for the wasted drinks and any other damage.

By most people's standards this should have been a salutary experience and a good lesson learnt but Smoker had other ideas. That afternoon he strode in to the café, cool as you like and asked for the manager. Then apparently instead of making it clear he was the culprit, he acted as though he was a representative of the school and had come to apologise and make good any costs. Clearly he wasn't recognised and the ploy worked a treat because apologies were accepted and he was treated to a free burger and coffee. Just goes to show that if you've got the neck you can get away with almost anything.

Sport was quite a big thing at St Peters and when I first went there we had to play rugby, which I absolutely hated, basically because I was terrified. I'd not had good experiences at primary school and being fairly slight of build and shy by nature was hardly a prime candidate for 'prop forward' or whatever it is rugby players are called. However it was obligatory and had to be endured so as a result I came to dread Wednesday afternoons.

Fortunately after the first year, for some reason I never knew, rugby was dropped in favour of soccer. But that was little better except that being marginally less of a contact sport I was able to avoid getting knocked about so much and used to just run up and down the pitch keeping as far away from the ball as possible.

The PE master would be shouting, "*Go on Simmons. Get in amongst it.*" and I'd say "*Ok Sir.*" and just keep running up and down. I was a real wimp on the sports field but then we are what we are I guess. I managed to exist in this way for three years when suddenly an escape route appeared.

It was announced that volunteers were being sought for the role of 'laboratory assistant' in the physics and chemistry departments. Duties would entail helping during break periods to set and clear up equipment in the laboratories and possibly from time to time having to miss games periods on Wednesdays.

I couldn't believe my ears and together with Michael Watson; (he of the horse shit cigarettes and another 'sports wimp'); I lost no time in presenting myself for what I thought would be a selection process and being one of the chemistry 'swots' I was hopeful of being chosen. Well I needn't have worried because there were no other takers and Watson and I became 'lab boys'.

It turned out to be a really excellent ploy for us. Especially useful as it quickly developed from being a couple of times a week and an occasional games period into a regular arrangement whereby more or less every break time and each Wednesday afternoon we disappeared to make the coffee for the two science masters Fr. Mac and Fr. Boulding.

This meant we also had coffee and biscuits as well as washing up a few test tubes and setting up experiments for following laboratory sessions. It probably worked well for the games master too because he didn't have to worry about trying to persuade or order a couple of unwilling boys to try to play a game they clearly were not good at.

Over the next year of being 'lab boys' we got to know the two priests as both teachers and friends.

Out of the classroom environment they were much less formal and with their guard down so to speak the odd expletive would slip out.

I recall one day when Fr Mac managed to hit his thumb with a hammer. "*Oh sod it!*" he yelped and suddenly seemed much more in my world.

Away from school both priests were interested in trains and trams and were happy to share their interest with us. On several occasions out of school hours we went with them to visit transport sites of either current or historic interest.

Such a relationship between teachers and pupils would probably be frowned on today as inappropriate. I hope I'm not being naïve but I don't believe there was anything of a dubious nature about it apart from perhaps an element of favouritism.

I believe that they honestly enjoyed sharing and encouraging our interest in a wider range of subjects. In addition the relationship encouraged my interest in the sciences that eventually led me to examination successes.

It would be wrong to suggest that Watson and I were alone in these extra-curricular activities. I knew of other occasions when masters who had some special interest had taken groups of boys on visits to one place or another.

For example Peter Boulding took about six of us on a visit he had arranged through a parent to Lloyds of London and the Stock Exchange where we had the working of both organisations explained. And on another occasion he took three of us to the Transport Museum at Clapham.

I just think that these days such activities would have to be far more formal in arrangement and officially sanctioned whereas then there were not the same anxieties or suspicions.

I mentioned previously that there was an old Morris van parked in an outbuilding within the school grounds and as Watson and I grew in confidence with the two science masters we decided to ask them if they would teach us to drive it. After initially dismissing the idea, when we continued to press them Fr. Mac eventually said, "*Ok. If you can get it going I'll think about it.*"

Obviously we didn't know much about how engines worked but we started by getting the flat tyres pumped up and I asked my Dad what to do about it.

"*Well,*" he said, "*The battery will need charging but if you're lucky it might not need much more than that.*"

There was a charger in the physics lab so we hooked up the old battery that amazingly took and held a charge. Father Mac gave us a gallon of petrol and to everyone's surprise after a few attempts the engine started.

It ran pretty roughly at first but by now the two priests had become more interested and after a bit of tinkering around between them the old van was running 'as sweet as a nut'.

Good to his word Father Mac said he would give us some lessons after school. So, having advised our respective parents that we'd be a bit late home, the following week driving lessons around the field and playground began.

The van was a bit of a wreck really and with seats that were scarcely secured to the floor it was difficult to get into and maintain a position that allowed proper control of the pedals so as you might imagine progress was not exactly smooth. This, together with excessively worn steering and the almost complete absence of synchromesh on any of the three gears made our lessons something of an adventure.

The brakes worked OK even if they pulled a bit to one side. The problem was you never knew until you hit the pedal which way the pull would be so it was interesting to say the least.

If this all sounds highly risky, it wasn't really as within the confines of the grounds we never actually got over about 20 miles an hour so there was never any real danger but it was the most tremendous fun.

We had quite a few lessons that I guess must have been beneficial when I came to learn properly a couple of years later but unfortunately, despite all our efforts, the experience was to be quite short lived. The school tractor broke down and the grounds-man hi-jacked the old van to tow the gang mowers around the playing fields and sadly that was the end of our driving lessons.

I was no star student academically but I guess I held my own more or less 'mid-field' as you might say, apart from Chemistry and English, both of which I enjoyed and was quite good at. My bete-noir was maths, which I couldn't understand and consequently hated.

Unfortunately as physics by this time had started to entail a fair amount of maths I had started to fall behind a bit there too.

In the fourth year it was the practice to enter students for a little-known public examination called The College of Preceptors, the idea being to give us some experience of public examination in preparation for the GCE 'O' levels that we would take the following year. I took eight or nine subjects and passed them all, three with distinction. The consequence was, for me at least, that I think it gave me a false sense of confidence.

As a result I didn't work as hard as I should have done and so when it came to the 'O' levels the following year I failed pretty dismally, only passing in Chemistry, English Language and Literature.

Following this performance there was no question of my continuing to sixth form and 'A' levels. I felt very demoralised and as I guess my parents were pretty disappointed too it was made fairly clear that the time had come for me to call it a day and enter the world of work. So in July 1960 I walked out of St Peters and full time education for the last time.

As I said, my friendship with Peter Boulding was to endure beyond my school years and some twelve years after I first met him he officiated at my wedding and then baptised my son. Years later when I was struggling to make an unhappy marriage work I often sought his counsel so he was someone quite special to me for many years. However, that is jumping ahead somewhat.

Chapter 7 - Meanwhile

Before I leave my school years behind completely it's probably pertinent to mention a few of the other things that happened on the home front during the same period.

I mentioned gangs earlier, but they were certainly nothing like those we hear of today with their violence and involvement with crime and drugs. No, these were just our childish affiliations that owed as much to the weather on the day or more likely to who had the largest bag of aniseed balls in their pocket.

That's not to say we didn't take them seriously though. There were some quite strong rivalries between for example, our little group of immediate playmates and the Simpkins and Jennings gang who lived at the top of the road.

I remember that one of the Simpkins boys was a bit of a bully who often sent me home with a bloody nose but who I got my own back on in great style one day.

I was about twelve or thirteen and had been playing with two of my friends in a copse a short distance from home and we were coming back across a field where there was a large hole. It was about six feet wide and a foot or so deep and because of recent rain was full to the brim with water.

As we headed home the Simpkins spotted us, and I assumed correctly that once again I was due for a smack on the nose. However, as Paul Simpkins closed in to have a go at me I somehow managed to turn so that he had his back to the hole. I can remember this so clearly it is amazing. I guess I was just so angry at his bullying that the worm turned and seeing my opportunity I charged at him pushing him in the chest.

He was so close to the edge of the hole that one step back was sufficient and he fell, arms flailing, backwards into the water and almost disappeared. Coughing, spluttering and dripping wet he scrambled to his feet and stood up and, wonder of wonders, started to cry.

We laughed of course and so did his brother because apart from a soaking there was no harm done but the loss of face was such that he never bothered me again.

Every November it was the practice for all the families in our part of the road to collect hedge trimmings and any other combustible rubbish for the Guy Fawkes bonfire that was built on some waste ground nearby.

As it was mostly us kids that built the fire it was more or less a requirement that rivalries were forgotten even if only temporarily.

On this occasion however with the fire built and with only a day or two to go before bonfire night we all fell out again and with cries of "*We want our wood back.*" the other kids started pulling the bonfire apart.

War was declared and a couple of us found ourselves a-top the bonfire armed with catapults and a spud gun repelling attacks by the Simpkins and Jennings boys until, unusually, the grown-ups intervened before any damage was done.

It was made clear by all the parents that the fire was to stay the way it was and we were to stop our scrapping, so hatchets were reluctantly buried.

A couple of days later the whole street turned out to light the fire and celebrate poor old Guy Fawkes' demise. As the fire took hold, first his chair began to burn followed by his donated clothes, his lolling head sporting one of old man Penny's hats and finally his total destruction as the cache of bangers buried in his innards exploded. The things we teach our kids!

Each family brought their own fireworks to let off, the parents gossiped and downed a few beers and eventually, once the fire had died down enough to approach safely, dozens of spuds were tossed into the hot ashes to cook. After what seemed like ages but was no time at all really, we'd all be sitting there with impossibly hot and black baked potatoes held tentatively in wads of newspaper happily scooping out the soft smoky flesh. Happy days!

I don't know what it is about fire but it has always fascinated me. Give me an excuse for a garden bonfire even now and I'm just a big kid again, raking the ashes together or down on my knees blowing on embers to get them going, rummaging in every corner for more fuel or simply staring into the flames. I remember Dad cautioning me about playing with fire.

"A good servant but a harsh master." He'd said.
There would come a day to remember his words.

It was around this time I think that I joined the scouts although I can't recall what prompted me to do so. The troop I joined was the 14th Epsom (St Josephs) that was affiliated to the Catholic Church so I can only imagine that if I'd begun to show interest in scouting Mum would have wanted it to be a Catholic troop and there wasn't one in Ashtead.

I loved the scout movement. The new friends, new skills, the adventure and fun of camping, cooking outdoors, and being away from home despite an element of homesickness that I managed to hide at the time although others didn't and were mercilessly teased for it.

The troop used to meet in a sort of Nissen hut on a piece of ground backing onto an old and much overgrown orchard along Worple Road in Epsom. Although water was laid on there was no electricity so we had this ancient generator that had to be fired up whenever it was dark enough to need lights. Created from an old army lorry engine and built into a little brick cabin, the 'Jennie' was a contrary old beast to start so I was still quite young when I began to learn the intricacies of flooded carburettors and other things mechanical.

Herbert Rowntree our scout leader was plain bloody marvellous. No spring chicken even when I first met him; Skip, as we had to call him, seemed to have boundless energy. Certainly enough to keep up with us youngsters.

He also had the charisma to inspire us and, when occasion demanded, his other life as a school teacher gave him the presence to keep us under control. It was a brave boy who would speak out of turn or answer back after one of Skip's serious looks.

You won't be surprised that the scouts also provided endless opportunities for pranks of all descriptions, one of the funniest being the doctoring of the scout master's cigarettes.

Skip was a heavy smoker, Players or Senior Service I think and it was his stock of fags that we decided were vulnerable for this prank. I'm sure that when father Mac demonstrated in chemistry class how the touch paper of fireworks was made he never dreamt how inventive this little boy-scout could be.

The process is simple. Paper is soaked in a solution of potassium nitrate and dried out. When lit the treated paper does not burst into flame but fizzes and sparks quite rapidly until the paper is consumed.

Surprising now perhaps, but back in the 50's it was possible to go to a chemist's shop and buy a wide variety of chemicals and it was especially easy if you took along a little jar labelled 'Potassium Nitrate' that clearly came from a toy chemistry set which is precisely what I did.

A few of my father's cigarettes were surreptitiously obtained and duly drizzled with the solution before being dried out under my bed.

At the following week's meeting one of the other boys had agreed to introduce the doctored fags into Skip's pack which was easy because he always left them with his lighter on a chair while he went around checking our knots or any of the other things scoutmasters do.

Halfway through the evening we used to break for cocoa, which was brewed up in a billycan, obviously not over an open fire in the scout hut but over a paraffin Primus stove that had to be pumped up to pressure. Once lit, the stove emitted this wonderful roaring noise that has remained an evocative sound throughout my life.

Usually at this break time we would sit around in a circle on a collection of funny old wonky chairs begged or salvaged from jumble sales over the years, drinking our cocoa while Skip or Pat McGurk the assistant scoutmaster would read stories or bits out of Baden-Powell's Scouting for Boys.

For the four or five of us in the know, when Skip reached for his cigarettes time stood still, as of course we didn't know whether he'd take out one of the doctored ones or not.

Whilst speaking, he slowly extracted a cigarette and then a lifetime seemed to pass as he twiddled it between his fingers while he finished an interminably long sentence before placing it between his lips. We were spellbound as he sparked his lighter into a flame and then, would you believe it put it out again when someone handed him a cup of steaming cocoa.

A few moments later Pat took over speaking so once again Skip struck the lighter and applied it to the cigarette.

Instead of gently smouldering as normal it immediately began to fizz and smoke profusely as it disappeared rapidly into ash almost before Skip could seize it from his lips and cast it onto the floor.

The whole troop fell about in hysterical laughter including Skip who after a moment realised he'd been had and fortunately saw the funny side of it too.

His attitude was that you could laugh at anything so long as no one got hurt and although it was a bit of a close thing at the time, he remembered and laughed about it with us for years and still left his fags lying around.

Scout camps were something I looked forward to enormously and they took place two or three times a year. There was a long camp in the summer holidays – usually a week or even ten days and a couple of short ones over long weekends during the Easter and other school breaks.

I can't imagine for a moment that it would be possible today to go off to camp the way we did then without major infringements of Health and Safety and goodness knows what other regulations.

For example, the transport for the whole troop of about twenty or twenty-five boys was a large removal lorry hired with driver for the day. Loading would usually begin early on departure day and the gear included several large tents that would sleep six or eight; four or five sets of kitchen gear, one for each patrol; a dismantled trek cart; any individual tents for those wanting to sleep solo and a canvas kit-bag for each boy.

Once all this stuff was on board the whole troop basically clambered aboard and settled down on the pile of kit bags. The tail-gate was raised and off we went, sometimes for a distance of 60 or 70 miles, jogging along in the back of the lorry with not a supervising adult or a seat belt between us because Skip and his assistant invariably rode up front with the driver.

One year we went in this fashion all the way to Ireland for two weeks although I think on that occasion it must have been some sort of self-drive hire because there was no driver with the lorry, just one of the parents who shared the driving with Pat. This trip meant a drive down to Fishguard where we got the ferry to Rosslare and then a drive up through County Wexford to Gorey where we camped in the grounds of a monastery. I can't remember how long this journey took but it must have been ages.

I was fourteen or fifteen at this time and leader of the Kestrels Patrol and together with some of the other older boys was up to a trick or two which included prioritising our supply of cigarettes and beer.

At the campsite, the monks from the monastery supplied us with water and milk from their farm but our other supplies had to be arranged from a local grocer called John Cooney whose shop was about a mile away. The monks had arranged an initial supply presumably based on a list provided by Skip in advance but shortly after our arrival, I and another older boy was despatched to the shop with a list of additional requirements plus we had our own list of needs too.

Situated on a crossroad and quite separate from any other buildings the shop was a revelation. Externally it had all the appearance of a small and pretty run-down general store plus there were two ancient hand-operated fuel pumps outside, - one for petrol and the other for paraffin. Inside, the shop was gloomy, smelled of bacon, soap powder and fertilizer and was fitted out with chocolate-brown wall to ceiling shelves all around. There was a post office counter in one corner and another longer counter along one side where Mrs Cooney served the customers.

However, and this was the surprise, at the end of the shop was a door marked 'BAR'. I had never seen the like before and was just so tickled at the idea of this wonderful multi-purpose arrangement.

We asked for John, and Mrs C. showed us through into the bar where there were a few locals supping their Guinness and who I must say were extremely friendly. John Cooney, a shortish quite dapper man in black trousers, white shirt and tie was behind the bar and was not in the least bothered by having two such young customers in front of him that I wondered whether it was the normal run of things

In addition to a range of groceries and confectionery required by all and sundry, our own private list included cigarettes and beer that we did not want to be seen carrying back to camp. To get around the problem we arranged that when John brought the delivery the next day he would give a couple of hoots just before he reached the main camp and we would nip out and collect our contraband. It worked like a dream. We had our illicit goods and no one was any the wiser.

In retrospect I bet Skip did know but so long as none of us came to grief then I think, especially as he was a heavy smoker, that it was a question of 'what the eye doesn't see etc.'.

In the middle weekend of the Irish camp my parents had arranged for Uncle Brian to come from Arklow just a few miles away and collect me to spend a weekend with him. I had to wait in the centre of Gorey town at a given time, which came and went – no Uncle Brian.

Anyway, twenty minutes later this old yellow Skoda came flying in over the bridge at the end of the street, screeched to a halt. I was told to hop in and hang on and in a moment began one of the hairiest drives of my life.

Apologising for being late and looking more at me than the road in front, he explained that being the weekend he was busy in the shop and had found it difficult to get away. However, we arrived very quickly into Arklow where Brian showed me to his optical consulting room. He had arranged a mattress on the floor and made up a bed for me where I was to sleep surrounded by huge coloured images of the insides of the human eye. .It proved to be perfectly comfortable but the eyes were a bit disconcerting especially first thing in the morning.

Anyway, for all his rushing about at first, Brian was a great host, taking me out for nice meals to his favourite local hotel and introducing me, resplendent in my patrol leader's uniform complete with khaki shorts, as his very special nephew over from England. I must admit that I squirm somewhat now when I think about the shorts but I was as proud as Punch at the time.

On the Sunday we spent the whole day together while he drove me around the beautiful Wicklow Hills and to the Vale of Avoca, a very well-known beauty spot immortalised in Thomas Moore's poem 'The Meeting of the Waters'. We also visited the moody Glendalough, a historic monastic site associated with St Kevin.

Brian had a shop assistant called Patricia who had been with him for years and was thought by the family to be his 'intended' or what we would now call his partner although Brian always insisted that there was no such relationship.

Personally I think he must have been daft because it was obvious to me even then that she doted on him and she was extremely attractive so why wouldn't he – if you know what I mean! Maybe it was to do with his earlier attempt to join the priesthood and wanting to maintain the celibacy thing or maybe he just didn't fancy her, although I certainly did.

I might as well conclude Brian's story while I'm about it although it means jumping forward many years.

Brian never did marry and as he grew older became something of a recluse once he no longer kept the shop.

I remember visiting him on a couple of occasions during the years and noticing how over time he gradually descended into that state of disorder and general scruffiness typical of the elderly but just short of squalor which was a real mystery as it was common knowledge that he was worth a small fortune.

An extremely devout Catholic all his life, Brian eventually took himself into a retirement home where he finally died amidst great speculation within the family as to what would become of his believed considerable wealth.

When the will was read it turned out that he'd left £360,000 to the church to have masses said for the repose of his soul. Well I've no idea what the going rate for a mass offering is these days but as one of my catholic cousins quickly calculated, that would have been enough to have a mass said every day for about fifty years. I couldn't help feeling very sad for him and thinking that for someone as devout and steeped in Catholicism as my uncle Brian, this was not exactly a great act of faith. As another cousin commented, *"He'd be better remembered if he'd helped a few of his young relations ease their mortgages."*

Because it relates to Scouts and camp fires and so on, now is probably an appropriate moment to recall my father's cautionary comments about fire.

"Where are you off to?" said Mum as I went to open the back door.
"How did she know I was going anywhere"? I thought.
She was standing at the kitchen sink facing the window into our back garden.
"Always knew she had eyes in the back of her head" I thought

"Out with Ray and Tony"
"Tell me something new." She said, *"But then where will you be?"*
"Oh. Up the park I expect".
"Well. Just be careful over the main road"

It was the late 1950's. I was about thirteen and it was towards the end of the summer holidays. The weather was glorious and seemed to have been so for weeks. On our back lawn the grass had all but disappeared leaving just a brittle beige coloured thatch that exposed veritable chasms in the hard-baked clay soil.

Dad didn't help as he persisted in mowing it weekly more or less regardless of need. Once he got out in the garden he sometimes seemed to be on automatic pilot. Amazingly the grass never surrendered and always came back for more the following year.

Although, as I've described, there were plenty of places to play safely near home, as we grew older we were allowed to venture a little further afield. This included going 'up the park' as we used to say, even though it did mean crossing the main A24 which, even in those days, was quite busy.

The park was in fact Ashtead Park that had originally formed part of the Ashtead Manor estate, the main building of which is now occupied by The City of London Freemen's School. I was delighted to discover recently that the park is now managed as a local wildlife reserve but at the time we used to play there it was very different.

The area had been pretty well neglected for years. A pot-holed stony track ran through the park from the school grounds to an enormous and ornate wrought iron gate that opened onto the main road. This would originally have been the impressive drive leading to the front of the big house.

The park was (and still is) quite wooded including many very ancient oaks, although there were also extensive open grassy areas. There were three ponds, one with an island that we used to get to by building up a causeway of old logs and brushwood. Beside one of the ponds were the remains of an old boathouse but the whole place was so overgrown that it was difficult to imagine how it would have been when originally set out in the 18th century. Spaced out along the track there were also five or six brick and corrugated iron buildings like small Nissen huts that had been built as storage for the anti-aircraft battery stationed there during the war. Two of the old huts and several hollow trees became regular camps.

It was a veritable adventure playground that would, with today's perhaps over-cautious attitudes be seen as potentially hazardous but for us it was heaven and what the hell, we survived although not without incident.

One activity that probably was quite risky, although we didn't see it that way at the time, was playing on the ice when the ponds froze over in winter. I don't know whether winters really were that much colder back then but I can certainly remember the ice being 4 to 6 inches thick during icy spells.

We didn't skate as such (although some posh locals did) but our fun was to create slides that I reckon must have been 70 or 80 feet long and on which we could reach significant speeds. Huge fun.

Tony was out with his parents so on this late summer day Ray and I set off adventuring towards the park and on the way picked up Adrian, another slightly older friend who had a bit of a reputation locally for getting into a variety of scrapes and who, to be honest, my parents were not keen on.

We'd spent probably a couple of hours just messing about and doing what kids do which on this occasion had included puffing on some cigarettes supplied, not surprisingly, by Adrian.

Sitting there in the long dry grass sending puffs of blue smoke into the air and, in my case starting to feel a bit green, we'd got to that dangerous point where, having run off our surplus energy we were at a loose end.
"I know. Let's have a camp fire," said Adrian fetching out his matches.

Ray thought it was a great idea and although a bit less certain I also joined in with gathering up dry grass into a heap.

I said, *"We need to be a bit careful and make a firebreak around it,"*

Being in the scouts I had earned my fire lighting badge, but rubbing sticks together or searching for tinder was not an issue here.

I'd also got my fire-fighting badge. This had involved a session at the local fire station where a display of how dramatically and quickly a fire can develop had made quite an impression.

We'd been taught to use a variety of extinguishers on wood fires, petrol fires and so on but had nearly come to grief when the instructor had been called away briefly. He left us to examine a CTC extinguisher and naturally being kids we couldn't resist giving the pump a couple of squirts and sending streams of this sweet smelling liquid into the air.

Carbon tetrachloride certainly has the ability to put out fires but as the fireman also discovered when he returned to a room full of distinctly groggy boy scouts, it can also put out people. Its use has since been discontinued.
We pulled up more grass in an effort to clear a space around what was by now quite a large heap of the stuff but Adrian didn't want to wait and striking a match stuffed it into the pile.

Whoosh! The grass was so dry it was instantly ablaze and we were forced back by the heat of it and saw to our horror that our feeble attempt at a firebreak had been a complete waste of time.

Vainly and at some risk to ourselves we tried to stamp out the flames as they spread to the surrounding dry grass but it was useless. Already the fire had started to roar. We looked at each other and ran.

Out of the park we ran and back over the road, scarcely slowing to even check for traffic. Adrian disappeared into his own house as we passed but Ray and I ran on. Looking back we could see a large pall of dark smoke billowing like an enormous mushroom high above the trees in the park. We were terrified.

Back at home we didn't dare tell our parents. Both nearly in tears we fled into my back garden but even from here we could see the wretched smoke. We needed to hide. There was an old chicken house in our garden, disused for some time it was perfect and we dived inside.

We sat there for what seemed like an age, trembling and speechless and then we heard the bells. It sounded as though there was a convoy of fire engines coming along the main road their bells clanging urgently as they approached the park.

By now we could hear my parents in the garden where they had come out to stare at the huge dark cloud of smoke spreading over the area. We could hear them talking to neighbours including Ray's dad.

A few moments later we heard Ray's mother who had just come back from Ashtead village on the bus. *"Peter there's a terrible fire up the park and seven or eight fire engines. Are the boys back?" "I don't know,"* he said. *"I haven't seen them"*
Then my mother was saying, *"Frank. Have you seen Brian?"*
I looked at Ray and said, *"We've got to go and tell them we're back."*
"Ok" he said, *"Back, yes. But nothing else or they'll kill me".*

If there were Oscars for wide-eyed innocence we'd have been first in line as we emerged from the chicken house.

"Did you call?" we said more or less in unison.

A couple of weeks later I was in the garden when Dad was chatting with Ray's father over the fence and I heard them talking about the fire. Peter Harris was telling my dad how he'd also set off a grass fire when he was a kid.

"Trouble was," he said. *"The common we set fire to was on top of a hill and wherever we ran we couldn't get away from the sight of it. Never did tell my parents. They'd have murdered me. But it taught me a lesson."*

"Me too." I thought

The more I think about that time of my young life the more terrible stunts I remember. It's embarrassing really.

One of my best friends both in and out of school was Nicky Hunt. Yes, he of the revolting cigarettes. We got up to all sorts of daft capers and I'm reminded of another thing we did which you certainly couldn't today, without falling foul of the dreaded 'health and safety' rules. Also because as I understand it, kids in school are not taught in such detail as we were about such things as gunpowder!

Probably just as well actually, but back then our science teachers really loved to bring the lessons to life. So this was how we came to know how to set things on fire with a magnifying glass, get coal gas to explode, make stink bombs and the proportions in which to mix sulphur, charcoal and saltpetre to make a version of gunpowder.

We'd also learnt that if you mixed a few grains of sodium chlorate with a little sugar and gave it a clout it too would explode.

Despite the fact that terrorists have been using chlorate weedkiller as an explosive ingredient for years, it is really only in the relatively recent past that its sale has been prohibited and as I said before, sulphur, charcoal and potassium nitrate were standard chemistry set ingredients.

Nicky and I had this sort of mini laboratory set up in his bedroom where we would grind and mix these things – it really is a wonder we didn't blow his house up.

Not far from where he lived there were the ruins of an old convent that had been bombed in the war. Not intentionally I'm sure but German bombers facing heavy flak over London would regularly turn tail and jettison their bombs over Surrey and Sussex.

These random bombings were often harmless but sometimes had serious results as in this case destroying the old St Andrews convent between Ashtead and Leatherhead. However, a few years later the site was well overgrown and very popular as a playground for us local kids.

Our theory was that if a few grains of the chlorate mix struck with a hammer would go off with a sharp crack, dropping a heavy rock from a good height onto a pile of the stuff should be very interesting!!

We'd found a location amongst the ruins where a large square coping stone that measured about two feet or more square was lying on the ground below a wall that was some six or eight feet high. Placing a small pile of our mixture – probably no more than an egg cupful, in the centre of the stone we clambered up onto the wall with a large brick – well more like half a breezeblock really. It took us both to manhandle it up there and hold it out far enough to be sure it would drop squarely on target.

I don't actually recall dropping it, just the explosion and the thump with which I landed on my back several feet away from the wall. I don't really remember what we said but probably something beginning with F and ending in 'hell' before we scrambled to our feet and ran around the wall to inspect our results, which was when it actually dawned on us, how daft and incredibly lucky we'd been.

The big coping stone, which was about two or three inches thick in the centre was shattered into about five large pieces but in the centre there was just a hole where hardly any fragment remained and of the rock we'd dropped there was no trace.. I always did like the practical sessions in school chemistry classes but I certainly think we went a bit far on that occasion.

So if our somewhat excessive enthusiasm for chemistry can be indirectly laid at the door of Father Mac then it was Peter Boulding our physics master who first got us into electricity.

He'd been explaining how by striking an electric spark between two carbon rods they could be drawn apart to produce a continuous spark or arc. Rather like a controlled lighting flash, this was one way in which the bright light of searchlights was created.

To be fair, when he did it in the class he had made us all use very dark eye protectors so I guess that was something, but not once did he say "Don't try this at home."

Well as you might imagine this experiment was one that rose fairly quickly to the top of our home laboratory list of things to have a go at. Big Mistake! Because there was another fact that either he hadn't mentioned or more likely that we hadn't registered and that was the fact that he was definitely not using the mains. I know now of course that DC electricity is required and that the school had a transformer that could produce high voltage DC for a short time from a car battery.

So there we were this evening in Nick's bedroom with two pairs of insulated pliers holding a couple of carbon rods extracted from an old cycle lamp battery.

We knew we had to be very careful and with extreme care we had connected each of these rods to one side of the domestic mains supply. So with Nicky holding one rod and me the other we very gradually brought the two together. Well in the same way that I didn't remember dropping the brick, I didn't remember touching the two rods, only the flash, another loud bang and then darkness.

Not only had we blown all the lights in the house, but also all the power was down in Nicky's street and several neighbouring ones. Obviously we weren't able to avoid responsibility for this stunt but I think Nicky's mother and the electricity people were more concerned that we were still alive than they were with giving us too much of a hard time. In my case as I was some distance from home my parents never found out about that one.

It would be unfair to put more than a half share of the blame for those two episodes onto Nicky but there was one occasion where his suspicious actions almost landed both my dad and me in court although ignorance of the law on all our parts was the main problem.

Dad had been clearing out an old coal shed behind the shop where he worked when he'd found the remains of an antique gun. It was part of an old rook rifle – just the action and trigger assembly minus both the barrel and stock and the whole thing was solid with rust. He brought it home and gave it to me.

I headed off to his shed where with a fair amount of sandpaper and elbow grease I cleaned the thing up but the internal mechanism was rusted solid and it was clearly never going to be anything other than a curiosity.

A few days later I tired of the thing and gave it to Nicky who was carrying it home when he saw a policeman. He must have had some vague idea that he should not have had it because he ducked smartly into a hedge to await the copper's disappearance.

After a few minutes he peered out to check all was clear only to be smartly collared by the police officer, who had likewise been waiting for Nicky to reappear.

Well, after a few questions the policeman elicited where Nicky had got the thing and sent him on his way with the promise of a summons. Later that evening the strong arm of the law arrived on our doorstep to tell both my father and I that we would be summoned for unlawful possession of a firearm – because any component part (working of not) is treated in law as a whole firearm

Dad, who had never had any sort of brush with the law, was devastated and set off to the police station where he explained the full circumstances; our collective ignorance of the law on the subject and the fact that in all seriousness this rusting relic could hardly have posed any sort of threat to public safety. Fortunately the Inspector took my father's view and shelved the matter urging a bit more caution all round in the future.

I used to spend a lot of time up at Nicky's house where the whole set-up was so completely different to my own home that I found it fascinating. Plus, Nicky had three older sisters, which in itself was a bit of a draw but his mother was the real star turn.

Mrs Hunt was very 'horsey' in that she had several horses, gave riding lessons and pretty well lived and breathed everything about them. She was really a bit eccentric which meant different in terms of both appearance – large with wild hair and clothes and none too clean; and attitude – she swore a bit and was very much inclined to call a spade 'a bloody shovel' or worse. However she was clearly a woman of some breeding to judge by her accent and some of the local people she knew.

Life in that house was certainly unpredictable. I remember one day being invited to stay for tea and we were sitting at the table where after some sandwiches a plate of cream puff cakes appeared.

Nicky took one and then just as he was gingerly attempting to take a bite his mum reached out and pushed the whole thing into his face where it spread out explosively just like the slap-stick custard pies used by circus clowns. She then nearly fell of the chair laughing. Nicky got really cross and I just didn't know what to do or think.

Nick went off to get cleaned up when suddenly there was a loud clattering noise from the hall.

The dining room door opened and one of Nick's sisters came in leading a horse which she brought past the table and out through the French doors into the garden that had been fenced off into a couple of small paddocks. I sat there open mouthed.

Confirmation that horses indoors wasn't that unusual came a couple of years later. Mrs Hunt used to buy groceries from Dad's shop and had said that if there was no reply at the house the van driver should just leave the delivery in the kitchen.

One day I remember Bill, the shop's driver, coming back to the shop in a real lather. Doing precisely what he'd been told, he'd opened the kitchen door at Nicky's house then was struggling inside with the heavy box where he came face to face with a horse. Apparently it was just standing there in the kitchen as if it was the most normal thing in the world and that he was the intruder.

I had another friend called Barry whose family were a bit outside my normal range of experience too. They were very posh or at least Barry's mum used to think she was. To me they were posh because they lived in a large house on Craddocks Avenue which was a world away from our small council house semi.

They certainly had a very nice car – a Jaguar Mk IX, and apart from the fact that it really looked expensive it had the coolest violet coloured dashboard lights which really impressed me (not, as I've said before that we talked about things being cool then). So when I was invited to join the family on a trip to the coast one weekend I was like a dog with two tails all week. The only trouble was the damn thing went and got a puncture on the way back and we ended up having to push it up the A29 and into a lay-by to change the wheel. Once that was done and we resumed our journey it was almost dark so at least I could enjoy those violet panel lights all the more. Funny isn't it the things that we remember.

Even at my relatively young age I did think it was taking 'poshness' a bit too far when Barry's mum used to get her husband to light up a cigar and walk around the house a bit before visitors arrived, just to get the affluent aroma of cigar smoke through the rooms.

In some ways my friends' parents were better value in the entertainment and interest stakes than my friends. This was certainly the case with Mrs McKye, art teacher mother of my friend Terry.

We all loved it around at her house because there were just no rules or at least none that we'd come close to breaking.

Mrs Mac as we called her was something of a hippy and as such a bit before her time. She wore floaty loose black dresses and had long grey hair that was either gathered into a loose and wispy bun or simply allowed to flow out behind her as she moved. She was so laid back as to be almost horizontal. She taught art in a local girls' school and I believe she did some private home-based tuition too.

There were no restrictions round at Mrs Mac's so we all gathered there to listen to music, smoke and use whatever language we liked within reason and that was self-imposed because I never did hear her tell anyone off.

Among the art work around the house was a bust – a nude self-portrait she had fashioned in black. Its nakedness initially caused a certain amount of sniggering among us teenage boys especially when seeing our interest she would caress the breasts and say, *"You boys like this don't you."* And we'd all snigger some more.

One day, there were some adult visitors to the house, possibly parents of a student or potential student. Mrs Mac showed them into the front room where we were all sprawled out listening to music. Next thing, she strolls over to the mantel piece and the aforementioned bust and announces to the guests *"The boys love this. They like to stroke my tits."* And with that she waltzes out of the room saying. *"Who'd like some tea?"* She just loved to shock.

I was still in the scouts at this time and the year following the Irish trip we went off to camp on a site at Pinhay near Lyme Regis.

By now I was dead keen on motorbikes so when the other assistant scout leader Vince Collins said he was going down on his bike and did anyone want to ride with him, I was first in line. I would regret it.

Vince had a virtually new DKW, a 200cc machine made by the German Auto-Union Company. Well, there was nothing wrong with the bike. It was fine and I was thrilled and enjoyed the experience for the first few miles.

However, 150 miles is a long way, especially perched on a small pillion seat and it seemed even further when the rain began. I don't know how many hours it took us to get there but it seemed like forever until we finally arrived at the site where Pinhay House and estate enjoy a superb cliff-top location a couple of miles beyond Lyme Regis.

Once the feeling began to return to my numb backside I started to feel more positive and set about organising my patrol in setting up our corner of the camp.

This meant unloading our large ridge tent from the lorry along with our patrol's share of the troop's cooking equipment and manhandling it between the eight or ten of us to our selected position on the site. Once the tent was pitched, because the site had a slight slope to it we had to dig a small trench around the tent on the uphill side to divert any rainwater past the tent thus ensuring we were all dry inside.

I can't honestly recall the situation with toilets at Pinhay but am inclined to think that being a well-established site there were probably some facilities already set up albeit pretty basic.

Sometimes however when we went to camp we had to dig our own latrines, which was when you really hoped for some soft ground. Ideally set well apart from the main camp area the latrine trench could be up to eight or ten feet long depending on the number of boys in the patrol and the duration of the stay. It also had to be about a foot to eighteen inches wide and about three feet deep. The whole thing was then enclosed by sheets of hessian sacking fixed to four corner posts and overlapping at the point of entry to provide a level of privacy.

At its most primitive that was it and in use one had to cast trousers and pants to one side and straddle the trench to do the business so to speak. A well-made latrine can work very well in dry weather especially if users are careful to toss in the required amount of earth after use.

However, having no roof covering, in bad weather going to the loo could require a great deal of courage, not just to face the muddy, slippery experience but to avoid literally ending up in deep doo-doo.

Over the years in the scouts I saw a number of attempts to improve the experience which ranged from poles to perch on, poles to lean on, a combination of the two and best of all was a large box designed to cover the entire excavation with six toilet seats set in the top.

I must say I thought that was taking togetherness a bit too far although I have seen precisely that arrangement in old Roman latrines in Pompeii. Perhaps we are just a bit too precious about bodily functions these days.

The tents slept six or seven boys lying across their width like a row of little sardines, plus two more length-wise down one side at the feet of all the others. This was the less desirable location and invariably fell to the weakest, youngest or less assertive members of the patrol and it's true to say that a certain amount of bullying took place over the issue of sleeping places.

One of the boys had brought his own small one-man bivouac tent and had thereby set himself apart from the rest. Well he was probably more comfortable in that he had his own space but his individuality brought its own consequences. Whenever anyone needed to go out for a pee in the night, the single tent provided the main target so I only hope it was thoroughly waterproof.

The Pinhay camp turned out to be a distinctly salutary experience in my young life and marked a significant watershed in my relationship with the scouts and Skip in particular.

I must have been just sixteen and had somehow managed to persuade my parents to allow me to go away with a friend on another holiday after scout camp.

The idea was that they would come down and collect me and my friend Peter from Lyme Regis a few days early in order that I could go with him to Butlins Holiday Camp at Clacton. So the last thing I needed was anything to spoil that hard won plan.

After about a week at Pinhay, together with Peter who was also a Patrol Leader and about six other boys I went off into Lyme Regis for the afternoon. It was only a couple of miles away through the fields and along the coastal path. After doing some shopping and general sight-seeing in the town we were heading back when there was a general consensus that a drink would be nice, but by that time we were some way from the soft drinks of the sea-front.

Someone suggested that we could go to a pub if we could find one somewhere in the back streets and after a few minutes we did. We all bought soft drinks and being in our uniforms soon attracted the attention of some of the locals who clearly thought it would be fun to introduce us to the local scrumpy cider.

My God what a mistake that turned out to be. The stuff was so damned drinkable and in no time at all we'd all drunk a pint or two each. Although we could feel it going to our heads a bit, it didn't immediately make a significant impact, until, that is, we came to leave and went outside into the air.

Several of the boys were immediately sick. They were the lucky ones because the rest of us, including me, who managed to keep it down, rapidly became exceedingly drunk and extremely silly. In this state we tottered off across the fields working our way through a repertoire of exceedingly vulgar rugby songs

When we eventually arrived back at camp the nonsense didn't stop and with me in the lead we apparently settled down in a corner and continued with the singing which very quickly bought the leader running. Our little gathering was instantly dispersed and I who was undoubtedly the ringleader was told in no uncertain terms that the next morning I could pack my bags and leave the camp forthwith. I had never seen him so angry.

Skip told me I had disgraced the troop, the scout movement and myself and that he never wanted to see me back at the scout hut again. The following morning with my first ever and the godfather of all hangovers the awful impact dawned on me that this was surely going to put paid to my Butlins trip. Fortunately for Peter, he was one of those who had been sick and was not seen as so blameworthy.

However, to present a front of solidarity with me he announced that if I had to leave he would go too and then incredibly one of the other older lads said the same as well. However, Skip was not about to back down so calls were made to our respective parents advising them of the train we would be on and we were ferried in the truck to the station.

As you might imagine it was not a happy homecoming. Dad was pretty angry although I think it was more that he felt I'd let my parents down. Mum however, was literally incandescent and couldn't bring herself to speak to me and in fact didn't speak to me at all for about a month.

From the conversations between them I was party to, I gathered that Mum's anger was much more to do with her and the shame I'd apparently brought on her with her friends at work, many of whom, as I've said, also had kids in the same scout troop. Of course the initial reaction was to put a full stop to the Butlins plan but after much pleading and apologising from me Dad eventually made the decision that it would be better for me to go than waste the money they'd already paid on the trip.

I was left in no doubt that I was expected to behave myself and so with severe warnings ringing in my ears and much relief, a few days later Peter and I set off by steam train from London to Clacton on Sea and the wonderful world of Mr Billy Butlin.

It may have been the aftershock of the Pinhay experience or more likely the extremely explicit warning from my father as to our behaviour that kept us on the (relatively) straight and narrow during the following week at Butlins. I also think perhaps that whilst Peter and I were among the older boys in the context of the 14th Epsom scout troop and therefore looked up to by the younger ones, here the absolute opposite was the case and our confidence level suffered something of a setback, at least for the first few days.

Looking back on it now, I find it hard to believe how lax arrangements were in the holiday camp. And I can very well understand how they came to get the reputation they did for booze, sex and rock and roll (drugs not having come to the fore at that time). For example, Peter and I were clearly not over 18, but were readily served with alcohol; in fact it was here that I discovered "Poor Man's Black Velvet" which at that time was the drink of choice for the teenagers.

Apparently, the original Black Velvet was a beer cocktail created in 1861 by the bartender at Brooks Club in London. Intended to mark the death of Prince Albert, it consisted of a dark stout beer cleverly layered in a tall flute with champagne so that the two did not mix. Nowadays (if it is ever drunk these days) it would be champagne and Guinness but in our case the poor man's version was stout and cider and never mind the layering nonsense.

Days were mostly spent posing around the pool or playing fruit machines in the arcades and of course dancing in the ballroom during the evenings. However, after 'lights out' (which meant that most people were expected to be back in their chalets and tucked up by around midnight); it was hilarious. Far from being tucked up there was more scampering about on the landings between chalets than during daylight hours. I remember the comedian Jasper Carrot talking about the Butlins experience and the security guards that patrolled at night.

Security guard pausing outside a chalet door, "Have you got a woman in there?"
Tremulous voice from inside "Er. No."
Security Guard, "Hang on. I'll get you one."

By the end of the week Peter and I had made up some ground and if not exactly out in front in the Casanova stakes we had regained a lot of confidence and managed to get a few dances in the evenings that led to some sweaty clinches but not a lot more if the truth be told.

So that was it really, lots of beer and cigarettes, dancing and a bit of inconsequential groping and the week was over, but at least this time we were going home on our terms with the first step of adolescent independence behind us.

I am the cool (not) guy on the right. And 'No' despite my best efforts I did not get the girl.

Chapter 8 - Family Life

Whilst I've been banging on about my fairly idiotic teenage escapades, it occurs to me that I've hardly mentioned my family and the life I shared with them at all.

I guess that in creating a memoir the inclination is to recount the highs and lows, the hilarious and the disastrous and overlook the days when not a lot happened. When; if you were fortunate as I was; everything was delightfully, boringly, happily normal.

The bottom line is that I was wonderfully fortunate to have, (with the exception of the odd hiatus usually created by me) a happy and tranquil family home. My parents were happily married, we were well housed and relatively speaking we were quite well off with Dad now in management and Mum back at work part-time.

My sister Angela and I got on pretty well for the most part and we both had our own circle of friends of whom we took very little notice until around the age of fourteen or so I started to take more than a childish interest in some in some of Angela's friends and she in mine.

Unlike some of my friends who were never able to go away on holiday, we could; and although they were never particularly extravagant I have very happy memories of holidays spent simply as a family. I can only remember a couple of holidays before we had the first car and they were to Littlehampton and Bognor Regis. (The Regis suffix said to have been bestowed by King George V following a period of convalescence in the area).

For Littlehampton we travelled by train down to the coast where my parents had arranged to rent a small wooden chalet close to the beach on the other side of the river from the town. I doubt we could have afforded a taxi so I imagine that Dad and Mum between them would have walked with the cases and us kids in tow across the swing bridge from the railway over the river Arun to the west beach.

Days there were spent happily on the beach and among the sand dunes where Dad would build us 'dug-out' camps fashioned from a few planks of drift wood and the odd sheet of old corrugated iron found abandoned behind the beach.

We always had the little methylated spirit stove sheltered from the wind in a biscuit tin where Mum would boil up a kettle for tea while Dad played ball with us on the beach or paddled along the shallows keeping an eye on us.

Dad never could actually swim. He could float for hours on his back but if he turned over he sank like a stone and of course Mum never exposed herself at all owing to her scarred arm.

In Bognor we stayed in a caravan but as the site was some distance from the beach the daily ritual of getting ourselves and all the beach kit organised became a bit of a drag.

It's curious how things stick in your memory. The huge grey gasometer near the caravan site remained there for years after we ceased visiting (may still be for all I know). So whenever as an adult I found myself driving through Bognor, the sight of the old gasometer instantly recalled those treks to the beach and I was rather inclined to the expression attributed rightly or wrongly to King George V – "Bugger Bognor".

Once we had the car, holidays became far more adventurous affairs and as Dad loved driving, trips to the West Country, Yorkshire, East Anglia and the Isle of Wight began to feature in our summer getaways. I remember going one year to the Isle of Wight where we stayed at a caravan site near Bembridge.

As well as the usual shop on the site there was also the club house. Every evening some sort of entertainment would be mounted and whole families including small children could go along and spend a convivial evening with a few drinks, some dancing and a bit of a sing-song. Around this time rock and roll was the big thing and I recall I had this really naff jumper. It was black with pale blue shoulders and a white band across the chest with bars and musical notes embroidered all over. I thought it was just so smart.

Angela and I had worked out a really great jive routine and so on these club evening we became something of a star turn. Me with my now trademark jumper, and Angie in her swirling dress as we rocked and twisted the evenings away. I think we may even have won a prize or two as the best dancers.

Mum and Dad in Anglesey

One year we went to Anglesey in North Wales and it wasn't just the journey that was adventurous. I had persuaded my parents it would be a good idea to camp and had borrowed a huge ridge tent from the scouts. Now these are nothing like the modern family sized tents that very nearly erect themselves. No this was an army surplus khaki canvas monster with poles almost 3 inches thick. We even had camp beds so Mum and Dad wouldn't have to sleep on the ground but one night was all we lasted.

It could not have rained harder if we'd ordered it specially and with the wind as well it was all too much for Mum who had been lukewarm about the idea from the start. "*Not another night*" she said and with that we went off and found a caravan in a nearby site. However we did erect the tent again for Angela and me to sleep in.

Anglesey has a particular significance for me though in that it provided the location for my first romantic kiss.

A couple of days after settling into the site I met this really pretty little girl from Liverpool and we palled up innocently enough to begin with for ball games, bathing and then walks along the cliffs which was where while we were sitting looking out to sea that she suddenly kissed me.

I was star-struck and instantly in love. The rest of the fortnight seemed to pass by in a sort of rose tinted haze and we spent all our time together until sadly both families had to go their separate ways. I'm just so sorry I cannot now recall her name but the Childwall area of Liverpool is permanently etched on my memory.

Another year we went to Ireland and did the tour of all Mum's brothers and their families. This was the time we went to stay at my Uncle Jimmy's guesthouse in Bray.

Jimmy was drinking fairly heavily then and I remember being quite scandalised by the way it seemed perfectly normal over there for everyone to come out of Mass on a Sunday and straight into the pub to get a 'skinful'. I was still a very religious little boy then.

After doing the rounds of the relatives in the south we headed up to Ulster and my Uncle Charlie's farm near Dungannon where Mum was originally born. They gave us such a welcome and I was introduced to Charlie's five daughters – my cousins.

My sister Angela with our five cousins on the farm in Northern Ireland

In anticipation of our arrival they had planned a ceilidh (dance party) and had the big barn all cleared out and set up for dancing with straw bale seats all around. There was even a doorman whose role (although I didn't know it at the time) was to keep an eye out for the police, as most of the drink being consumed was the illegally home-produced poitin (pronounced potchin).

Mum with her brother Charlie

Another year we went by air to Jersey. This was a real first for the rest of the family although not for me as I'd been by air previously on a school pilgrimage to Lourdes. On that occasion we flew from Blackbushe airport in an old unpressurised Douglas DC8 with doors that fitted so loosely you could see down to the ground. No wonder I was airsick. However, I did get my fevered brow stroked and gently soothed by a rather delicious stewardess that made all my mates as jealous as hell.

The Jersey trip was by Vickers Viscount, which was a relatively new aircraft at that time, and got Dad quite excited as he tried to explain to me the principle of the turbo-prop engine being a cross between a jet and the old fashioned propeller driven plane. We flew from the old Art Deco 'Beehive' building at Gatwick, which accommodated both the air traffic control and the terminal from 1936 until the modern day Gatwick began to be constructed in the 1950's including a new control tower which itself has since been superseded by today's lofty structure.

The Beehive is now a listed building and is apparently still considered an internationally important example of early airport terminal design.

In Jersey our destination was a holiday camp that comprised numerous individual chalets built around a central clubhouse and dining/ball room. The whole complex was spread over a hillside above the cliffs overlooking beautiful Portelet Bay with its island and tower connected to the beach by a causeway at low water but totally cut-off at high tide. The semi-circular bay was a perfect suntrap and there were daily warnings advising caution because with the light reflecting off the granite cliffs the beach really was like being in an oven.

It was here that I finally learnt to swim. I had been splashing about all week with a rubber ring and Dad had been trying to help by supporting me in the shallows. However, the day before we came home I was clambering about on the rocks above some quite deep rock pools when I missed my footing and fell in. I was completely out of my depth and there was no one around to help so I simply had to swim, which I did sufficiently to get myself out of the water. Fortunately, far from unnerving me, the experience proved I could do it and over the rest of the summer in the local pool at home I became quite confident and from then on was always happy and confident in the water, - a bit of a show-off even.

The only other foreign holiday that I went on with my parents was to Italy when I was about sixteen I think, in the summer before I started work. We went by train – certainly not a TGV – down through France overnight, then through the Swiss Alps where we stopped at Basle to change the engine. It was dark and misty in the early morning and I remember thinking how like a scene from a black and white spy movie it all seemed. Not at all like a train full of holidaymakers chartered by Thomas Cooke.

Arriving at last in Milan we changed to a local train for our final destination that was Pesaro near Rimini on the Adriatic coast. It was the first time any of us had experienced a beach holiday with such style or such a smart hotel and the sound of the lyrical Italian language being spoken all around made it seem so exotic.

It was also my first introduction to the wonderful world of ancient civilisations when we went to visit the amazing buildings and mosaics of Ravenna.

In Pesaro Dad and I went to get an Italian haircut and what a different experience that was compared to Charlie our regular 'short back and sides' barber in Leatherhead. I recall the thing that impressed me most, apart from his apparently casual use of the fearsome cut-throat razor, was the way the barber actually looked to see he was trimming our sideburns to precisely the same level. Now that was professionalism.

With Dad on the beach at Pesaro

Following the Lyme Regis debacle I really believed that my scouting days were over so was surprised when after a few months Vince Collins, the assistant leader that I'd travelled to Dorset with came to see me.

He explained that he was going to start a Senior Scout troop. He said that clearly the previous drinking episode was a mistake on my part and he would be pleased to forget all about it if I'd like to join the Seniors.

Truth to tell, it was probably as much about getting the numbers up as anything else but I was happy to get back into scouting again.

Sometime later someone gave the senior troop an old motorcycle combination. It was a former military machine, a 1949 Norton 500cc single cylinder and the idea Vince had in accepting it was that its restoration could become an interesting and educational group project. I learnt recently at a vintage vehicle gathering that the old Norton would now be worth £10 – 15,000. Sadly it's long gone. Such is life.

Well, as you might imagine everyone was keen as mustard to get stuck in and dismantle the old thing, whilst learning in the process a good deal about how engines work. However, there was a significant enthusiasm failure when the time came to put their hands in their pockets (in reality their parents' pockets) and come up with some money to buy the necessary spare parts before the rebuilding could begin.

The project stalled and for other reasons too it was soon apparent that the senior troop didn't have the numbers to remain viable so reluctantly the decision was made to wind it up.

This left the problem of the old motorbike so when Vince said, *"Look Brian, You've put most into this project why don't you have the bike."* I jumped at the chance.

So that's how I found myself the owner of the Norton, which in reality, consisted of no more than a frame, an engine and several boxes of miscellaneous bits and pieces. It certainly didn't look anything like a valuable gem of auto history. Auto-jumble, yes.

I was still very keen though, and as I had been given the old bike for nothing I was convinced that I was on a free lunch. In reality, Vince was almost certainly delighted to have off-loaded the pile of junk onto such a willing and gullible recipient. This, at least is how my Dad saw it, and as I learnt over the years he was right more often than he was wrong.

To be fair, my parents weren't against me taking it on but were more concerned with where it would go whilst I pursued the restoration. My father was actually quite keen having been a motorcyclist himself and so suggested that together we build a shed to house the bike and carry out the work. So Dad and I built the shed and in the process I learnt the basics of carpentry, awakening another life-long interest that has served me extremely well.

One sees things so much more clearly with the benefit of hindsight. It's only when I look back that I realise what a huge influence my father was. And how so many of the things that I can do and now take so much for granted I owe to him and the interest he took in me in those early years. That's real parenting and he certainly didn't have to go to classes to learn it. Interesting how things change isn't it.

Another really strong memory I have of family life at home in Ashtead is around Christmas and that most basic of festive detail – the turkey.

Because of the family connection with the farm at Coolmaghery in Northern Ireland there was a long standing tradition of uncle Charlie sending turkeys to his brothers and sisters including those in England.

As a consequence, in the week or so before Christmas my sister and I would be forever at the front window looking out for the Carter Paterson lorry.

Long before 'white van man' arrived in his various guises the Carter Paterson company had existed as one of Britain's premier road haulage firms since the 1860's. If I recall correctly their lorries were all finished in an olive green livery and most had canvas tilts with kind of drop-down canvas curtain across the back.

When the lorry finally arrived there would invariably be a driver and mate. Then the driver would hop up behind the canvas curtain and appear a few moments later to hand the turkey down to his mate. I've no idea why these things stick in my mind but I can so clearly remember the mate striding down our front path clutching the hessian clad turkey by its poor dead legs while its poor dead head hung out the other end with congealed blood on its beak and unseeing eyes.

Now clearly this was not the sanitized, oven-ready shrink-wrapped Christmas turkey of today. Far from it. These where complete in every respect. Heads, feet, feathers innards, the lot. So it was a great blessing that Dad had the history he did in the grocery trade that enabled him to do the necessary which of course my sister and I observed with great fascination and a good deal of nose holding when it came to removing the smelly entrails.

Mum and Dad always threw a family party around Christmas time that over the years also became something of a tradition. The gatherings included any relatives that could come, some of the neighbours and usually two or three of Mums friends from the hospital and their husbands. Angela and I were also allowed to invite a few friends as well so it wouldn't have been unusual for 20 or 30 people to be crammed in to our house.

Fortunately the two connected living rooms lent themselves perfectly to such a gathering. With all the larger furniture pushed back to the wall and as many extra chairs as possible added it was usually possible to seat most people and leave some space in the centre for circulation or dancing.

In the back room Mum used to extend the dining table along one end of the room and then load it with all the Christmas food. This included platters of cold meat, sandwiches, cheese straws, vol-au-vents, mince pies, trifles and jelly and of course her home made Christmas cake iced by Dad (just another little skill picked up somewhere along the way).

My great pleasure and privilege was being allowed to be barman for the evening. My family were never great drinkers so the first thing to do was to get out the bottles of gin and whiskey that had probably not seen the light of day since being put away after last year's party.

I would put a plastic cloth over the sideboard before setting it out with rows of glasses according to their size and purpose then adding the drinks. New bottles of various spirits, martinis, port, vodka and brandy were set up at the back like generals while in front the other ranks of Babycham, tonic and dry ginger took their places. There was always a place left at each end for a soda siphon while all the bottled beers were stacked on the floor.

An insulated plastic container for ice cubes in the shape of a pineapple took its place beside a dish of sliced lemon, the bottle opener and a corkscrew; although in those days we were more a beer and spirits gathering than wine drinkers. This was my domain for the evening (or at least until the party got going and I lost interest) and so even here and at quite a young age my parents were introducing me to the way things are done so that later in life I never felt socially ill-at-ease due to ignorance of such matters.

Christmas Party – Bramley Way 1960

I recall that one year Dad bought a wooden keg of beer that had to be set up a couple of days in advance and how he decorated the round end of the barrel with a white beard and red hat to look like Father Christmas. He even added a twist of cotton wool to the tap so that it looked like he was smoking a pipe.

Mum was by nature very sociable and had made many friends through her work at the hospital and through the church both of which provided the opportunity for seasonal social events.

Around Christmas there was always a parish dance at the Peace Memorial Hall in Ashtead village. Certainly not a riotous affair but great fun and good education for Angela and I. It was here and at similar events in the hospital that Angela and I learnt by example from Mum and Dad how to behave socially and how to dance a little too.

Mum would help me with the first tentative steps of leading her in a waltz or foxtrot while Angela learnt the same by standing on Dad's feet as he whisked her around the floor

If as you read this you think *"Well what a lucky devil he was."* you'd be absolutely right. We were indeed very fortunate. Much more so than many others. However, because it was all so good I believe I simply assumed many years later that all I had to do was follow my father's example and I too would have the perfect marriage and live happily ever after. You'll have to wait and see if I was right.

Me with Angela and friends Piers Connor and Nicky Hunt (right)

Chapter 9 – Girls

Following the little holiday romance in Anglesey it had started to dawn on me that there was more to girls than met the eye although it was probably what did actually meet the eye that mainly attracted my interest.

This was apparently true of my mates too as it was noticeable that the gangs of boys I was familiar with had gradually morphed into mixed groups of friends who used to hang around, or 'hang out' as they say today, on our estate.

Inevitably this was when little romances began to develop and the first tentative explorations of sexuality took place. This might have been public 'snogging for a dare' or something a little more intimate and clandestine which is exactly where I came to grief.

I'd had this little 'thing' going with one of the girls for a while and on this occasion we had disappeared together into one of the partly built houses to pursue our romancing. To my great joy inside the house we came across this pile of what in the gloom seemed to be wonderfully soft mattresses into which we sank.

All was going fine and I must say she was slightly ahead on points, which kept me distracted for some time. However after a while we both became aware of severe itching in some seriously uncomfortable places caused, we discovered, by the fact that our soft bed was in fact a pile of fibreglass insulation material. With our ardour substantially cooled we abandoned the house and headed off for a bath, a change of clothes and a lesson well learnt that things are not always what they at first appear.

I always reckoned the church youth club had a lot to answer for with regard to my emerging sexuality although I'm not sure that Father Maxwell, the then parish priest at St Michael's, would have wanted to think of it that way. The club was held in the presbytery on Friday evenings and I imagine his main motive in setting it up was a pragmatic solution to a potentially problematic situation. Without a controlled venue in which to gather, the local adolescents were going to gather anyway without any adult presence and get on with doing what comes naturally.

So by providing a venue with space (the two downstairs rooms in his house) to dance, drink soft drinks and generally socialise he would be meeting a need and ensure that for Friday evenings at least we were not led into temptation. Well, that was the theory and basically it worked quite well.

Father Maxwell himself had the good sense to realise that his continued presence would probably be too much of a damper. So he managed to delegate the general supervision of the club to a spinster of the parish whose face comes readily to mind but whose name I can't for the life of me remember. It's a shame because she deserves the credit for doing a sterling job in walking the required line between understanding the need for a certain amount of teenage canoodling and ensuring on the other hand that things never went too far to be acceptable given that we were after all on church premises.

There were times however when things developed into a bit of a pantomime.

Of the two rooms, the larger was kept for dancing whilst in the other there was table tennis and refreshments and general gathering space. Now all the while the music was up-beat she had no problem but as soon as there was a smoochy ballad someone was bound to switch the lights off and Miss 'Whatever her name' had to casually amble round and turn them on again only for the switch to be flipped off again as soon as her back was turned. And so it went on. I kid you not; to anyone standing outside the house there were times when it looked as though we were running Morse code classes rather than a youth club.

Fourteen is a funny age. You have all these strange feelings that swing between elation and depression, supreme confidence and a complete lack of the same. You can go between being a complete pain in the backside and the perfect child in moments and the trouble is you know you're doing it, how it hurts people and you do it anyway. As my dad used to say, "Not a man nor yet a boy."

He seemed to understand which was just as well a few months later when I came very close to getting arrested for burglary.

I almost fell off the windowsill when he spoke.

"Good morning Sir."

I jerked round, clinging frantically to the window frame, and looked down. Below, shining a torch up at me, was the policeman.

"I can explain everything," I stammered. *"Well young man, I suggest you come down and try."* He replied, not sounding too convinced.

What I didn't tell the copper was that my situation was really all down to hormones. Let me explain.

It was the hot summer of 1959. The year Buddy Holly died and Cliff Richard topped the charts for eleven weeks with 'Living Doll' and Travelling Light'. I had just turned fifteen and my greatest birthday present seemed to be the rush of testosterone that arrived with the warm summer days.

Every day for the last week I'd been cycling with my friend Jeremy to the Fetcham Grove open air pool at Leatherhead where we'd met these two girls. They were real stunners, and as we watched them running and jumping around in their bikinis I'm sure our eyes were popping.

Of course they weren't the miniscule modern thong type of bikini that amounts to little more than string and sticking plasters as far as I can make out. Not that I've made a study of the subject (or not that I'll admit to) but these were certainly revealing enough to raise our blood pressure.

Jeremy knew one of them slightly as she lived not far from him. Her name was Helen and her friend Theresa had come to spend the summer holidays with her. I guess they were about the same age as us or perhaps a little older and were the classic double act – blonde and brunette and about the same height with lissom tanned bodies slick with sun oil. They certainly knew what they were up to and it was working a treat on us.

For a change it wasn't the usual situation where there's one good looker and her, well let's be charitable, 'less attractive' friend. These two were both gorgeous and what's more they really seemed to fancy us.

We'd been chatting to them for a couple of days and had played a bit of badminton as well as just lounging. Thinly disguised posing I guess you'd call it.

There was the predictable sky-larking about of course with us chasing each other around in and out of the pool and us picking up the girls and tossing them in the water and then diving in to swim under the water and through their legs etc. etc. I'm sure you get the picture!

The interesting thing, and for our raging hormones, the most exciting, was that any 'accidental-on-purpose' touch on the soft and curvy bits was not repulsed, so you might imagine we thought things could only get better.

And better they did get when the following day Helen said *"We're sleeping in the summer house tonight. Do you want to come up"?*

Well "Is the Pope Catholic?" – Certainly we wanted to. So that was how I came to be creeping out of my front door at half-past midnight and riding my unlit bike through the moonlight the half-mile or so to Jeremy's house.

He was there as agreed but to be honest as neither of us had ever done anything like this before, we were both a bit wobbly about taking it any further especially as it was looking as though we both might be 'real men' before the night was out if you get my drift.

I don't think either of us wanted to exhibit any lack of nerve but I guess perhaps I was because Jeremy said *"Are you really up for this then?"* and I said, *"Yes. What about you?"*
He said, *"I am if you are." "Ok then"* I said. *"Let's do it"*

So with our joint hormone level pretty well through the roof, we set off along the footpath that led to Helen's house where we had to scramble through a hedge and then following her detailed instructions, creep furtively through the deep shadow around the lawn's edge to the summer house. Moving stealthily forward we could see the light of a torch in the summer house and there, true to their word we found the girls waiting for us.

They were in their sleeping bags when we arrived but I could hardly believe my eyes when in order to let us in Theresa got up and I saw she was wearing these short, more or less see-through 'Baby Doll' pyjamas. They had certainly tried to set the scene because there was beer that they had smuggled out of the house, cigarettes and, of all things, packets of Digestive biscuits. I've never been able to look at a digestive biscuit since without being transported back to that night.

Well after a drink and some cigarettes and amid a lot of giggling I got into Theresa's sleeping bag where I discovered to my shock and delight that she had surreptitiously slipped out of her 'baby dolls'.

I had never even seen a naked woman before apart from in the odd magazine, much less have one pressing herself against me. Well I was so innocent and really didn't have a clue. A certain amount of kissing and general groping about took place but in the event it didn't go any further.

Not so much because sexual athletics is a bit difficult in a sleeping bag but because between us we didn't really know or perhaps were a bit afraid of the next move

Quite what Jeremy and Helen achieved (if that's the word) I couldn't tell at the time although I discovered later it was also what you might call a 'no-score draw'. I guess we just weren't quite ready for group sex or perhaps all those deeply held taboos so firmly established by the church and school somehow managed to hold us in check. After all it wasn't even the swinging sixties – quite.

Now for the anti-climax. Not literally of course.

It was about half three in the morning when we left the girls and so just before four o'clock and with the first traces of dawn light streaking the sky I was back at my front door where to my horror I discovered that in my lust-fuelled haste I had come out without the door key. I couldn't believe it.

At first I simply didn't have a clue what to do then as I calmed down and started to think straight I realised there was a possible way in.

My room was the small one over the front door and I could see that the little top window was open, but the problem was how to reach it.

I reckoned that if I dragged the dustbin over to the door I should be able to climb up onto the porch and get from there to the window sill but I couldn't at first see how I would be able to open the big side window and get in. I needed something that would enable me to reach in and down far enough to lift the lower catch.

I went into the outbuilding on the side of the house where I hoped to find something in Dad's shed but it was locked so I just started to look around and eventually in the outside loo found what I hoped might do the trick. The lavatory brush had a loop of string on the end of the handle that I thought might just let me reach the catch by holding it upside down. Unfortunately this did mean I would have to hold it by the business end, the thought of which almost stopped me but then 'needs must'.

Tucking the loo brush into my belt at the back of my trousers I half slid and half lifted the dustbin towards the front door and managed without much difficulty to get onto the porch and from there to the window-sill where I had to perch on my toes in a sort of squat position.

Hanging onto the window frame with my left hand I reached behind me with my right, and trying not to think about where it had been I grabbed the spiky well-worn brush and pulled it from my belt. Inserting it through the little window at the top I was in the process of trying to lasso the window latch with the string when the policeman spoke.

I clambered down desperately thinking how I might explain myself, not just to the policeman, but also to my parents.

"Look sir." I said, *"It isn't what it looks like. I live here and I forgot my key. I really don't want to wake my parents so can't you just let me carry on."*

The copper was quite understanding really, but even I could see his difficulty.

"Look son. I probably do believe you but unless you can prove you live here we're going to have to knock someone up to confirm it. What were you doing out at this time of night anyway" he asked.

"I just went out for a bike ride. I've never been out in the middle of the night before and the moon was so bright I thought it would be exciting.

"OK" he said. *"Let's get this over with."* And he rapped on the doorknocker.

Silence; and then the hall light came on and suddenly Dad was standing there in his dressing gown looking down at me through sleep-filled eyes.

"Brian? What the devil's going on? What on earth have you been up to?"

"I'm sorry Dad. I forgot my key"

He was pretty irritated at the time but the following day both Mum and Dad admitted to seeing the funny side of the situation with me being caught on the windowsill. However, that was on the basis of me just going out for a moonlight bike ride. They never did know the real story.

This growing interest in the opposite sex got me into trouble on a couple of other occasions too.

At the top of the road in Merrow where I went to school at St Peters was a girls' school called Merrow Grange and a number of the girls travelled to and fro on the same buses as we did. Well naturally over time little friendship or in this case an imagined friendship developed between me and this girl called Hilary Kemp who lived in Epsom.

I guess I'd imagined a shy smile or some similar signal that I thought indicated my interest was reciprocated. So one day having made a show of getting off the bus at my stop I hopped back on and went inside on the lower deck until Hilary got off a couple of stops later when I cautiously followed her to discover where she lived.

Armed with this knowledge on the following Saturday morning I rode to her house and concealed myself in a hedge opposite her house in the hope of catching a glimpse of my 'beloved'.

However as time passed and nothing happened I grew impatient and started to whistle in the hope that she might look out and see me.

Well whether she saw me or not I never knew but what happened next was that two exceedingly large brothers looking like a couple of rugby forwards came out and headed directly for my hiding place so I can only suppose they had worked out beforehand where I was. Anyway I didn't wait to find out but a bit like years before when the policeman was after us after the firework incident, I was on my bike and away like some sort of Olympic cyclist.

Writing this now, I'm amused to remember when, many years later I had to chase off a young Romeo who'd actually clambered on to our garage roof in an attempt to make contact with my own pubescent daughter. Apparently not a lot changes does it especially when it comes to teenage hormones.

The other event, which did actually land me in trouble, and was certainly not my fault, concerned once again one of the girls from Merrow Grange.

In the fifth year and in order to economise on staff and facilities an arrangement was reached between the two schools that involved some of the girls coming down to us for sciences and some boys going up to the Grange for maths. Well, you might imagine what this did for the testosterone levels around the place.

I honestly did nothing to encourage her but it seems that a pretty girl called Mary Ford had taken a fancy to me from a distance. And she was also pointedly ignoring the attentions of a Belgian boy in my class called Jacques who was far more handsome than anyone had the right to be and certainly much better looking than me.

So, if I'd had any idea that he fancied her I would have made a point of actively discouraging her coy looks in my direction believing that I couldn't possibly compete. However I was in complete ignorance of the jealous anger brewing in his breast or at least I was until he punched me in the face at the end of classes one Saturday morning and sent me home with a bloody nose.

Chapter 10 - Pocket Money

It was around this time too that the need for some extra pocket money began to make itself felt if I was to keep up with better-off friends who always seemed to have not just pennies but even pounds in their pockets. And it wasn't just for a few gob-stoppers from the tuck shop – no, cigarettes were the thing.

There was huge 'street-cred' in producing a packet of fags even if they were only Weights or Woodbines. Mine always were Woodbines because that's what Dad smoked, which enabled me to pinch the odd one or two to top up my own pack.

Most of us could only ever run to buying our cigarettes in packs of five (which should never have been sold to us of course) but for those who could somehow manage to produce a pack of ten or even twenty the cool factor was off the scale. Not that 'cool' or 'street-cred' were terms I actually recall from the time. Come to think of it, I can't really remember what we would have said when seriously impressed.

I remember Mum used to smoke a bit too; just the odd one now and again or at parties and her brand was Mills Filter Tips that came in a smart red and white pack. Well, they say imitation is the sincerest form of flattery but she was far from flattered when she discovered a packet of Mills in my school blazer.

"They're a present Mum." I blathered. *"Oh that's nice,"* she said. *"Pity someone seems to have pinched a couple."*

However, back to the fund-raising.

Unlike some of my friends I never did do the paper round or earn a few shillings helping the milkman. Mum and Dad thought that on school days we kids needed our rest in the mornings and time to do our homework at night which only left the weekends and school holidays. We did get a little pocket money but it was nowhere near enough for my developing needs, which is fortunately where the scouts came to the rescue.

Skip asked us boys if anyone wanted to earn some pocket money by cutting his grass and as I was quickest off the mark I got the job which paid me half-a-crown (12 ½ p) an hour – not a bad rate in those days at least for pocket money. However there was a spin off. One of his neighbours saw me doing his lawn and I found myself doing another couple of hours there for the same rate so I was well happy.

There was a further bonus too. My new employer, a widow by the name of Mrs Danvers was a great cook so my efforts were not only rewarded financially but with large wads of fruit cake or marvellously oaty flapjacks which have been my downfall ever since.

She lived with her brother who had a couple of BSA motor bikes and when he saw how enthralled I was with them he paid me another shilling each to polish them although in truth they never needed polishing as he always kept them immaculately. So, although it was some distance, I never grudged the Saturday bike ride to and from Epsom even if the return trip was mostly uphill and a bit of a slog.

By this time Dad had become the assistant manager of the grocer's shop called Baldwin's in Ashtead village and during school holidays he arranged for me to work there with him. Baldwin's Bros is just on the right by the white sports car.

Photo – The Frith Collection

It was a traditional grocer's shop offering personal counter service, as supermarkets had not yet arrived in our part of the world although it wasn't to be long before they did.

My father and the two or three other assistants who worked there moved around so fast fetching items from shelves out in the shop or passing and re-passing each other behind the counter that they were almost a blur.

Items stacked up in front of them until at last the customer said, *"I think that's it for today thank you."* And then began the wondrous adding up process. Now you need first to think about the level of mental arithmetic that our schools turn out today and then remember that this was prior to decimalisation when prices were in pounds, shillings, pence and even halfpennies, (farthings were gone by this time – if not forgotten).

I used to watch transfixed as Dad and the others added up these stacks of groceries faster than I could think and certainly faster than a good typist could have punched them into a calculator.

Once behind the scenes at the shop it was like entering another world a million miles away from the orderly presentation of the public area.

Stacks of boxes were piled along the walls containing all manner of goods from cans of Australian peaches to Fray Bentos corned beef from Argentina. Huge cases of Kellogs corn flakes vied for space with sacks of rice, Demerara sugar and sultanas. The smell was exotic rising to knockout level when someone had to open a fresh sack of coffee beans from Brazil or sticky dried apricots.

This was to be my domain. My principal job on most days was to weigh and bag these wonderful bulk commodities into 8oz; 1lb or 2lb paper bags and then get them out onto the shelves.

Beyond this stock room there was a tiny staff room with a sink beside the back door that led to the rear yard and staff toilet, a small shelf with a gas ring and kettle for brewing tea.

There was also an ancient sofa that had seen much better days with frayed maroon moquette cushions resting on springs that could be seriously life threatening of you didn't sit down carefully. Here the staff took their breaks, and on occasions I even had to set up my scales for lack of space elsewhere.

At the back of the shop there was a long narrow yard some 100 feet in length surfaced with the sort of stone setts used for stable yards, which it almost certainly had once been, for along the length of one side was a row of six or seven brick sheds with corrugated roofs some of which still had stable-doors. These were the main storage areas for the shop, each dedicated to its own particular purpose.

My favourite was the cheese store. Whole cheeses were stacked here in their waxed muslin skin waiting to be undressed and cut. The largest were the English Cheddars; so weighty that even Dad could scarcely lift them. Then there were the Caerphillys, red Leicesters, Wensleydales, the tall and seriously smelly Stiltons, red skinned Edams and the flat Dutch Goudas.

Dad taught me how to skin the cheeses and how to use a cheese wire to cut them into wedges for counter display.

Other stores housed cereals, canned fruit and vegetables, biscuits from Huntley and Palmer, Peek Frean and McVitie & Price that came in large metal boxes from which they could be weighed out on demand.

Then there was a soft drink store where crates of Corona lemonade, ginger beer, Tizer and soda siphons were kept. In those days bottles were returnable and another of my jobs was to sort through the crates of empties to ensure they were in their correct crates or risk the wrath of the drayman when he called to find he had to sort out a mixture of Tizer and Corona bottles.

There were two other stores. At the far end of the yard was the huge walk-in refrigerator that I hated and not just because of the claustrophobia it engendered. In order to retrieve a case of butter or lard from the stack along the back wall you had to duck and dive between whole sides of bacon hanging from overhead hooks while attempting to avoid the odd pool of blood on the floor only to be startled out of your wits by the fridge unit kicking in loudly overhead.

The last unit I remember was Dad's special 'baby'. It had been his idea to introduce home cooked hams to the product range and in order to do this a huge boiler had been installed in the first of the sheds closest to the shop. This was about the size of a large chest freezer and made from stainless steel with thick heavily insulated sides and a screw-down top. Electric elements in the base provided the heat.

Dad and his colleagues used to bone and roll whole gammon and shoulder joints that would then be packed as tightly as possible into the boiler. Cold water was introduced by turning a direct feed valve and once covered they were left to soak overnight. This had the effect of drawing the salt from the joints. In the morning this brine was drained off, the unit refilled and brought to the boil. The heat was then turned off, the top closed and tightly clamped shut and the bacon left to literally 'stew in its own juice'. Timing was critical.

Over-cooked and the joints would fall apart and be impossible to slice. Fortunately Dad had this off to a fine art and the shop developed a well-deserved reputation for its delicious ham. What the customers didn't see was my role in all this, which was the only job I really disliked.

Once the boiler was opened the revolting fatty brine solution, bacon juice, whatever you want to call it, was run off with God knows what effect on the drains! I then had to unload the hams onto a shelf to cool completely. Skinning was the next stage, and if you've ever done this you'll know it is no mean feat hanging onto a greasy ham joint that perpetually threatens to slither off onto the floor (as some indeed did).

Most of the fat was then trimmed off and they were coated in bright orange breadcrumbs that transformed them into the delicious home-cooked hams that became much praised in the village especially around Christmas time.

I remember one day I was struggling with one of these horrid hams when Dad went striding briskly past towards one of the other stores. He must have crept up on me because I hadn't heard his footsteps returning when his voice from the door said, *"How's it going son?"* I looked up only to be hit squarely in the face by a well-aimed squirt from a soda siphon.

"Sorry." he said laughing, *"Couldn't resist it."* Even when busy he had a sense of humour.

Dad and his colleagues taught me how to bone out a side of bacon and cut and tie it correctly into joints. I also learnt how to use the bacon slicer. Some will remember the machines before they were electrified that required you to turn the operating handle with one hand while taking the slices off the huge rotating blade with the other. A bit like that game of patting your head and rubbing your stomach at the same time; it's not as easy as it looks. Can you imagine the uproar in our modern 'healthy and safety' world if a fourteen year old was handed a foot long razor sharp butchers knife and allowed to do such things.

Not that I escaped entirely unscathed. I did get a cut one day when I foolishly went to stop a knife from falling off the bench. *"Won't do that again will you."* said Dad as he bandaged my finger.

By the time I was about fifteen or so I started to look for holiday jobs that were actually 'on the cards' so to speak as I needed to earn a bit more than Dad could pay me out of petty cash and I went to work for a firm of nurserymen and landscape gardeners. My word what a contrast!

Initially I was put to work with a landscape gang as a labourer, which involved more heavy work than I knew existed. One day I'd be wheeling barrows of soil, stone, or fresh mixed concrete around until I thought my arms would drop off. Then it would be humping railway sleepers or bags of John Innes from A to B only to take them back again when old Harry decided he wanted them somewhere else.

Old Harry was one of four full-timers in our gang of six. Two of us were holiday workers. I can't now recall the names of all the others but there was Wally the foreman, two other regulars and Harry. He had pretty well been there, done it all in the landscaping business and whilst he certainly did know the job he was mainly distinguished by the strength and obscenity of his language.

However he taught us youngsters a lot about the job, always ribbing us in a reasonably light-hearted way with his favourite expression *"What sort of f**king mess do you call* that?"

You know what it's like when you are fifteen or sixteen going on twenty-five and think you know a few things. Well I certainly discovered pretty rapidly that I didn't know that much at all; although in retrospect there could have been gentler ways of finding out.

I worked with the gang for three or four weeks that first summer, ate like a horse and almost overnight my body changed from that of a boy to a man. I became so fit that in no time it seemed I was almost throwing around the bags of John Innes that I could scarcely lift off the ground at the beginning. We did several jobs together and even today I can drive around the area and say with some pride *"I made that garden."* or *"I planted that tree"*. There is definitely something special about creating things that last. Imagine how Capability Brown felt!

For the remainder of that holiday I worked in what was called the JI shed. This was a huge sort of overgrown Nissen hut where the different formulas of John Innes composts were produced and the process was interesting in addition to being extremely physical.

At one end of the shed there was a mountain of top-soil that was replenished by the lorry load a couple of times a week.
Fresh top-soil not only contains desirable humus and chemical nutrients but also vast numbers of undesirable weed seeds, bugs, bacteria etc.

The first stage in the process then was sterilisation which was to say the least, not subtle. The soil sterilizer consisted of a large steel tube about 15 feet long and two feet in diameter that was mounted almost horizontally in a frame on sets of rollers that allowed the cylinder to rotate when driven by an electric motor. It was set at about shoulder height and as I said was slightly inclined with a large hopper or funnel at the high end with its upper opening about six feet off the ground.

Inside was mounted a kind of Archimedean screw and at the lower end a jet that emitted a blast of flame that extended the length of the cylinder. I can't recall now whether the flame was provided by oil or gas but whichever it was the roar and heat were intense.

In operation soil was thrown by us labourers up over our heads into the hopper. As the cylinder revolved with the fire blasting up its centre it caused the soil to continuously fall through the flame as it was driven along by the screw until it fell out of the other end hot and thoroughly sterilised. So sterile in fact that absolutely nothing would grow in it without further treatment.

Working on the sterilizer in ten-minute stints was certainly the most demanding job I've ever done. Not only in the physical sense but also because of the noise, heat and dust. In a way it was not unlike those images you see of men sweating away in the red fiery glow of an iron foundry.

The next stage was a kind of reconstitution process that involved putting back all the humus and nutrients in controlled proportions according to the purpose of the compost, i.e., JI 1, 2 or 3.

The process was remarkably simple and utilised an old fashioned concrete mixer with a large hopper that lay flat on the ground to be loaded and was then raised to pour the ingredients into the rotating mixer.

Once again the physical element was significant. We had to wheel barrows of sterilised soil, peat (not much used these days I'm pleased to say), sharp sand and a variety of chemical fertilisers into the hopper and once mixed we had to pour it into ½ cwt hessian sacks which by that time I really could toss around as if they weighed nothing at all.

It was a strange time really now I think back on it. It was as though I were several different people. At one level I wanted life to go on in its simple homely way with Mum, Dad and Angela but then there were times when I just deliberately went out to be a complete pain and enjoyed the annoyance it caused them. Curious then that in the next moment I was in the shop working alongside Dad and loving it.

I was very interested in girls but didn't know what to do about it. Other friends at home and at school seemed to be so much more confident in that department and now even though I had some money I couldn't seem to push through my shyness.It was all simple adolescent angst of course but you don't see it that way at the time.

Around this time too fashion started to become important. Looking back it seems so ridiculous but there was a trend for brightly coloured fluorescent socks that my parents flatly refused to buy or allow me to wear but as I now had some of my own money that was no problem.

I remember I bought this bright lime green pair that I kept in my school bag and used to change into on the bus to school and strut around in all day at school like a dog with two tails. It was forbidden being a non-uniform item and we were forever in lunch-time detention but I think after a while the staff decided that it was easier to ignore the socks and naturally without any attention the fad died out in no time.

This was the back end of the 1950's when Teddy Boys and their drain-pipe trousers had pretty much been and gone except that I hadn't had my share. To feel part of it all I desperately wanted tapered trousers that once again Mum and Dad refused to countenance.

However, I was determined to have them but even my new earnings weren't enough for new tapered trousers so I decided to take in a pair I already had.

One day home alone I got out Mum's sewing machine and turning the trousers inside out stitched a wedge of material down the inside of each leg with the result that the trousers were more like a pair of tights than drain-pipes. They were uncomfortable too as I'd left the wedge of material in place so undaunted I grabbed the scissors and lopped it off so at least they fitted more comfortably.

So there I was in my new Teddy Boy pants like some kind of bizarre Max Wall look-alike. However, with no-one around to see them I needed to get out so I hopped on my bike and pedalled off to Epsom where I wandered around feeling really the 'bee's knees' and probably looking like nothing on earth. After a while, not having met anyone I knew to show off to I decided to head home and the long climb to the top of Epsom Hill.

Just before the top I felt something give around the crotch of my pants and as I crested the hill and started to pick up speed there was a loud ripping noise as all the stitching gave way and the trouser legs flew out behind me like a pair of sails.

I think I might have died of embarrassment if I'd been spotted by anyone I knew but fortunately even as I turned in to Bramley Way there was no-one about and I managed to get indoors with my dignity if not exactly intact at least partially so.

It was an everlasting mystery in our house how a pair of trousers can simply disappear or at least it was until many years later when I eventually admitted to my parents what I'd done, by which time it was just another one of Brian's hair-brained stunts to laugh about.

Although like most kids I undoubtedly took them for granted I was blessed to have wonderful parents whose patience and tolerance was really above and beyond, even if it wore a bit thin at times.

With me around fourteen or fifteen and starting to be more of a teenager than her little boy; and Angela, catching up fast as girls do in maturity if not in years; Mum arranged to have some studio photos done. Perhaps this was the way she wanted us to stay. Some hope!

Mum and Dad share a quiet moment in the garden at Bramley Way

Chapter 11. - The World of Work.

Work!

What, real work? Not just holiday jobs for pocket money?

Well, that really was a jolt. It shouldn't have been of course because I'd been used to holiday working for several years. However, the fact is that during the school years you don't really think that seriously about them coming to an end. So, when after my poor 'O' Level results my parents start talking about proper jobs and especially about my housekeeping contributions it brought me up a bit short to say the least.

There had been a point when I thought I might try to go into dentistry but that had waned somewhat as I started to find physics more difficult and in any event I had never done any biology. As a result I was pinning my hopes on doing well in chemistry because an acquaintance of my father, a Mr Lemmon who was the research director of a company in Ashtead had said, *"If he gets chemistry he can come and work for me."*

So, in the summer of 1960 with 'O' level passes in just Chemistry, English Language and Literature I entered the world of work aged 16 and became a trainee laboratory technician at The McMurdo Instrument Company in Ashtead.

McMurdo's occupied Victoria Works in the village. This was a substantial but rather wear-worn red brick factory building but with an interesting and varied history. Dating from the late 1800's the building had previously been home to Cadett and Neal Photographic, early pioneers of colour film processes who were eventually bought out by Eastman Colour and then merged into the Kodak empire.

In 1908 Stanley Steam Cars took over the works and it was one of their vehicles that achieved the world speed record in 1906 for covering a mile in twenty-eight seconds (128mph) which was pretty phenomenal at the time.

When the first war and the rapid development of the internal combustion engine eventually put an end to Stanley's enterprise the factory was taken over by Ashtead Pottery.

The Pottery had a sadly short life, being in business for just 12 years from 1923 to 1935. The factory was set up with the laudable aim of providing employment for disabled ex-servicemen at one point employing forty two men. The main driving force behind the creation of the company was Sir Lawrence Weaver, a highly influential local man of the time.

The company produced a vast array of wares in the Art Deco style, ranging from figures and commemoratives, designed by leading artists of the day, through to everyday crockery. The great depression, increased competition and the untimely death of Sir Lawrence led to eventual closure of the pottery in January of 1935. (Credit www.ashteadpottery.com for info. and above text) However the company's products have since become quite collectable today.

After the pottery closed, the works was occupied from 1937 by Celestion Ltd, radio engineers and makers of loudspeakers (still in business today). In 1946 The McMurdo Instrument Co. took over the works where it installed a large plastics moulding shop to manufacture items such as valve holders, plugs and sockets, electrical connectors and model railway parts.

When I arrived on the scene McMurdo were still producing moulded plastics but there was a great deal more going on 'behind the scenes' as it were.

By then the company had begun developing and manufacturing a more sophisticated range of components for the rapidly expanding electronics and communications industries and were pushing the boundaries in the development of batteries for everything from rechargeable shavers to guided missiles.

My position was in the chemistry lab working under the Chief Chemist John White. The laboratory was included within a very large open plan building with Crittal style metal and glass partitions about eight feet high so there was never any sense of privacy or quietness especially as a corridor ran the length of the building.

Of the many things we were working on, electro-plating of components was one of the most important initially.

We were responsible for monitoring and improving the quality of the gold and silver plating on the thousands of small contact pins that were fitted every day into the plastic housings produced by the moulding shop.

Without going into boring detail one of my tasks was to take random samples from batches produced and measure the thickness of the gold that was deposited in a layer only a couple of ten thousands of an inch thick.

Laborious as it sounds, and indeed was, this was achieved by cutting a section through the pins and then measuring the layers of gold visually under a microscope.

This monotonous and repetitive task was the introduction to my new career in chemistry. What a far cry it was from the chemistry of the school lab with all its fizzes and pops, bubbling flasks, coloured smoke and wonderfully foul smells.

In addition, I was on a part time day-release course at the local technical college that would, (hopefully) lead to a National Certificate in Chemistry which was somewhere between 'A' level and a degree. To this end I had to attend college for one full day and two evenings a week and horror of horrors there was more, much more, maths.

However there was more to McMurdo's than boring routine.

Girls!

I had probably only been there a couple of weeks when I fell head over heels in adolescent love with Blondie.

She was one of about thirty women who worked on a pilot assembly line in an adjacent building where we used to set up small production runs for items under development in the labs.

She was about twenty-two to my sixteen years, shortish, with an hour glass figure, mini skirt and short blond hair and she used to walk up and down the corridor past the lab several times a day apparently oblivious of my existence and the palpitations she was causing.

Very occasionally when I could justify going to the assembly building, after a quick visit to the cloakroom to check hair etc. was in order, I would make a point of walking near her position and, joy of joys, one day there was a piece of paper on the floor under her chair.

Seizing this heaven sent opportunity of making contact I picked up the paper, leaned over her shoulder and said, with a mouth so dry my tongue would hardly work, *"Excuse me. Is this yours?"*

She turned around smiling and said *"Oh yes. Thanks very much"*

I thought my heart would burst. But sadly I was far too shy and tongue-tied to extend the conversation. Turning to walk away, I stepped right into the path of Mr. Lemmon, who was carrying a cup of tea that went straight up in the air and came down soaking the pair of us. Now I could have died.

The old man was fine about it but I just wanted the earth to open up and swallow me.

It's funny though how these things can work in your favour because in an instant I'd gone from invisible to known. Known; yes, as the idiot who drowned the director but known nevertheless. It also meant that the ice was broken and that now I was on speaking terms with Blondie, or Dorothy to give her correct name and the whole bunch of women who worked with her. I carried a torch for Dorothy for a few months as you do but it was never going anywhere as she had a fiancée so that was that.

The poor ladies on the assembly line had another reason to remember me a few weeks later when I had an accident that caused them all to walk off the job for a couple of hours.

Kipp's apparatus is a piece of kit many will remember from their school days that was used, among other things, to produce a gas called hydrogen sulphide, famous for its revolting smell of rotten eggs. At McMurdo's we used this gas in a special building outside of the factory to test the corrosion resistance of our plated components and it was my job from time to time to bring it into the lab for cleaning and on the way in one day I managed to drop it.

The whole of the assembly line area was suffused with this terrible smell but not only is it revolting it is also quite poisonous so had they not all walked out we would have had to evacuate until the gas dissipated.

Although the toxic levels reduced quickly the smell lingered for several days and there was a fair bit of grumbling before it all settled down again and I certainly took a bit of stick every time I walked through their building.

We all take very much for granted these days the tiny rechargeable batteries that power so many of our electronic gizmos but it was here at McMurdo's in the sixties and a few other places I guess that the prototypes were being devised and tested.

Early versions of nickel cadmium batteries had a propensity to explode unexpectedly so we had built a sort of brick bunker in the corner of the lab where these things could be tested safely. However some of the projects were very much more trial and quite a lot of error as you might say.

One such project related to the development of a fairly large battery that would be used for powering missiles and we had to devise a test system that would somehow simulate the firing of the missile.

Without going into too much detail the battery comprised alternate metal plates with spaces in between into which hydrofluoric acid, a particularly nasty chemical, would be forced by the acceleration forces of the missile being fired. However we needed a way of doing it in-situ so that we could measure and monitor the power output of the battery.

We hit on the idea of forcing the acid plunger down with an explosive charge but of course had no idea and no means of calculating in advance what size of charge would be needed. A metal housing was made up to encase the battery and the charge which we felt should be sufficient to contain the forces concerned but to be safe it was decided that we would remain at some distance and behind some form of protection.

What we eventually arranged was that the battery and charge would be on the ground on some waste land behind the factory and that we, the test team would be in a room inside the building with the device connected to our monitoring meters and so on by wires. In hindsight it was a pretty dumb plan but then that's research – if you don't know, you guess.

I was responsible for firing the charge electrically by just touching a couple of wires to a battery while three colleagues were there to record and monitor the unit's performance.

"Ok Brian." said John *"On my mark – three, two, one, Now!"* I touched the wires and saw a tiny spark jump.

There was the most almighty bang, the whole building shook, the window shattered and then silence. Someone said *"Holy Shit!"* and we all rushed to the broken window.

There was nothing there apart from a damn great hole in the ground.

I said *"I don't think we'll need the missiles, just use the batteries."*

"Back to the drawing board." said John, *"A bit less powder next time I think."*

Another thing we were involved in was the development of water activated batteries. Anyone aware of a bit of basic science will know that dissimilar metals and a suitable electrolyte can give rise to an electric current and we were charged with refining this principle to produce batteries for lifeboats and lifejackets.

The idea was that they should operate automatically and show a light as soon as they were immersed in water. So to this end we spent quite a few days floating about in the Solent lobbing these floating lamp units into the sea and measuring the output. The sun shone and it was most enjoyable. I'm still not sure why we couldn't have done it in a bucket of salty water behind the factory in Ashtead but it was great fun and a few good days out.

Then some bright RAF type said *"What about doing something for pilots that have to bail out over land or even in the desert – not much water there."*

So we put our thinking caps on and realised the only water to hand might be the pilot's own water – urine to be more specific.

As a result, every time we needed a pee we'd trot off the loo with a glass flask and bring back our own urine for the little test rig we'd got running in the fume cupboard at the back of the lab. I'm pleased to say the experiment worked and hopefully may have resulted in the odd flier being picked up just that bit sooner.

Nowadays the latest batteries don't have to rely on liquid electrolytes. Just as well for me as I certainly can't pee on demand any more.

I learnt a lot at McMurdo's. It was the first time I had worked as part of a team where my input was to any extent valued and it did a lot for my self-confidence. I had my own projects – albeit small - where I had to write reports and proposals for further research.

I also extended my knowledge both in the lab and at college and not just in the chemical field.

Electrical and mechanical engineering both featured to an extent in our work when it came to designing new plant and systems and in devising solutions to the problems that arose. As a result I also learnt to use a lathe and how to do basic welding.

The other thing you learn very quickly when you step into the real world of work is about people and how they interact. It didn't take very long to work out the personalities. John the chemist was fairly young and married to a girl who also worked there in the offices so he disappeared every lunch time to spend time with her. He was a pleasant guy but not really a manager, in fact I don't think he'd been responsible for anyone before I came along. We developed a relationship that worked but wasn't close.

Then there was John Fuller who was in the adjacent lab where they were concerned with designing the batteries that we were testing. He was a joker and always up to some prank or other.

His passion was photography and he apparently had quite a successful home based business doing weddings and such like.

There were several other guys that I worked quite closely with but whose names I don't remember. We all got on together and they treated me well, young and inexperienced though I was.

At lunch times I used to go to the canteen and there got in with another group of chaps who were mainly from the other side of the business. They worked in the plastics moulding and machine shops and their great love in life was the half size snooker table in the canteen where they played every lunch-time in a very serious league. Needless to say I soon got involved too and actually became quite a dab hand at both snooker and billiards.

The thing I never did succumb to though was the fruit machine or 'one armed bandit' as we called it. I have watched on a Friday as people put virtually a whole pay packet into it and walked away in tears.

What a mugs game. I've never understood gambling like that. The odd flutter yes but not to that extent.

Of course you don't get a bunch of people working together without having a few laughs which was just as well because the pressure of work was quite intense at times.

Some of the biggest jokers worked in the moulding shop – a horrible hot and noisy environment where you certainly needed a sense of humour to remain sane. But it was a bit of a trial for anyone else who had to walk through the area to get to the main offices because they had to run the gauntlet of shouted remarks and wisecracks that allowed no quarter in those days for consideration of racist or sexual discrimination. Anyone was fair game but that also included their own too if the opportunity presented itself.

One of the press workers really fancied himself with the women and as his machine was right beside the alleyway through the centre of the shop he was ideally placed to lean over, chat-up, grope or otherwise harass any pretty but luckless female that had to pass that way.

What this guy didn't know however was that it was common knowledge among his colleagues that he wore a toupee – well coloured and well-fitted no doubt but false hair none the less.

One day he was in the process of seriously embarrassing one of the secretaries who was new to the company and not accustomed to the banter. He had managed to detain her for some moments when one of his colleagues reached over behind him with a high pressure airline.

Well-fitted it may have been but the toupee certainly couldn't withstand the ninety pounds per square inch jet of air that lifted his hair piece and lofted it high across the workshop. Everyone gets their just desserts and this was his day. Sad in a way because he was totally mortified but if you dish it out you have to be prepared to take it.

Christmas was an interesting time at McMurdo's and in anticipation of doing not a lot on Christmas Eve the assembly line girls used to save up all year and arrive at work laden with bottles of booze – mostly gin and vodka plus baskets of mixers and party food.. The theory was that they should work up to coffee time and that after eleven o'clock management would capitulate and the party could begin.

Well that might have been the theory but the reality was that serious drinking began soon after arrival at 8.30 so that by coffee time any man who was foolish enough to venture anywhere near that end of the building was almost guaranteed to lose his trousers. All in complete fun for sure, but highly embarrassing if it happened to be you although anyone unlucky enough to get captured was expected to take it all in good part and laugh it off.

For our part in the lab we didn't need to bring in alcohol, just a few mixers because we had alcohol aplenty in the form of Winchester Quart bottles of pure Ethyl Alcohol. Highly dangerous it's true if you don't know what you are doing but then we were the chemists and I'm still here to tell the tale.

Following this nonsense the entire factory adjourned to a pre-booked back room in one the Ashtead village pubs for sandwiches provided by the firm and a lot more drink.

This was where, whilst I was engaged collecting a Christmas kiss from one of the office girls, a supposed friend emptied a bottle of brown ale into my back trouser pocket.

After a distinctly uncomfortable and wobbly ride home on my bike I had to explain to Mum how I'd come by a dark brown stain from my back-side to my turn-ups.

It was during this time that I had come into possession of the old motor bike from the scouts and became heavily into anything to do with motorcycling although to be truthful I was being less than successful in the restoration programme.

This was mostly because the realisation had dawned that however much time or money I spent I was only going to finish up with an old relic and certainly something a million miles removed from the shiny new Triumphs and Nortons I used to read about in magazines

It was hardly surprising then that when I met a guy called Dave at work with similar interests we became friends despite quite an age difference.

He had a Norton Dominator 500 cc bike that in those days was quite a 'beast' and I was just so thrilled when he took me out on it one lunch time. We went down the A24 through the Mickleham bends and the cutting at almost 100mph. I was just so excited although to be honest I was also a tiny bit anxious about slowing down enough for the roundabout at the foot of Box Hill.

We weren't to know that we were trailblazers for the many who were to come after us when Rykas burger bar at Burford Bridge became the weekend 'mecca' for motorcyclists from miles around. Sadly this friendship was interrupted when Dave decided he'd had enough of McMurdo's and announced he was leaving to join the merchant navy. I must say I did feel a bit envious.

On the work front I was quite enjoying life in the laboratory but in all honesty I hated the studying side of things because I was really struggling with the maths component of the course.

This aspect was not helped by my developing social life that seriously conflicted with the two evenings a week I had to drag myself off to Ewell Technical College College, not to mention the time I should have been putting in studying for impending exams.

After I first learnt to swim in Jersey I'd got really keen, joined a swimming club at Epsom Baths and became a regular during the summer months at a little private outdoor pool in Ashtead. This was in Ottways Lane and was called Littlewoods which was the name of the family that owned it. Sadly that eventually closed down and we migrated to the Fetcham Grove pool at Leatherhead where we'd meet the two girls of the midnight assignation. So as I enjoyed swimming it's hardly surprising that it continued to feature in my spare time.

By the time I'm now describing, my out of work social life was largely associated with Gilmais, a nice little private open-air swimming pool and club at Bookham. During the summer months, which in those days seemed to be both long and hot, we spent as much time as we could swimming, tanning, weight-lifting and posing around the pool in the daytime and dancing in the social club at night.

There were also weekend dances at various village halls in the area and as I was not yet driving I seemed to spend interminable hours pedalling my bike around the district in the hope of getting off with the current female of my heart's desire. Believe me it's not that easy to look suave and attractive when you've just sweated the 5 miles from home to the latest venue.

It was around this time that I first fell for the gorgeous Paula in common with several others in our group. Her house backed onto the Gilmais site so the pool and club were pretty much her second home as a result of which she was able to slip into her bikini and top up her tan whenever she chose.

Paula was extremely attractive and whilst not in any sense a classical beauty she had a gorgeous figure. Also, there was just something about the way she moved and behaved or looked at you that was so sexy that she had pretty well all of us boys at her feet.

I was never promoted to 'boyfriend' status but did go out with her a couple of times. She was inclined to share herself around between her adoring admirers allowing us to spend a few pounds on her whilst all the while remaining just a little reserved. You might just manage a kiss or a little more and there it stopped – well it did for me at least.

Paula (right) with another friend Rosemary - sadly no longer with us.

Meanwhile back in my Ashtead circle my friend Barry had become a base guitar player with a little local rock band called The Cosmos (sounds naff now doesn't it).

They had become very popular locally and much in demand for playing at functions such as private parties and the above mentioned village hall dances. I had somehow worked my way on board as a sort of 'roadie' lending a hand with the lugging of the weighty loudspeakers and other assorted kit that was apparently required and as such found myself at a number of interesting venues.

One evening the group had been booked to play at a dance for 'Young East Africans' somewhere in Bayswater. We'd got ourselves lost or otherwise delayed on route and were joking that we'd probably be met by a crowd of angry tribesmen with bones in their noses all shaking spears at us. We were so wrong because the gathering was more like a Young Conservatives gathering and they were in fact all the pampered offspring of British ex-pats working as diplomats or similar colonial functions.

I jumped out when we arrived, apologised for our lateness and asked where they wanted us to set up. They must have assumed I was the manager because at the end of what turned out to be a very successful gig the organiser pressed a wad of cash into my hand with much thanks for giving them such a good time.

By this time the poor old Norton in the shed at the bottom of our garden was becoming more and more neglected and even my interest in fancy machines like Dave's and motorbikes in general was beginning to be eclipsed by my approaching seventeenth birthday and Dad's promise of my first car driving lesson.

Coincidentally with this developing interest in cars I got to know a chap called John Bowyer who had a very much modified Austin A35. Now this might seem almost laughable today but at the time minis had not yet come into their own in the world of motor sport and believe it or not the modest little 'teapots' as they were known could hold their own against many more powerful cars like Mk 2 Jaguars and others. Indeed they still do at historic race meetings held at Goodwood which was where I first saw John race his car.

The little Austin had been lowered for track use, and had most of the interior trim removed for weight saving along with serious modifications to the engine. It also had a straight-through exhaust system which made it a bit difficult to ignore particularly with the race numbers in circles on the doors. All of which made it the ideal vehicle to meet two travelling nuns at Heathrow Airport.

What happened was that my aunty Peggy, who had become Sister Hildegarde when she escaped from Ireland years before, was due some home leave from the convent in Zimbabwe (or Rhodesia as it then was) and Mum had offered her a few days at our place. Unfortunately on the day she arrived neither parent was able to go and meet her so John volunteered for the job.

John had never met a nun before and what's more there were two of them as in those days they were not allowed to travel alone. So he was somewhat apprehensive to say the least especially at the prospect of squeezing them into the back of the little Austin with virtually no suspension and an exhaust that would totally preclude any conversation.

In the event, Peggy and her companion took it all in their stride and far from sitting in the back praying for safe arrival they were positively crowing with excitement by the time we arrived at home.

It must have looked so incongruous to see (and hear) John's car pull-up outside our house only to decant a pair of holy sisters in their black habits and headgear.

The race-prepared A35 doing its stuff at Goodwood

Chapter 12- My First Drive

There are many moments in life that one always remembers and in my case one of the most memorable was my first driving lesson. Of course there had been the sessions with the old van at school which undoubtedly helped a bit with the basics like clutch control but I'm now talking about driving officially and on the public road.

Once again I have my father to thank because he had promised that on my seventeenth birthday he would give me my first driving lesson. The year was 1961 and the family car was a red and cream 1958 Hillman Minx with a bench seat in the front and the gear change lever mounted on the side of the steering column.

On went the L plates and after a pretty brief verbal description and demonstration by Dad it was my turn. Well kangaroos had nothing on me. We leapt and lurched and zig-zagged off down our road – yes the public road – watched and waved off by Mum, my sister, my mates, and it seemed to me almost all the neighbours. Such was the community in those days that rites of passage like this were a big deal and went round the bush-telegraph like wildfire.

We were thankfully soon out of sight and I settled down to driving 'straight and level' after a fashion until after a couple of miles we arrived in Leatherhead and Dad said *"Ok son. Turn left here and stop"*. As soon as we made the turn I knew what he was up to. The road was Park Rise, the steepest hill in the area.

I looked at him and said, *"You must be joking"*. He said, *"Am I laughing? If you can do a hill start here you can do it anywhere and we're not going anywhere else until you can"*

"Feel the engine slowing" he said. *"Gradually ease the clutch until it starts to bite. A gentle squeeze on the throttle, handbrake off and Bob's your uncle"*
Engine screaming – lurch – stop.
"Ok start it again," he says calmly for what seemed like the hundredth time *"and this time very gently"*

Yes! We're rolling and I'm set to wave goodbye to Park Rise when he says, *"Ok stop again". "What?"*

"Once is no good. You've got to be able to do it every time and no rolling back into the bloke in the posh car behind. Hang on a minute."

At this point he started fishing about in his pocket. Out came his Woodbines and I thought, *"He's going to give me fag as a reward."*
In my dreams!
Now he had a box of matches and he said. *"They used to do this in the army. I'm going to stick it behind the wheel so you'll crush it if you roll back even a fraction"*
"OK" he said. *"Off you go"*

A few seconds later as we turned out of Park Rise onto the flat he said *"Stop"*
"What now Dad?" I said and glared at him impatiently as I yanked the handbrake on. He said *"I'm going to check the match box."*

Getting back in the car he said, *"I should think you need a cigarette now don't you?"*
This really was a first and as he lit my cigarette I smiled at the perfect un-marked match-box.

We drove miles together over the next few weeks, often with Mum and Angela on board as we explored the back roads of Surrey and Sussex and all the time I grew in confidence. Too much as it turned out.

Dad had never taken a driving test and was so indignant when I failed mine. It was like a reflection on his driving and his teaching but obviously he didn't know the finer points that the examiner was looking for. Basically he'd done too good a job because I was too confident and as a result drove too fast and according to the examiner with insufficient caution.

I had six lessons with a local driving instructor, passed the test and the door opened to what has become one of the loves of my life; the world of cars, motor sport and driving in general.

The instructor was a former police sergeant and we chatted quite a bit about his time in the job and, who knows, that may have been where the seeds of a future career were sown.

The evening after I passed the test I was due to go to college and Mum said, *"I suppose you'll want to drive now won't you?"* Naturally I did.

I shall never forget that day and I have always believed it is 'going solo' for the first time that either makes or breaks a driver and possibly for the rest of their motoring life. A bad experience on that important occasion could so damage one's self-confidence that it might be hard to recover. Happily in my case it was fine. I drove off up the road grinning like the proverbial Cheshire cat and I'm sure if anyone had seen me they'd have thought I was some kind of nutter.

Of course the problem for me now was that I didn't have my own car and not much hope of saving enough in the short term to buy one.

Although Dad allowed me to use the family car to go to college he drew the line at allowing me to take it over as my own so for the time being friends' cars or my trusty bike remained my principal means of transport.

It was probably around this time that I met Ken Thorn although I don't now recall precisely how. It was most likely to have been through the swimming pool crowd. Ken was from Leatherhead and from a somewhat different background to me.

He lived with his widowed mother in a rather select development of flats and although his father had died around three years previously there was clearly no shortage of money probably due to the fact that they had sold a substantial house in another part of the town and moved into the flat.

Apart from becoming a close friend, Ken was also a particularly useful friend at that time because he did have a car, a Triumph Herald if I remember correctly that I think was subsidised or perhaps even provided by the estate agents he worked for.

It was the ideal job for Ken because he was a pretty suave and smart guy and to be honest as time went on I came to understand that he didn't have that many scruples as far as business was concerned, nor for that matter in his attitude towards women.

He was a good looking chap too and had a way about him that meant he had no trouble finding female company but also no problem moving on. He said to me once *"I'm the one they go to bed with and it's you they fall in love with. I know which I'd rather be."*

He was quite right. I've always had a bit of a conscience about treating people fairly and although I guess I wouldn't want it otherwise it has been a bit of a hindrance to progress over the years. Also in the dating game I was still carrying a lot of the hang-ups from the religious teaching at school so whilst I really wanted to get some sexual experience I was also half afraid to do so.

At this time the 60's had hardly started to swing in the permissive sense and there was still the notion around that "nice girls don't" so for me losing my virginity seemed a bit if an uphill struggle.

I wouldn't like to say that I picked up too many of Ken's attitudes but I made a point of trying to emulate his style to some extent and in those early years we really were a pair of posers in our smart gear and his flash car.

On special occasions, as in he just felt like it, or we had a couple of girls we really wanted to impress, he would manage to borrow his mother's car which was a Wolesley 16/60. It had real leather seats that smelled wonderful and polished walnut dashboard and door caps that just looked so luxurious or so we thought as we set off to pick up the latest dates.

That car was so much more spacious than the Herald that it really was the perfect 'passion wagon' if you weren't too worried about making out in the back seat with your mate trying to do the same just a couple of feet away in the front.

As we all came of age and either got our driving licences or better still our own cars, one of the Gilmais crowd had the idea of starting a car club based, not on the swimming pool but would you believe, on the local pub. Probably not the ideal combination but this was in the pre-breathalyser era so somehow the idea didn't seem quite as odd as it does now. The Oak Motor Club was born and we set about organising a programme of meetings that involved a fair amount of drinking and events that involved a lot of driving one of which was to be a treasure hunt. And this was how I first got to go anywhere with Paula who had the use of a car belonging to her parents.

As not all the members were car owners (yet), it was suggested that owners and those without cars pair up as driver / navigator teams for the treasure hunt which predictably enough very soon started to take on the nature of a rally rather than a pleasant run in the country.

Somehow or other I managed to get myself teamed with Paula who turned out to be a really great driver and I wasn't in the least nervous as we spent a great afternoon thrashing around country lanes looking for clues. I can't recall now how we faired in the competition but it was great fun and it really threw us together. A few weeks later when I invited her to my firms New Year dance she agreed and so I put my bike on the train from Ashtead to Bookham, pedalled up to her house and went off to the do in her car.

When we got back to Paula's house everyone was in bed so she asked me in for a coffee which as I'd hoped turned into coffee and a cuddle but nothing more despite my best efforts so at about 2 am. I set out to pedal back home.

A couple of days later I phoned to say Hello and was answered by Paula's sister who said something like *"My God, you really put the cat among the pigeons the other night."* So I said *"What are you talking about?"*

She explained that after I had left, Paula had gone to pick up our cups from the sitting room, sat and down and promptly went to sleep on the sofa where during the course of the night she apparently slid down dragging her dress up over her thighs. When her parents came down in the morning and saw her there all déshabillé they jumped to all the wrong conclusions that I'd had my wicked way with her right there under their noses so to speak.

Obviously Paula was able to put them right but there was apparently quite a ruckus until they accepted she was telling the truth. I stayed friends with Paula but my hoped-for romance never got off the ground. Shame, as I was really quite smitten with her.

Doing the double handed thing with Ken did become a bit of a pain after a while and it must have looked as though we were practically joined at the hip. Terrible twins. That would have been about right at the time but it was all to come to grief eventually and precisely because of the closeness between us the break up when it came would be all the more painful. However, that was a few years ahead.

Despite all this working together I did have other friends from my school days and was still in touch with a few of the kids from the Church Youth Club one of whom was a pretty little girl called Sue Stevens.

I had been out with Sue a couple of times and had become quite fond of her in the half romantic, half lecherous way you do at seventeen. But, as my bike was my only mode of transport our assignations were not exactly that romantic being confined to a bench in the corner of Ashtead 'rec' or the back doorstep of her house before her old man came out and called her inside. I really needed a car so once again driven by my adolescent hormones, a plan emerged.

By this time Dad was an area manager for what in those days was quite a large supermarket chain. The company was Keymarkets, part of the Fitch – Lovell Group that Dad had found himself working for when the grocery shop he used to manage in Ashtead had been taken over by the group along with the butchers on the other side of the road.

Sadly but predictably I guess, the old style grocery shop had been closed down and Dad was appointed as provisions manager at the shiny new Keymarkets branch that was opened in Epsom. This was on the site of the old Granada cinema – yet another scene of much back row shenanigans in my earlier teenage years.

Dad – the area manager

Within quite a short time it seemed, he was offered the job of branch manager which he held for a couple of years before he was promoted again to area manager for what sounded like most of the south-east. In addition to financial rewards the job came with a car, also a Triumph Herald although unlike Kens, this was brand new.

I don't really know why may parents decided to hang on to the old Hillman Minx apart from the fact that whilst old it was in fact more spacious and comfortable for family outings than the new Herald. In any event it was this that became the focus of my plan to impress Sue.

At the time most people on the estate that owned cars either parked in the street, in the estate car park just around the corner from our house or had rented a garage in the same car park which was what my parents had done. So the old Hillman Minx was tucked away in the garage while Dad was using the firm's car.

I arranged to meet Sue on a day when I knew my parents wouldn't be around to ask so in their absence I simply went to the garage and took the Hillman. She was well impressed when I turned up with the 'wheels' and off we went, to Box Hill if I remember correctly. Well we had a lovely walk

then stopped off for a drink at a pub on the way home before pulling into a layby not far from Sue's house to say our 'goodnights' and I must say the old Minx with its bench seat was a great deal more comfortable than the places we had to resort to previously.

In fact this turned into the hottest experience I'd ever had with a girl and only stopped short of full sex because neither of us really knew how. On reflection this was just as well because I hadn't given a thought to any form of protection.

Both somewhat surprised and exhilarated by the intensity of what had happened neither of us knew quite what to say so we kissed goodnight and I saw her to her house. I then set off to return the car with the idea that what Mum and Dad didn't know about me borrowing the car wouldn't harm them.

Driving into the car park I was furious to see that I'd left the garage doors wide open although the full import of this fact didn't hit me immediately. I drove into the garage, locked the car and turned to leave then stopped dead.

Parked there right opposite the wide open doors, was Dad's Triumph Herald. He could not have failed to see the Hillman was gone. I couldn't believe I had been so stupid and now what the hell was I going to say?

By the time I'd walked round to the house a few minutes later it was just before eleven o'clock and I'd decided that a straight cough and apology was going to be the best approach and then take whatever storm that unleashed. My story was that the opportunity to take Sue out had come at the last minute and there had been no chance to ask permission to have the car. I knew it was thin but it was the best I could come up with.

Going in the front door I could see that there was still a light on in my parents' room so any idea of sneaking furtively in and deferring the showdown until the morning clearly wasn't an option. I climbed the stairs with my heart pounding but for very different reasons than an hour before. Dad and Mum were both sitting up in bed. Dad reading a book and Mum her nightly prayers from a little pile of prayer cards that she kept beside the bed. Situation normal.

I was puzzled. They were obviously going to leave it to me.
"I'm so sorry Dad." I blurted out. *"I know I should have asked but you weren't here."*

I was about to go on and develop the story and justification when Dad looked up and said *"What on earth are you talking about Brian?"*

"Oh SHIT!!!" I thought. *"He didn't notice. Shit! Shit! Shit!"*

So then to my huge embarrassment I had to start again, confessing to what I'd done, how sorry I was etc. etc. I was blathering away when I suddenly realised that they were both smiling and suddenly the whole tension of the moment was broken because they were just so amused at the mess I'd got myself into and probably the worse mess I was making of getting myself out of it.

In the event apologies were accepted, we all agreed it was a daft, and worse, a dishonest thing to have done but so long as I understood that, then it was all over as far as they were concerned. Sometimes they really were quite amazing.

One thing the whole episode did do though was to emphasise how much I needed a car of my own, not just for one off occasions like this but also to be less dependent on Ken. The problem was that on the paltry amount I was earning at McMurdos this was going to be a very long haul.

Meanwhile, and probably because my mind was focused on other things mainly below my belt, I was falling further behind with my college course and wondering how I might extricate myself when I ran into Dave. He was the one who had left McMurdo's to go to sea and was home between trips. It was when he told me of the exotic places he'd already seen in just a few short months that an idea began to germinate.

If you're wondering what happened to Sue, I did see her for quite a while longer. But for the same reasons as previously – lack of location and therefore opportunity – we never did manage to recreate the passion and magic of the night in the Hillman and eventually went our separate ways.

Our red Hillman Minx circa 1959

Chapter 13 – Off to Sea

It must have been so hard for my parents when I decided to throw up my studies and a secure job to go off to sea, especially as Dad had been so influential in getting me the job in the first place. So why wouldn't they be shocked and disappointed? Well of course I can see it now. With the benefit of hindsight and the experience of navigating my own two kids through their 'interesting' teenage years, I can understand only too well.

I mean, here I was, the elder child on whom they had spent significant resources to provide a private education that I had signally failed to make the most of as evidenced by my three paltry 'O' levels. And now apparently I wanted to chuck it all up completely.

Actually disappointed is something of an understatement. Horrified would be a more accurate description of their response although I think Dad did get what was going on. Mum however absolutely did not and bearing in mind the priority she placed on education, apoplectic would be a better description of her reaction. You could have cut the atmosphere with a knife.

"How could you do it?"
"After all we've done for you."
"What about your career?"
"What sort of future do you think you'll have"? Etc. etc.

For my part however the decision was made and this was my way out. I was off to see the world and at someone else's expense. What could be wrong with that? I could catch up later with my scientific career (or not, as it turned out) and if I'd been a bit older I would have been in for a couple of years National Service and anyway isn't it right for a young man to want to stand on his own feet – so my argument went. They didn't see it that way.

However, and in retrospect quite surprisingly for one as young and immature as I was; I stuck to my guns and said I was going to do it anyway and sorry if they didn't like it.

Within a few days I found my way to Leadenhall Street in the City of London and the offices of P&O, or to give its full title the Peninsular and Oriental Steam Navigation Company.

Although attracted by the idea I must have known even if subconsciously that this was not going to be my career for life. In my friend's case it was. He had joined as deck crew and was planning to work his way through a cadetship and ultimately to a seaman's ticket.

All I wanted though was to escape what I saw as the drudgery of work in the lab, or more particularly the evening classes, combined with the chance to see a bit of the world, so I asked what they could offer on the catering side of things. Yes they wanted stewards, and if I passed a medical they could offer me a job. As it happened there was a doctor on the premises so to my surprise within an hour I'd been passed fit and taken on as a Utility Steward.

To anyone who recalls the post war years 'utility' as in 'utility mark' meant sound but basic and basic was the bit that applied to my new post, but more of that later. Effectively U.S. is the first rung on the ladder in the catering side of life at sea and can be a bit mucky as I was to discover.

"Go home." they said *"But don't give your notice in until we find you a ship"*
In the meantime I had to get a union card which entailed a trip to London's docklands armed with a couple of passport size photos and where, after signing on the line I became a fully-fledged member of the Seaman's Union. Not knowing quite what to expect I went back to work when amazingly within about a week later I had a call to report to the SS Himalaya at Southampton in two weeks' time.

At home the recriminations went on right up until the day of my departure when it all disappeared in floods of tears and hugs and fond goodbyes and promises to write as I climbed on board the train for Southampton docks where I was due to sign on with the SS Himalaya.
And so it began.

I met a couple of other guys on the train who by complete chance also happened to be heading for the same ship so we shared a cab from the station to the quay where the 700-foot, 28,000 ton liner was being provisioned for the cruise.

The journey of a lifetime as far as I was concerned, that was going to take me to all of the places I had only read about. I felt I'd burst with excitement and not a little trepidation.

Although certainly not large by today's standards, Himalaya looked absolutely enormous to me. Towering above us like the cliffs of Dover, the white painted hull glistened in the morning sun and emitted a hum of activity that hinted at imminent departure.

Processions of lorries came and went as load after load of all manner of stores were fed up three or four conveyor belts and disappeared into the bowels of the ship. Next a large refrigerated lorry pulled up and half a dozen white clad porters emerged from another gangplank and began almost sprinting on and off the ship whilst carrying impossibly large sides of beef, lamb and pork. Meanwhile further along the quay a crane was busy swinging nets of cargo off the dock and into one of the large deck hatches.

The fellows I'd met on the train were also new recruits so we had each other for moral support as we dragged our cases up the steeply sloping gang plank marked "CREW" that disappeared into a hole in the side of the ship about 20 feet above the quayside.

High above our heads a level covered walkway festooned with bunting extended from the passenger terminal to A deck. That was the way the paying customers arrived. It seemed to emphasise that we were very literally "below stairs".

Entering the ship through a hatch I later learnt was known as a 'gun-port' we found ourselves in front of a makeshift desk of old packing chests behind which were two smartly uniformed officers.

The Staff Captain, responsible for all ships personnel seemed a bit young for the job but smiled a welcome, shook our hands and introduced us to the Second Steward, responsible to the Chief Steward for all catering matters including staff.

The contrast could not have been greater.
"Names?" he demanded. No smile or handshake here.
"Books" he glowered, holding out his hand for our Seaman's Books and passports.

Checking us off against a long alphabetical list he eventually turned to a nervous looking boy standing behind him and said
"Peak 18 for these" and addressing us
"Sign-on is at half six in the morning in the galley. Don't be late"

The nervous boy who only looked about 14 motioned us to follow and set off briskly along an alleyway that sloped gradually upwards. After what seemed a very long way and a few corners he indicated a narrow door on the right bearing the figure 18.

"This is yours." he said pushing the door open and standing back to let us pass.

"What does peak mean?" I asked as I squeezed past.
"Short for forepeak. Sharp end to you. You'll soon get used to it" he grinned.
"I'm a bellboy – name's Robin - basically a gofer but it's fine. You've got the rest of the day free so you'd better make the most of it. Have a good look around, don't get in the way and get drunk tonight but not too drunk 'cos you've got an early start in the morning."

Dave, one of my fellow rookies said, *"Where's the best place to go for a drink?*

"Horse and Groom's a good laugh and it's only a short walk" said Robin and was gone.

We now had the chance to look around and get the measure of our new surroundings.

Well, to be honest it certainly wouldn't have taken much measuring as the cabin was only about 12 feet square and contained not three but six beds. The three double bunks were only about 2 feet wide and with two passages effectively filled the width of the cabin while the remaining space was occupied by a small table, two chairs and a row of six steel lockers.

On the wall (sorry – bulkhead) alongside or behind each bunk was a small lockable cupboard.

The cabin was basically a steel box painted in a sort of dull buttermilk colour whilst the steel framed bunks were or rather had been a kind of grey-blue colour although mostly it was chipped to reveal the grey metal beneath.

Two circular ceiling lights with wire framed protective guards were somewhat reminiscent of a prison and smaller wall mounted versions provided reading lights for each bunk. The only natural light was provided by two brass-framed portholes set in the inch thick steel hull and was all there would be between us and the might of the ocean. Scary!!

However we were undaunted, (if privately I at least was a little disappointed at the sparseness of it all), and set about settling in. Being the first arrivals and able to take our pick of the bunks and lockers that we deemed best, we staked our claims and got organised.

I chose the top bunk against the inside wall and unpacked my case, carefully putting my toiletries, writing materials and a few other personal items in the little wall cabinet.

The other two chaps did likewise. Dave, the older of the two was about 25 and an East-ender; a real Cockney, bright and breezy with a ready smile and a really sharp wit. I liked him immediately on the train and we'd found an easy rapport. Tim was younger. Just 20 but still older than my eighteen years, He was more reserved and I judged by his voice that he'd been well educated.

Both claimed the same reason as me for heading off to sea – a quest for an adventure and an opportunity to see a bit of the world at someone else's expense. Once organised in our cabin, we set off for a wander around the ship and thence to the Horse and Groom to do as instructed.

Now what we didn't know was that The Horse and Groom was the gay centre of the city although of course in those days the word was not gay but queer or camp. In our naïve innocence we were inside before we realised it and the sight was truly something to behold, as indeed our faces must have been.

The place was heaving with a shoulder to shoulder crush of customers many of whom seemed to be in full drag ranging from micro minis to gowns that would not have disgraced the foyer of a London theatre.

There were wonderful wigs, false eyelashes, pouting red lips and fishnet clad legs in 3-inch heels all bumping and grinding to a heavy rock-n-roll rhythm but above all the atmosphere was unbelievable. It seemed just so happy and blissfully uninhibited and incredibly the only real women in the place were the two behind the bar.

Everyone seemed to know each other yet we newcomers whose wide-eyed innocence must have stuck out like the proverbial sore thumb were simply absorbed, swallowed up until in what seemed like moments we felt we belonged. It really was the most incredible experience given that until then my only knowledge of what in those days we called 'homos' had been gleaned via smutty jokes and seemingly impossible graphics on toilet walls.

After an hour or so I suddenly remembered that Dad had asked me to phone home and tell them I'd arrived safely. Well, I had certainly arrived but quite how safe I was, I must admit I was beginning to wonder.

Dad answered the phone and after the first re-assuring words to confirm my arrival on board the ship, naturally, it all started to pour out.

'Dad, you should see all the queers

"Shh! lad – your mother's here"

This was our 'best' uniform. Day to day gear as I was to discover shortly was much more basic. The cap was only ever intended to be worn for 'boat drill' so that in the event of an emergency and everyone having to report to muster stations, passengers would be able to identify crew who would 'look after them and see them safely on board lifeboats.

(If they didn't jump in themselves! I reckon that would be a tough call. I'd like to think I might have been heroic but who can tell)

Chapter 14 –All at Sea 1

At the time, SS Himalaya was pretty well up there in the pantheon of luxury cruise liners. Launched in 1949, she was the first major post war project out of Barrow in Furness and at the time of her launch was the fastest and largest ship ever owned by P&O. So when we met in 1962, she was still pretty much 'state of the art', which, as I was shortly to discover, was far from 'state of the art' as we might define it today.

Himalaya offered First and Tourist class accommodation and with around 500 crew to serve the needs of 1100 passengers one can get an idea of the standard of service provided. However it was to be some time before we new recruits saw much luxury.

Not all the crew were European; quite a number were of Indian origin, mostly from Goa just south of Mumbai. They were employed in both the catering and deck functions of the ship and were generally speaking very good at their work as many of them had been 'on the boats' for years. However, there was discrimination and the accommodation allocated to the Indian crew was definitely inferior to ours which doesn't say much considering ours was pretty basic.

Known as Lascars (from the Persian word for sailor) the deck crew lived in what were in all honesty pretty squalid conditions below decks at the stern of the ship – and certainly the noisiest part owing to the propeller rotation. The catering crew were virtually all table stewards and mostly employed in the Tourist Class saloon although I think there were one or two in First Class.

It was probably just as well that our accommodation was separate because they never dined with us in the crew mess, preferring to cook up their own traditional dishes and eat communally, all squatting around large dishes of curry and rice on the floor and eating with their fingers. I must say it smelled wonderful as I passed their quarters but I wouldn't have wanted it in my nostrils all the time.

As I said, they were good at their jobs by virtue of long experience but the table stewards were particularly exasperating as they appeared to have only two speeds – slow and stop. Nevertheless they always finished their sittings, got their passengers out and were away long before the other stewards.

I also learnt quite quickly that the Goanese crew were useful in other ways. Being mostly Muslim they were abstemious with alcohol, also careful with money, which they saved to send home and so took every opportunity to earn a bit more. This included providing a laundry and tailoring service to us Europeans, many of whom, like me, didn't have clue about such things.

Without relevant previous experience in the hotel or related industries new recruits to the catering section always joined as 'Utility Stewards', which in the case of Dave and I, meant we were assigned to the plate house – i.e. dish washing. However this was not the only thing we would have to do as we discovered when we clocked on in the galley at 6.30 the following morning.

Here we were issued with the uniform and tools of our trade that comprised two pairs of loose denim trousers, Wellington boots and a couple of blue and white striped cotton jackets.

Not that it occurred to me at the time, but looking back it was almost exactly the garb (apart from the boots) that one sees worn by prison inmates. In addition we were each given a galvanised bucket, scrubbing brush, metal scraper, wire wool scourer, a large block of hard soap, a couple of loose-weave cloths and several tea-towels.

The Second Steward then marched us off, back towards the crew accommodation where he stopped in the alleyway outside our cabins. Each of us was responsible for an area of the floor that was to be scrubbed by hand each morning after we had clocked on and would have to be inspected before we could go to breakfast.

The alleyway, which was about 10 feet wide, was marked off along the edge in 8-foot lengths and each was given a code.

Mine was S9, which translated as section 9 of the working alleyway that ran through the starboard side of the crew's quarters; starboard being the right hand side when facing the front or bow of the ship, for those of us that didn't know, which included me.

"Ok" he said *"Get changed, fill your buckets with hot water over there in the 'heads' and back here in three minutes"*

"Right. Get on with it then" he said *"Let's see what you're made of."*

So while he lolled against the wall smoking and flicking ash on our floors we got down on our knees and started.

Well, you can imagine what sort of a job an 18 year old made of scrubbing a floor. What to do first? Soap on the brush or soap on the floor? How much water? And God knows what was in that soap because at almost took the skin off my hands.

"No that's no good," he'd say. *"Look there's a scuff mark here"* or *"This looks like chewing gum – use the scraper"*

How we came in the space of about three days to loathe that man! I'd have cheerfully scrubbed the floor with his face.

However, we eventually got the way of it. By watching the older hands we soon realised that the trick was less water and less soap too. In fact less of everything seemed to make the whole process faster and with vigorous use of the scraper or scourer for stubborn marks the job could be accomplished quite easily. As time went on we learnt from the older or more experienced stewards that less is almost invariably more and I think the same holds true through much of life.

Once "the old bastard" as we came to call him realised that we'd got it sussed he got bored with bullying us and only showed up for weekly inspections.

So that was how our days began. This was followed by breakfast which I have to say was always excellent and whilst not served in the same style as it was to the passengers, we were able to choose more or less anything we wanted from the Tourist class menu. However, leisurely it was not, because we had to resume work at eight o'clock.

For the first couple of days before we sailed, we were employed to do a whole range of fairly menial tasks that mostly included fetching, carrying and cleaning jobs associated with readying the ship for the boarding of the passengers.

My first trip was to be a two week mini-cruise to the Mediterranean calling at Casablanca, Naples, Palamos and Gibraltar, all of which sounded the most exotic and romantic destinations imaginable to us new recruits, most of whom had never been out of the country.

Boarding was scheduled for the Friday afternoon and was planned to give passengers the opportunity to settle in before Himalaya sailed at six and to be clear of the Solent and well down the Channel by the time dinner was served at 7.30.

In those days the departure of a big ship from its berth in Southampton was always something of an event and even when only leaving for a short cruise could be relied upon to give rise to a fair amount of razzmatazz.

Although the 'back-room' crew such as we Utility Stewards were supposed to keep a low profile and very much away from the passengers we all managed to get up onto the fore-deck which was the crew's designated recreational area to watch the goings-on.

As the appointed sailing time approached, Tannoy announcements were made on board reminding friends and family to go ashore and were accompanied by strident sounding of the ship's siren to indicate its imminent departure. Then a local military band came marching along the quay and entertained all and sundry to a medley of popular tunes whilst the last stragglers left the ship. Finally, as hundreds of coloured streamers were thrown between the passengers along the rails and the well-wishers on shore the bunting-draped gangway was swung away and the ship secured for sea.

Huge capstans whined as the thick steel hawsers securing Himalaya to the mooring bollards were released and drawn in-board whilst on the sea-ward side a couple of powerful tugs gently eased the great white lady away from the quay until she was able to start her own engines and set sail down the Solent. From this point on, life for the crew, and especially for us 'untouchables', dropped into a routine totally associated with mealtimes on board the ship.

The early morning job didn't change apart from the fact that it simply became so much a part of routine as to be unnoticed. However 'plate-house' duties whilst equally predictable really were something else.

There were two dish-washing areas serving the Tourist and the First Class restaurants. Whilst the work in each area was effectively the same, the First Class dish-washers among whom I found myself had this fanciful notion that we were a cut above the others.

Perhaps this was because we were disposing of a better class of left-overs from plates emblazoned with a posh logo. Now that was snobbery above and beyond but I guess if your life is washing dishes you need to find your self-esteem where you can.

The plate-house consisted of a square area with stainless steel surfaces all round, one side of which fronted onto the alleyway between the galley and the doors out of the restaurant. It was onto this surface that the waiters or 'wingers' as they were known would deposit all the dirty plates and cutlery on their way out of the restaurant and en-route to the galley before returning to the restaurant along the opposite leg of this one-way system.

Along this surface of some 12 or 14 feet were three equally spaced holes through which we had to scrape all the left-overs into metal dustbins underneath the surface. Large rubber grommets around each hole served to prevent plates from getting chipped.

With plate-scrapings comprising a revolting mixture of moist food detritus, fish-bones, sauces, gravy etc. the dustbins were extremely heavy and as they had in due course to be disposed of overboard this presented quite a challenge in itself not to mention some interesting adventures.

The restaurants on board were located quite low down in the ship and not that far above the water line, and while the restaurants themselves were air conditioned after a fashion, the galley and plate-house area was not.

I guess it stood to reason really that with all the heat generated in that area any form of air-conditioning would have had its work really cut out to make much impact. As a consequence the working conditions were at best too hot and at the worst indescribably awful.

Except in the roughest of weather we always worked with the portholes open and in order to further improve the ventilation someone had invented the 'air-scoop'. This was similar in effect to sticking your hand out of an open car window while in motion and diverting a cooling draught of air inwards. This metal blade protruded out of the porthole and most of the time worked very well to improve the ventilation.

However, just occasionally; and you're probably ahead of me by now; being fairly close to the water the blade would catch the odd higher wave and direct not cool air but a deluge; not just a little splash, but gallons of cold sea water onto whoever had the misfortune to standing in the wrong place.

This always caused huge hilarity to everyone but the unfortunate victim, although the bottom line was that we all suffered because with the floor inches deep in water we were all slithering around all over the place. It wasn't until I experienced this for the first time that I understood why we'd been issued with 'wellies', although we rarely wore them, finding flip-flops or even bare feet more comfortable. Looking back at the situation through modern 'health and safety' eyes it is almost impossible to believe but at the time we didn't give it a second thought.

There were six of us in the plate-house. Three receiving and scraping, two loading and unloading the dishwashing machine, and the other stacking up the crockery for collection by the wingers, which brings me to another little curiosity about the job.

As I was to discover some weeks later, a key element of the waiting job is to be able to get your passengers served as quickly (within reason) as they want to eat, thereby giving yourself less time at work and more time off duty. To achieve this you need to have available a ready supply of clean plates. Stands to reason I know, but once a meal sitting begins, the supply of clean hot plates in the galley soon dries up.

Then each waiter has to fall back on the supply that he has, if wise, put by in his own 'dumb waiter' – the little heated locker near to each serving station in the restaurant.

This in turn relies on the relationship he has built up with the guys in the plate-house, which in reality means how much he pays them.

So you have this interesting little bit of graft going on. Passengers tip the waiters to get that bit of extra special treatment and behind the scenes the waiters are paying off the dish-washers, the chefs, the locker men and so on so that they can actually provide that extra special service to the passengers. As everyone's favourite meerkat says "Simples!"

I guess the clever waiters are the ones who actually manage to pay out less than they receive so leaving a small margin for themselves.

There was one memorable day when I did come to regret wearing the 'wellies' although to be honest, with or without, the result would have been equally revolting.

As I mentioned, disposal of the food waste presented something of a challenge, mainly because of the weight of the bins when filled.

A few yards from the plate-house there was the disposal chute (I never could understand why it was not actually inside but there you go!). This was a tube about 10 or 12 inches in diameter that widened at the top into an aperture about 2 feet square with a metal cover that was screwed firmly down closing the chute.

About 12 feet long, the tube dropped vertically before bending and opening out of the side of the ship more or less on the water line.

On the day in question, Dave and I had struggled to drag one of the bins over to the chute. Having opened the cover, we'd managed between us and with some considerable effort to up-end the bin into the chute but unfortunately for some reason or another, the contents jammed in the chute and of course the weight on top of it meant that it was well and truly blocked.

Apparently this was not an unknown occurrence because to one side against the wall there was a long wooden pole and as one of the chefs nearby pointed out to us, all it needed was "a good poke".

If we had noticed the small crowd of onlookers that was gathering, albeit at some distance, we might have had some inkling of what was about to happen. However between us we were so busy jointly ramming away with the pole that we didn't pay any heed.

Once again here, you may be ahead of me. Suddenly the ship gave an unexpected roll, and forced upwards by the sudden ingress of a large volume of water into the bottom of the tube, the entire contents of the now tightly packed chute exploded volcano-like into the air and cascaded down onto the pair of us accompanied by whoops and shrieks of hilarious laughter from the assembled onlookers.

Further description is probably superfluous but with regard to the wellies, they were full to the knees with a revolting mixture of plate scrapings and seawater. I never wore them again.

There were few benefits to dishwashing even allowing for the dubious honour of handling first-class leftovers, apart perhaps from the sheer basic nitty-gritty of it. By this I mean it is a leveller and does not allow any silly pretensions because when a group of people are all doing the same rock-bottom job and are all equally wet, filthy and at someone else's beck and call there is no room for attitude.

However, there was one little perk in addition to the tips from the waiters.

At the end of each session there was this unwritten but generally understood agreement that because it was such a rotten job, on the way out of the galley we could help ourselves to the odd item from the cold pantry. This was on the basis that the activity went unnoticed, so yes it was a tacit permission to steal.

For me, the cold pantry meant fruit and as much as I could reasonably secrete in my bucket beneath a pile of tea towels.

Dave and I had just left the pantry, me with grapes – my great weakness and he with bananas and were on our way back to the cabin when he got waylaid chatting to someone on route.

Now, as I said, grapes are my weakness and so by the time I'd got back to the cabin I'd already munched my way through quite a few and as he didn't arrive for some time I simply carried on eating. In my own defence it was probably as much to do with the need to re-hydrate myself after the shift as anything else like greed for example - surely not!

As I mentioned previously, Dave was an east-ender with an original cockney accent and I'll never, ever forget his outburst when he discovered that I'd eaten almost all the grapes.

"You bleedin' gannet you" he railed.
"Free pahnds. There must 'ave been free pahnds of bleedin grapes and you've scoffed the bleedin lot. Don't fink you're 'avin' no bananas"

I had no defence but I'm pleased to say he didn't hold a grudge although he wasn't slow to remind me of the occasion during the months we were to be shipmates.

The episode earned me the nickname 'Grape Gannet'

Chapter 15 – All at Sea 2

I must admit that the two weeks of that first trip passed in a bit of a blur – mostly alcohol induced. I wasn't at that time of my life very experienced and certainly not a hardened drinker, but there was a certain pressure, particularly amongst us rookies to "keep up" so to speak in the boozing stakes.

That was probably the reason, apart from the headaches, that I don't remember that much about the trip with a couple of notable exceptions.

The first of these occasions took place on the second night at sea. It was September and we were heading for Casablanca, our first port of call. We'd been lucky with the weather through the Bay of Biscay and it was a balmy evening as we cruised south, off the coast of Portugal towards North Africa.

Once off duty after the evening dishwashing session it was normal for the catering crew to sit around chatting and drinking in the crew's bar or if the weather was good in our outside recreational area. This was right up in the bow on the fore deck above our quarters and about as far away from the passenger decks as it was possible to get as off-duty fraternising with passengers was strictly forbidden.

Someone had a guitar and I'd had a really pleasant evening, smoking, singing along, having a few pints and basically getting to know some of my new shipmates.

One of these was a guy called Raymond that I'd met in the bar the previous evening. He was a waiter in the tourist class restaurant and had been on the ships for a few years since he ran away from an unhappy home life.

What I didn't realise though was that these occasions were also seen by the gay fraternity on board as the perfect opportunity to start sizing up us innocent newcomers with a view to establishing future relationships.

I mean, how naïve can you be! After all, we'd seen the goings-on at the Queens Head pub. As the evening had gone on some of the obvious queens had started really camping it up and even some that we hadn't sussed out up until then had really started to come out.

I don't know what it is about the camp homosexual but they can be just so incredibly funny. Of course we are used to it nowadays and this sort of camp or suggestive entertainment is the norm but back in the sixties it was risqué and quite exciting.

Sharp as nails and so quick-witted, they were a source of huge entertainment and yet so disarming that one quickly forgot about their sexual proclivity and the fact that to them the performance is simply part of the mating game as I was about to discover.

By about one o'clock in the morning it would be fair to say we were well mellow and the party started to break up. Several of us stood up, if a little unsteadily and amid a certain amount of general banter started to wander back towards our quarters, arms around shoulders and so on in a generally pleasant albeit inebriated intimacy.

I was shuffling along with Raymond who I'd been chatting to on and off most of the evening when, just as we were about to descend a short flight of stairs from the open deck to our cabins, he pulls me towards him, says *"You know I love you don't you?"* and kisses me smack on the mouth.
Well, shock wasn't in it. I was absolutely horrified.

I pulled away and without thinking, punched him straight in the face.

Now this really is not me at all. I've only ever hit, as in seriously punched, one other person in my life and that was at school and to be honest I would much rather avoid any potentially violent situation than confront it. On this occasion however, his action so repulsed me that I'm afraid it was a virtually automatic response.

I don't remember if he looked surprised or not because as soon as I hit him he disappeared from view. Unfortunately for him he was on the edge of the stairs and as he went back with the force of my punch there was nothing behind him but space and he finished up flat on his back at the bottom of the, thankfully, short flight of stairs and out cold.

The next thing is someone has grabbed me shouting, *"Christ! Brian, What the F*** was that all about?"* and I'm shouting back *"The bastard snogged me. Right on the mouth"*

Mercifully for everyone concerned his alcohol induced relaxation must have saved him from any serious injury and he soon came too and was all over me again but this time full of apologies. *"I'm so sorry. I thought you liked me too. Please forgive me."* Well, apparently 'like' had a whole new meaning on board ship and definitely more than it does on Facebook!

Apart from feeling guilty at having assaulted a shipmate, albeit justifiably in my view, I also felt embarrassed that he had seen me as being possibly amenable to his advances. And I spent hours mulling over whether I'd done or said anything to give him the wrong idea.

Fortunately one or two others had seen what happened and as I later discovered were not surprised, as this was apparently Raymond's normal MO. No messing, just straight in. I just wish that someone had given me the nod.

However, as the dust settled over the next couple of days I discovered that the episode had worked to my advantage. I learned that I was seen, if not exactly as a hard man then certainly not someone to be messed with.

I also discovered that on board ship there were two types of homosexual. There were the "queens" – often outrageously camp and effeminate but usually with hearts of gold and then there were the "black market queers" as they were known, like Raymond, who hide their inclination and were seen as potentially dangerous.

Over the next few months I had to make my own decisions about whom I chose to befriend and thankfully there were no more unpleasant incidents.

Over time I found to my surprise that many of my best friends on the ship were gay and that as long as they knew where I stood there was never an issue. Well let's be honest, after that kiss incident there couldn't have been many on board in any doubt. Thinking about the incident as I have many times over the years I can't believe how incredibly lucky I was. If Raymond had fallen harder or hit his head on something I could so easily have finished up on a charge of GBH or even manslaughter.

Chapter 16 – Foreign Parts

Embarking on this new way of life was a real eye-opener, given that apart from a few scout camps and a couple of weeks at Butlins with friends I'd never really been away from home - certainly not seriously AWAY, as in hundreds or even thousands of miles. So, while that first trip was just a two-week cruise, to me it was no less exciting for that.

After three days at sea and with memories of the disastrous deck party beginning to fade, we arrived at the port of Casablanca in the early morning with an apricot glow silhouetting the outlines of the nearby town. Observing the scene as the ship berthed I heard for the first time in my life the eerie sound of at least four muezzins calling from nearby minarets while below I could see what my wife has always called 'men in long dresses' bustling about on the quay prior to the gangways being connected.

There were dozens of camels tethered in groups, some with their front and rear legs hobbled whilst being loaded with goods landed from the many smaller and clearly local cargo vessels.

However a lot of goods were also being loaded into lorries so it was soon apparent that most of the camels were actually there to lend an air of exotic authenticity for the arriving passengers. Many of whom were almost falling over themselves with excitement to get ashore and pay the smiling 'men in long dresses' for the privilege of riding what looks like the world's most uncomfortable mode of transport. Meanwhile, the less adventurous but perhaps wiser ones ran feverishly about with their cameras recording it all for posterity or at least the family album.

Once the passengers were ashore the ship seemed strangely deserted and although we crew had to work a rota of duties to ensure everything was suitably spick and span for their return we were also allowed off the vessel for strictly controlled periods of shore leave.

Casablanca was fascinating and although I've been back there since as a tourist I'll never forget that first visit. The thing that struck me most of course was the heat, even close to the water. Also, the frenetic activity associated with our arrival and the pervasive smell of fish in the port area mixed with the occasional whiff of exotic spices. Less exotic though was the incongruous odour of diesel fumes as the wind veered around to bring the exhaust emanating from the ship's funnel back on-shore.

Being a predominantly Muslim country it was obviously far more difficult to find alcoholic drink so it was here that I first tasted mint tea.

Now this wasn't out of a packet or tea bag but was actually concocted by the infusion of a generous bunch of mint sprigs in boiling water and usually included an even more generous quantity of sugar.

Often mint tea was available right on the street served in small thick glass cups, which you can hardly touch because they're so hot. The locals though seem to have developed asbestos fingers.

Much nicer and far more atmospheric are the tearooms frequently tucked away in odd corners and where the tea ritual is more respected. Here the tea is brewed in silver or pewter teapots with felt cosies and the glasses are often contained in metal holders. Far more seemly, and what's more you are even allowed to add your own sugar.

I remember one we found was actually on the top of the old city wall and accessed via a narrow and well-worn stone staircase within the wall itself. There was an arrangement of small booths of different sizes screened by wooden slats painted a wonderful cobalt blue but now mostly faded by the north African sun to that soft pastel shade much favoured by the Homes and Gardens fraternity. Canvas tent-like canopies provided shade and the seating was brightly coloured cushions on low stools or banquettes. The small booths were clearly intended for more intimate tête-à-têtes, although at that time in Morocco tea and coffee shops customers were mostly male. Some were occupied by larger groups playing cards or dominoes and others appeared to be having serious business meetings.

The bustling Medina in Casablanca

We also made the almost mandatory visit the medina, the old walled town with its dark, mysterious and slightly intimidating souks. The Arabic word souk originally refers to an open street market, a major feature of which is the absence of any fixed prices.

This is where tourists are so often found locked in intense bouts of bartering with local traders while they argue over what amounts to a couple of pence. And all this for something that in other circumstances they wouldn't have given a second look. Funny what holidays do to us

If time ashore in Casablanca was limited for the passengers it was more so for the crew and it wasn't long before I was back in the plate house as dinner service got under way and Himalaya slipped her moorings on the next leg of our trip to Naples.

I regret not making more of the city but I don't suppose I'd ever heard of Pompeii or Herculaneum, either of which would have been worth a visit, as I now know having visited them both in later life. What I do remember is that with the exception of the impressive old Art Deco Ocean Terminal building I didn't much like what I initially saw and decided to use my day off on a trip to Capri. I've no idea at all why I did that apart perhaps that Mum used to sing a song about Capri or perhaps because I knew Gracie Fields lived there.

None of the other guys wanted to go so I found myself virtually alone on the little ferry heading out into the Bay of Naples beneath the looming cone of Vesuvius. The day was blistering and still, with only a few horsetails of cloud in an azure sky. And below, the only sound above the low hum of the engine was a gentle hiss as the bow sliced through the glassy water. I was transported and delighted beyond words. Wonderfully alone but not lonely.

On landing I immediately found a small bar and nursing a cold beer I honestly believed I was in heaven.

A few brightly painted little boats danced on the sparkling clear water while on the jetty a couple of old fishermen repaired nets. Three black clad grandmothers stood gossiping nearby and, gesticulating wildly to make a point then collapsing into gales of cackling mirth at some joke which judging by the sidelong glances at the old men on the jetty was largely at their expense.

I set off to walk up from the port following narrow paths that climbed steeply between pretty houses. Passing stone walls, terraces of vines and heavily laden fruit trees I found myself remembering the Wordsworth verses about "wandering lonely as a cloud". I was very happy.

Ambling up the hill behind Capri town that hot September morning was one of the most blissful experiences of my young life. Apart from the family holiday on the Adriatic coast a couple of years before, I had never been anywhere so caressingly warm and to me, so idyllically beautiful.

By the time I left the bar it was almost eleven o'clock and the temperature was rising rapidly. Crickets were chirping madly in the olive trees and among the grapevines planted on the steeply terraced hillside. The heady smell of Mediterranean herbs hung heavily in the hot dry air while the scent of lavender wafted up from the self-sown seedlings accidentally crushed underfoot as I followed the winding stony path behind and now high above the old town.

It was the sense of being apart but not lonely that was so entrancing and I just loved the idea that no-one I knew had any idea where I was. It was incredibly liberating and has been one of the great joys of travelling ever since.

After perhaps a mile or so of climbing, the enclosing walls ceased and I reached something of a plateau where the disintegrating terraces of bygone times were neither tended nor mended. And the orderly and luxuriant planting gave way to rough scrubby vegetation and dry gravely soil. Here the view opened out and I turned to take it in.

Immediately below, the terracotta tiles and white walls of the old town toasted in the sunshine while beyond, the shimmering blue water of the bay stretched away towards the hazy port where, in a few short hours, I knew I must re-join the ship and the real world.

However, I was far from done with Capri. Following a scarcely discernible route across the scrub I eventually picked up a downward path, larger this time and more suited to a donkey and cart than the narrow path I'd come up. I imagine that these days it's more likely to be used by the four wheel drive fraternity heading for the hills. That's assuming that the scrubby plateau hasn't been developed into an extension of Capri town. I'd rather not know.

The route down was less tortuous and consequently steeper so that I very quickly started to feel it in my knees and thigh muscles which by the time I was back in the town were on the verge of letting me down. So once again I sought out a little bar, this time in a shady back street, where I took on board some more fluid, this time of the non-alcoholic variety, a salad Niçoise and some lovely crusty bread.

I also picked up a discarded tourist map of Capri from which I learned about the Blue Grotto that could only be entered from the sea. How fascinating!

Half an hour later I was back down at the port and quickly traced the little jetty with signs for boat trips to the Blue Grotto. Apparently it was a sea cave with a very restricted entrance that could only be entered from the seaward side but then only when the weather was calm, which thankfully, it was at the time.

There were just two other people interested in taking the trip; a couple of Australian girls, backpacking their way around the world which I guess in the early 60's was quite unusual.

Within a few minutes we were chugging our way out of the harbour where to my surprise I discovered that even on a glass smooth sea a small motor boat can bob about in quite a lively fashion. I imagine the distance was barely ¾ of a mile but that can take quite a few minutes which was time enough to discover a bit more about the 2 girls. They were both 22 and had been travelling for just over a year and to my great envy were actually staying in a little pension on Capri itself, not just for a day, but for a whole week.

Suddenly we had arrived at what looked at first, just like a cliff face until our skipper pointed out a dark shadow that was the cave entrance. Cutting the engine he took up the oars and with consummate skill brought us closer to the cliff. I could certainly understand why this would not be possible in anything but the calmest weather

The cave mouth was barely 3 feet or so above the water and we had to virtually lie down in the boat as it slipped from the brilliant sunlight into what at first was total darkness accompanied by a dramatic drop in temperature. After a few seconds passing under the rock (although it seemed longer) the boatman told us to sit up and I will never forget that first sight and understood immediately why it was called the Blue Grotto.

It was as though the little boat was floating on a lake of quicksilver, in area probably about the size of a couple of tennis courts. So not exactly vast, but quite significant.
The water was the most amazing iridescent turquoise colour and as our eyes became accustomed to the light we could see it was not dark at all because the whole of the water surface was a light source that illuminated the cave roof with an eerie pale blue light.

At the boatman's suggestion we reached out and slowly dipped our arms in the water. The effect was remarkable. They turned silver. By immersing them slowly, the tiny air bubbles that remained trapped by the small hairs on our skin caught the light transmitted by the water from outside the cave and lit up like thousands of tiny bulbs. It really was the most amazing sight and was of course the reason why the whole lake surface shone with sunlight transmitted through the water into the cave from outside.

Our boatman explained that the effect was even more dramatic if you swam in the water which I unfortunately couldn't do as I didn't have a costume, but the two girls happened to have bikinis on under their dresses and without any hesitation they stripped off and were over the side in a moment.

The effect was indeed spectacular and extremely attractive as these two shapely young girls swam around like a couple of silver mermaids to the delight of both me and our ferryman. I smiled as I wondered how many times a week he managed to pull that off.

I had a drink with the girls when we got back to the port and then reluctantly took my ferry back to Naples and a pile of dirty plates.

Our next port of call was a relatively short hop in an almost straight line west from Naples and through the straits between Corsica and Sardinia to the Balearic Sea and the Catalan resort of Palamos.

In the late 1950's tourism had begun to discover Spain and by the early 60s the development of the Costas was under way and destined to continue pretty much to the present day.

Apart from bringing with it much needed income from tourism it also began what in the view of many Spanish, and foreign observers too, was the ruination of a way of life along the Spanish Mediterranean coast. It was less clearly seen in those early years but the rampant over-development of the Costas is now regretted almost unanimously by those with any sort of environmental or social conscience.

By the time I'm talking about, Tossa de Mar, L'Escala and Estartit were already quite well known Costa Brava hot-spots so I cannot imagine what on earth possessed P&O to choose the tiny fishing port of Palamos.

It could perhaps have been an attempt to prove that there were still some relatively unspoilt places that were worth a visit. I guess it's the classic conundrum. Tourists want to visit the original and unspoilt places, which very predictably then become rapidly spoilt and unoriginal.

Palamos was quite a pretty little town at that time. Little being the operative word as the port was too small and not deep enough for Himalaya to tie up so this great white monstrosity, (for that was to my mind exactly what it looked like in that context), had to anchor off the beach.

Passengers were then ferried ashore in funny little boats that had a gangplank mounted on the bow rather reminiscent of a pelican's beak. The boats were run up onto the beach and you simply walked on and off. No Problem. Well no problem if you were sober!

Now bearing in mind my immature eighteen years and relatively sheltered upbringing, certainly as far as alcohol was concerned, what occurred that afternoon was hardly surprising. Until then (apart from the Lyme Regis cider and the Butlins 'black velvet'), a couple of half pints of brown ale had been the usual limit of my experience

So when I went ashore with a bunch of hard drinking new-found ship-mates the result was pretty much a foregone conclusion. My downfall was the local St Miguel beer. Not especially strong in moderation but pretty toxic taken in excess.

And I guess that in trying to keep up with the others whose alcohol tolerance I later discovered was staggering, I probably drank seven or eight bottles plus some brandy. Oh, and of course we simply had to sample the local wine too.

After the teeth started to go numb I just sort of went with the flow as you do and I didn't really remember much until I hit the water when I fell off the gangplank. I vaguely recalled being hauled in over the side of the little boat amid a fair amount hysterical drunken laughter and dragged back to the cabin. It was only the following morning when, nursing a huge hangover, I got a roasting from the chief steward who, to be fair, was mostly concerned with the fact that I could have been seriously hurt. I guess that he'd seen it all before with young and foolish recruits.

I'd recovered enough by that afternoon to join my mates for a swim but as there was no crew pool on board and being anchored off-shore the sea had to be our pool. The issue was that the lowest part of the ship from which it was possible to get in the water was the well-deck which itself was twenty or thirty feet up. So to get a dip one had to muster the courage to leap off the ship into the sea.

The routine was then to swim forward, climb a few feet up the anchor chain, wave victoriously and then swim back alongside the ship to get back on board. One then had to scramble up a rope ladder to the gun-port from which the little beach ferries left.

Then you'd run around and do the whole thing again. Seems a bit pointless in retrospect but was fun at the time.

Whilst we were thus engaged a couple of English guys came out from the beach on a speed boat to have a look at the ship and in the course of conversation were complaining about the local cigarettes.

We were getting ours on board for 11d (pre-decimal) for 20 Senior Service so I shot back to my cabin and got them a couple of hundred which I sold at a profit but they were still so grateful that they let me have a go on their water skis. Given my sporting track record (not) I was totally useless but it was great fun.

Our final port on the cruise was Gibraltar, which unfortunately I didn't get to see as I was rostered to remain on board. Have been back there since and I must say it is a distinctly odd experience to cross the border from Spain and find yourself suddenly in this little bit of England basking in Mediterranean sunshine.

However some of us had to stay on watch in order provide a slightly scaled down service to cater to those passengers who had chosen not to go ashore. A few days later we were back in Southampton and my first trip was over.

Our stay in Southampton was to be short. We had just ten days before the ship was due to leave on a five month trip that would circumnavigate the globe. This meant that shore leave would be very limited as a great deal of work was involved in provisioning and deep cleaning.

Some of the older hands weren't worried about heading home for such a short time but we younger ones were actually encouraged to touch base with parents for at least a couple of days, a policy I thought was surprisingly sensitive. I took about five days off but then came back to work-by as it was known in preparation for the next departure. It was also an opportunity to earn a bit of extra money.

The itinerary for the next trip was very exciting and involved a quick cross-Channel hop to Cherbourg to pick up some more passengers followed by a trans-Atlantic run to Trinidad. We were then scheduled to pass through the Panama Canal, up the west coast of the USA stopping at Los Angeles and San Francisco, continuing to Vancouver before dropping down to Hawaii then across to Japan and Hong Kong. We would then head down to Manila, Fiji, New Zealand and then to Sydney our southern terminal port.

The schedule then included a Pacific cruise back around the same places returning to Sydney before commencing the return leg around the south of Australia, across to Colombo, Bombay and home via Suez.

I quite forgot to mention the princely sum we were paid by P&O.
My salary was (wait for it!) £36.50 per month. It is necessary to bear in mind that this was 'all-found' meaning all my food and accommodation was provided and if this still sounds very little a quick conversion to today's value comes out at £640 which while still not a lot was not such bad pocket money for an 18 year old.

In common with most of the crew I made an allotment of £20 that was sent home to my bank so that after 5 months I had £100, which in today's money equates to almost £1800. So I knew that when I got home I would at least have a little nest-egg which was already earmarked for the purchase of a car.

I fully expected to be continuing with my plate-house duties and indeed that's how the trip started, at least as far as Cherbourg when one of the other utility stewards was sick and had to be taken off the ship.

His job had been as a 'locker man' meaning he was responsible for the silver-ware used in the First Class saloon and it was his task to keep it in good order and dish out items of cutlery and tableware as required by the waiters.

I must have impressed someone because this poor guy's demise turned out to be my escape route from the grotty dish-washing when after just a day into the trip I was given responsibility for the silver locker.

One of my new tasks, which I found very rewarding, was burnishing. Apart from some highly polished centre-pieces, tableware such as cruets sugar basins, milk jugs and the cutlery had a semi matt finish but being silver was also liable to tarnish.

The process of burnishing involved tumbling the items in a large hexagonal barrel together with the burnishing medium. This comprised thousands of stainless steel shot and some mild abrasive powder. Just a couple of minutes in the machine restored quite knocked-about items to virtually new condition – most satisfying.

One slight downside to burnishing was that it wasn't a lot of good for knives as they would come out with almost no edge, which necessitated re-sharpening. I quite enjoyed that too if I had the time but usually the silver knife handles were very satisfactorily polished by up-ending them in a mildly caustic solution for just a couple of minutes and then buffing them to a nice bright shine.

Apart from maintaining the condition of the company's silver-ware it had been made very clear to me that I was also responsible for keeping records of what I issued and to whom.

It was well known that items of cutlery were sometimes used by dishonest waiters to trade for goods in some of the locations Himalaya was likely to visit around the world. (Really? Who'd have believed such a thing!!)

I was expected to report suspicions I had about any individual waiters to the Second Steward, which talking of knives, as we were a moment ago, left me having to walk that knife-edge between loyalty to the company and my crew-mates. In order to avoid ever having to blow the whistle on a friend I became the tightest and most 'by the book' locker man P&O ever had.

However, I can't in all honesty say I was quite so careful of the company's property a few months later when I needed some negotiable items for a trip ashore in Manila, but maybe more of that later!

For that first leg of our trip, our passenger list comprised a wide variety of individuals. There were Brits emigrating to the US, Canada or Australia who had decided to build a couple of months cruise into their travel plans and they were mostly travelling Tourist Class.
There were also the better-off Brits who were simply holidaying plus the 'money-to-burn' American tourists who were the largest contingent in the First Class section of the ship. Finally there was a relatively small group of other well-heeled business and leisure travellers comprising a mixture of nationalities most notable and noticeable of which was a bunch of extremely noisy and greedy Greeks.

One way or another we had a quite a laugh at the expense of the passengers and it has to be said, especially the Americans who were particularly gullible. They'd believe pretty much anything you told them.
The first little joke, and I understood that it worked on every trans-Atlantic trip was in relation to the Panama Canal.

Within a couple of days of leaving port the waiters and bedroom stewards would have built up a friendly rapport with most of their passengers who came to regard the crew as the source of all knowledge by virtue of their experience and time at sea. They would question avidly about all aspects of the trip and pretty much hang on their every word.

As something quite outside most passengers' experience the ship's passage through Panama was a topic of great interest and in answer to their questions passengers were often advised to save a few bread rolls for the mules that would pull the ship through the canal.

"Gee. That's incredible. This huge ship is pulled by mules?"
"Sure is." came the answer and good as gold on arrival at the canal all the yanks would turn up on deck with bags full of bread rolls.

What their new 'friends' had omitted to tell them was that they were diesel-engined 'mules' each one amounting to several hundred or thousands of horsepower. They usually took it in good part and had a laugh at their own expense.

On another occasion when the ship was hundreds of miles from the nearest land one of the passengers (also American) happened to glimpse a splash of spray blown past the window. You need to know that this was in one of the public rooms at least thirty feet above the water.

"Wow! Was that a bird" she exclaimed.
"Yes. Penguin actually." Came the poker –faced reply.

"You guys are so interesting." she said *"I always learn so much on these trips."*

After a quick hop to Port of Spain in Trinidad the ship headed for Panama, which, as I've always had an interest in things even vaguely technical, was a really fascinating and amazing experience.

Firstly the geographic orientation needs to be understood as the general assumption would be that transiting Panama from the Atlantic is an east to west journey. Not so. The way the Isthmus of Panama is located means that the journey is actually north to south.

Some of the diesel-engined 'mules'

Secondly, based on most people's experience of canals there would be a certain expectation of how it might be. Panama is absolutely nothing like one might expect.

The scale is awesome. With lock chambers more than thirty three metres wide, almost as deep and at 320 metres in length they can accommodate all but the largest of modern cruise liners and tankers, indeed such is the strategic importance that American warships have been specifically designed to be able to pass through the locks with literally inches to spare.

Thirdly, it is so much more than a canal. The fifty mile journey through Panama includes six locks that lift vessels almost 100 feet above sea level to cruise across man-made Gatun Lake surrounded by pristine tropical rain forest. It was unbelievable and I was still only a few days into my trip. What more could lie ahead?

Leaving Panama behind, Himalaya sailed north towards Long Beach – in effect the port city for Los Angeles, where we picked up many more American passengers who were joining the ship for the pacific cruise.

My abiding memory of Long Beach is how enormous everything seemed. Also how, when running to cross the road before the lights changed, I caught my jacket pocket on a fire hydrant and ripped it out sending a cascade of small change all over Ocean Boulevard. Well, money's money so there I was trying to pick up my hard earned pocket money with huge gas-guzzling American cars whizzing by and doing their best to avoid splattering me across the tarmac.

Long Beach also marked the end of my 'locker man' days. With the increase in the number of First Class passengers they were short of waiters in the saloon so I was offered the opportunity to become a 'winger'. It's probably as well that I didn't think too hard before agreeing or I would almost certainly have declined because it turned out to be one of the most nerve-racking things I've ever done before or since.

Training was non-existent.

"Just ask the others," they said, *"You'll be alright."*

I was allocated a 'four', as in a table of four people who had paid for and were entitled to expect First Class service and I didn't even know how to lay the table. There were eleven pieces of cutlery per person for Heaven's sake. The most I had ever seen over and above the basic three was a soup spoon! Another ever-so slight difficulty was that we were not allowed to write down orders. This meant that I often had to go hot-footing it back to the galley for something I'd forgotten, or just as likely, I could end up with a couple of spare courses if not whole meals in my dumb waiter at the end of the sitting.

First Class Dining Saloon

Dumping them in the plate-house was an option of course but seeing good food wasted has always irked me so I was much more inclined to smuggle them back to the cabin and as a result got very used to eating cold posh food. At least I got to know what the various dishes tasted like and was able to give later passengers a bit of guidance around the menu which even for many of our first class travellers was a bit haute-cuisine.

One thing that did appear on the menu from time to time were sautéed frogs' legs but the name in French (Cuisses de Grenouille) gave absolutely nothing away and if I said they were frogs' legs some passengers wouldn't believe me so I had this little trick to help.

If they were on the menu I would get a pair that had not broken up in the cooking process and put them to one side so that if required to explain exactly what the menu item was I'd take the little pair of legs and dance them on the table. It was a bit 'make or break' as some passenger though it hilarious and others were put off completely.

Long Beach was followed by San Francisco and I'll always remember arriving there. There is a strange optical illusion as you approach the Golden Gate Bridge. We were all up on the crew's deck from where the foremast rises and standing there as the ship headed towards the bridge you'd swear it's never going to get under but literally in the last moments the mast appears to telescope down on itself as the ship passes below the deck of the bridge with room to spare. Odd that.

The other major thing of note on entering San Francisco was Alcatraz Island. Known as The Rock, the island was a high security prison for years but I notice now on Google maps that there is a visitor centre and residential apartments so clearly The Rock was not destroyed by the combined efforts of Nick Cage and Sean Connery in the film of the same name.

More passengers joined the ship in San Francisco and then in Vancouver so that as we set off on our Pacific cruise Himalaya was carrying very nearly her full complement and life on board was busy although unlike the Tourist Class saloon we only ever had one meal sitting so things were a little less hectic for us.

Next stop was Hawaii. How exotic that sounds. Well so it may, but as I was beginning to discover, for crew members, ports of call tend to blur one into another. This is largely because, with little time available, it is quite hard to avoid being swept along with the crowd to one bar after another and then back to the ship to start over.

Of course I did the obligatory visit to Waikiki the famous surfing beach and was so disappointed to discover that much of the golden sand had actually been shipped from California and dumped there to replenish the beach. However this practice ceased in the 70's after technology was developed to enable off-shore Hawaiian sand to be dredged from deep water and pumped onto the beaches.

It was probably around this time that I started popping a few pills. Known as 'Dexies' (Speed nowadays); as far as we were concerned they were just pep pills that enabled us to stay awake enough to enjoy a good night out after a day's work and then do another days work before crashing out.

I was so naïve I didn't even know they were illegal but it seemed there was very little illegal once on board and outside UK waters. In retrospect it was pretty daft because although I didn't know it, Amphetamine is addictive. I just used them socially as and when required and it would seem never got to the point where I was at risk of getting hooked although of course I'll never know how close I may have come.

Unfortunately my parents found out about the pills quite by accident when I got home as some were floating about loose in the bottom of my case which Mum unpacked for me. Being a nurse she recognised them as Dexedrine and flew into a real panic in case I'd turned into a junkie.

After Hawaii the trip started to get really interesting as we headed for the Orient where our first port was Yokohama. It is however a sad fact that although I travelled right the way around the world, in reality I saw very little more than the inside of a lot of sleazy bars within a mile or two of the port and to be honest they are pretty much of a muchness.

Dimly lit, pounding music, scantily clad or topless waitresses and hostesses desperate to part you from your hard earned cash.

This in exchange for meaningless conversation and ridiculously expensive drinks that were not much more than thimble sized shots of crème de menthe or something similar. No wonder I soon tired of them and found the best way to avoid that experience was to head for a decent restaurant if you knew where to find one and that is where the experience of some of the older hands came in very useful. The only slight problem was however, that a very high proportion of the older and more experienced hands were gay and being seen in gay company usually resulted in the charge, even if in jest that you'd "gone queer".

Group outings were fine though, and this was often the way it worked out with whole groups of mixed gay and straight guys going ashore to paint the town and because they knew where to go we had some really great times.
I remember one evening, I think it was in Yokohama, when a group of us arrived at a really superb Japanese restaurant where all the waitresses were dressed in full geisha costume with the kimonos and obi sashes, and ornately styled hair with decorative hair pins.

Not only did they look beautiful but they greeted us wonderfully because, as we discovered, our gay friends were regulars there. Locals were rapidly shoved off the best table to make way for our party of honoured guests and in no time at all a lavish spread of food and drink appeared. It was only about half way through the meal that someone tipped me off that the beautiful geishas were all in fact males in drag and that once again unwittingly we'd found our way or been taken on this occasion to the best gay restaurant in town.

A few days later in Kobe I unusually had free time in the afternoon and another steward had asked if I wanted to go ashore with him. Jimmy was an older man who'd been on the boats for years and what he didn't know wasn't really worth knowing, but he was, as Dad would have said "*Queer as a nine bob note.*"

One or two of the other guys had raised a cautionary eyebrow at this. However by this time I felt quite confident that everyone who needed to know was well aware that I had no homosexual inclination and to be honest I found the experience and wit of the older gay stewards really interesting and often extremely entertaining.

Jimmy was brilliant and really did know some interesting bars that were pretty far out in the gay stakes but which never for a moment left me feeling ill at ease. We also visited some museums and temples that I probably wouldn't have found without his help and later on we ended at a really great restaurant.

It was totally traditional and we decided on the Sukiyaki meal at Jimmy's suggestion. With much bowing and kneeling we were shown into a small private room with translucent paper screen walls and one low table beside which were three cushions. Our attendant was a diminutive and strikingly pretty young Japanese girl for whom etiquette required that she had to do virtually everything on her knees.

For example when she brought items to the room we would see her form appear on the other side of the wall. She would kneel, put down the items, slide the door open, stand up and step through then kneel again to close the door before shuffling on her knees the 3 or 4 feet to our table where she knelt on the third cushion.
The first thing she introduced us to was the etiquette associated with drinking sake. This is Japanese rice wine, and the process couldn't have been more different from slinging back the shots in the way we'd become accustomed to do in the bars.

Although referred to as 'rice wine', sake is more akin to a spirit where a mash of the raw material (in this case rice) is fermented. It is not however distilled but even without that stage it reaches an alcohol level of 18 – 20% so it is to be treated with some caution.

Sake should be served slightly warm so a small prettily decorated porcelain carafe was allowed to stand for a few minutes in a little matching bowl of hot water until just warm. Etiquette requires that one never helps oneself so it is important when sharing a meal or drink with someone that you are mindful of the needs of your guest.

Over the years I've eaten a few unusual things but the starter on this occasion took some beating. A small dish of circular slightly rubbery meat (or was it fish?) turned out to be raw slices of baby octopus tentacle.

The centre was white with a dark brown skin on which it was just possible to discern the tiny suckers. Yes, I must say I swallowed a bit hard but more at the thought of it than the flavour which was actually quite pleasant and delicate. I guess these days when we're all eating sushi the notion of raw fish is not so strange but believe me for a council house kid in the 60's it was.

Sukiyaki consists of thinly sliced meat- usually beef – cooked at the table in an iron dish with a little oil over a gas burner

However each course, and there may be many comprising perhaps only a mouthful, has a completely different flavour. This wondrous trick is achieved by the use of a different type of vegetable, grass or seaweed that is added to the cooking of just a couple of pieces of meat.

These are then served by dropping them piping hot into a dish into which a raw egg has been broken. The hot food instantly cooks a thin coating of egg onto itself, which sets by the time it arrives at your mouth. Served with light and fluffy rice it was superb and an experience I'll never forget.

Hong Kong was our next port and I have to admit that here I reverted to type and set off with a bunch of others to hit the town. There was quite a long walk from the ship's berth to the security gates beyond which the town proper began. Here were all the vendors, the rickshaw boys, the pimps and the bar touts in their dozens (if not hundreds it sometimes seemed) dishing out their cards depicting naked females engaged in a variety of interesting contortions.

"Hello. You want rickshaw.– Special price?"- *"No thanks."*
"Hello Johnny. You want jig-a-jig?" - *"No thanks."*
"Hello. You want fuck my sister?" *"No I don't."*
"Ok. You want fuck me?" *"No! Fuck off."*

At last something seemed to work, but only until the next time.
Actually you learn after a while that the best trick is to completely ignore them which is hard for us English who are taught that it's rude to ignore someone who speaks to you. Avoiding eye contact is important and makes it easier as you can kid yourself you don't know who's talking so it's easy to ignore.

That first night in Hong Kong was crazy and within an hour or two we were all pretty well plastered so as we fell out of one heaving club onto the street about one o'clock and someone said *"Hello. You want see dirty film?"* we almost in unison said *"Yea. Why not."*
I may have been well gone but I remember it as one of the strangest experiences and I'm talking about just getting to this film show.

"OK. You come. You follow." So off we went through the back streets to the foyer of a very smart modern looking office block. We followed up the marble steps to some glass doors that were open and rather looked as though they'd been forced, but some time ago because despite its modernity the place looked dusty and unoccupied as though abandoned by builders who'd gone bust.

"Ok You come. You come." bleated our guide as he led us to the lifts and pressed a button to open the doors. Inside the lift it was clear things were not right because the interior trim was missing and we were standing in what was effectively a mesh cage not unlike those that take miners down

their pits. Even now we didn't realise how wrong things were because we were still in the lift shaft but a moment after our Chinaman pressed the button and the lift began to rise we saw it all. Literally!

Above the ground floor foyer there was no building to speak of apart from a steel framework through which our lift was rising. Not unlike a visit to the Eiffel Tower, except that instead of the lights of Paris laid out before us we had Hong Kong in all directions. As far as we were concerned the next stop could have been the moon.

Why hadn't we noticed the state of the building? Well; one, because we were all smashed; secondly it was dark and I guess we were just too busy keeping our balance and looking down as we climbed the entrance steps that we simply didn't look up.

Interestingly in retrospect, and I guess this is the dulling effect of excess alcohol; no-one flew into a panic, rage or anything. We just waited and I don't believe anyone even spoke.

Within a few seconds we had passed through the skeletal structure and were once again surrounded by the fabric of a building and in a few seconds more the lift stopped. We tipped out into a lobby albeit looking more like a building site where once again our friend took the lead and guided us through some double doors to where unbelievably, at the top of this two part building a film show was actually in progress.

Obviously it was dark and only illuminated by light from the screen where three or four if not more people seemed to be copulating with great enthusiasm. In the flickering gloom, we realised there were at least another eight or ten people already seated.

The hugely funny thing was that as our eyes adjusted further we saw that they were almost all the senior officers from Himalaya. Realising that it was a bunch of their own catering crew that had arrived they attempted to cover their embarrassment at being discovered by much pulling up of collars and sinking deep into their seats. They must have wished the floor would swallow them.

I had never seen a pornographic film before, the limit of my experience in that regard having been the odd magazine such as 'Health and Efficiency' which was titillation masquerading as Naturism and possibly one or two others that today wouldn't even be competition for an underwear advert.

What I did discover though was that watching porn is a great leveller. It doesn't matter if you are the Chief Steward, First Officer or a dish-washing Utility Steward, you can't stand on your status or have any pretention about rank if you're sitting together watching a blue film. It is also very sobering or at least it worked that way for most of us.

The drunken bravado quickly evaporated and apart from the last ditch efforts of one or two who's attempted wisecracks fell pretty flat we all subsided into silence privately hoping I'm sure that the experience would soon be over.

When it eventually finished the group of officers literally scrambled for the doors looking pretty sheepish and with the odd remark about 'Mum' being the word and suggesting that we all forget we'd bumped into each other.

Clearly only one of the lifts was working so we had to stand about for a few minutes which in our now much sobered state gave us the chance to take in the surroundings a bit more.

The place was indeed pretty much still a building site littered with empty plaster bags, off-cuts of timber and odd sheets of the trim panels that were to be fixed to the wall as a final finish.

There were however no tools and the general feeling was that work had certainly, at least for the time being, come to a halt. Beside the lift shaft was a pair of doors opening to a staircase with steps both up and down so clearly our floor was not the only one. However, I remember thinking that you'd need to keep your wits about you if tempted to descend via the stairs because certainly in a few feet they must come to an end in open space!

After a few minutes the lift came back and Mr "*You follow*" herded us inside and in a moment or two we were back on the street and for my part wondering whether it had all really happened at all.

Somewhat deflated and with post- inebriation torpor setting in we shambled our way back to the ship and that as they say was that. However we were not finished with Hong Kong as Himalaya was due there again in a few weeks as part of our pacific cruise itinerary.

Next stop was Manila in the Philippines, a heaving cauldron of humanity and superb example I thought of religious tolerance. More than 90% Roman Catholic since the times of the Spanish rule the population also includes other variations of Christianity, Islam and Buddhism not to mention a variety of other minor creeds and all apparently without any of the inter-faith conflict we see today around the world.

Manila Street Scene

Manila City was a great stop for passengers and crew alike as there was loads to see and in the two days we were in port there was also time enough to fit in both cultural sight-seeing and shopping. Oh, and in the case of the crew a fair amount of bartering too.

Manila is one huge market where anything and everything can be bought and sold so it was the ideal place to give in to the temptation to purloin the odd item of P&O gear and test the market so to speak.

As I said previously, the company was well aware that a certain amount of pilfering went. However, as I now discovered once we tied up in Manila it would be no exaggeration to say that an avalanche of P&O property found its way ashore to be exchanged for local produce mostly in the shape of the Manila rum and cigars for which the place is famous.

As a smoker in those days I can say that I was well pleased with my cigars and suspect that at least one Filipino was delighted with his posh new bath towel. Enough said I think!

After Manila there was quite a long hop to Suva in the south Pacific Fijian islands with their long palm-fringed beaches. Slightly more off-putting though were the sharks cruising around close to the ship in the port where they had apparently learnt to scavenge among the human detritus.

Fiji – Classic South Sea Island beach scene

Our next port of call was a brief stop at Aukland where the 'must-see' attraction was the new Harbour Bridge.

The 'pre-clip on' harbour bridge at Aukland

Opened just a couple of years previously in 1959, the bridge carried a four lane highway across the harbour mouth although it had already attracted much criticism for lack of imagination by not including provision for either rail or pedestrian traffic. Worse however was to come as I discovered when I visited New Zealand again years later.

Dramatically increasing vehicular traffic made it obvious that more capacity was needed and so in 1969, only ten years after opening; two-lane box girder sections were clipped on to each side, doubling the number of lanes to eight. The sections were manufactured by Ishikawajima-Harima Heavy Industries of Japan, which led to the nickname 'Nippon clip-ons'.

The selection of the company was considered a bold move at the time, barely 20 years after the war and with some considerable anti-Japanese sentiment still existing.- The costs of the additions were much higher than if the extra lanes had been provided initially.

A few days later Himalaya arrived at her terminal port of Sydney where we were due to remain for about a week whilst the ship was re-provisioned. Hooray! Now for some worthwhile shore leave.

The ship berthed in Circular Quay almost underneath the iconic Sydney Harbour Bridge and not much more than a stone's throw from the site where the now equally iconic new Opera House was being built.

Started a few years previously in 1958 the project was to suffer innumerable setbacks and near cancellations before its final opening in 1973. How tragic it would have been not to finish the job.

The good thing about a longer visit was that whilst we did of course hit the sleazy clubs and bars of the Kings Cross area there was also an opportunity to explore attractions a bit further afield.

One such trip was to Luna Park, the vast fun fair or what I guess we would call a theme park these days that was situated (and still is) just across the bay from Sydney Cove and Circular Quay were we were moored.

There was also a great day spent with a couple of lads out at Manly beach, famous for its surf and the many beautiful people there enjoying Australia's enviable open air life-style. We did have a swim there; however, I must say that it concentrated the mind somewhat to see the shark nets across the beach.

This was especially so when a bit of on-line research during the course of writing this showed the number of sharks caught that might otherwise have been responsible for beach attacks.

Lovely beaches and lifestyle though and with emigration passages at just £10 back then, small wonder there was such a rush to apply.

Sun lovers and surfers at Manly Beach

Chapter 17 - Pacific Cruise

Departing from Sydney the ship was setting out on a circular Pacific cruise although for many of the American passengers it was in fact the return leg of their cruise begun several weeks earlier in San Francisco or Los Angeles. This time the route was clockwise starting with Manila and returning to the USA via Hong Kong and Japan before a long fast sprint via Hawaii back to Australia.

Running a virtually full First Class saloon required some re-arrangement that resulted in me getting a six table instead of my easier 'four'. However the four that I'd got to know had left the ship in Sydney so I quite relished the idea of meeting a new group of passengers, three of whom I was to become very fond of.

Winkin, Blinkin and Nod

These three elderly widows were all from Los Angeles and had been touring in Australia for a month prior to boarding the ship for their return trip back home to the States. I christened them "Winkin, Blinkin and Nod" on account of their mannerisms. The first two because they both had this way of screwing up their eyes every so often and Nod because that's exactly what she did. It was quite confusing when she was saying *"No"* whilst nodding her head up and down at the same time.

My other three passengers were an American doctor and his Yorkshire born wife plus her sister also from Yorkshire. The one married to the doctor had lost a good deal of the accent but her sister's accent was still so broad that I had a problem on occasion understanding her so it was small wonder that there were a few communication issues across the table.

After a brief stop in Manila we arrived in Hong Kong where we were scheduled to stay for several days to give passengers a real opportunity to explore the city and for the more adventurous to take up the excursions offered to visit The New Territories on mainland China.

However there was another reason too for the longer stay in port. Presumably because of the availability of cheap labour, P&O had arranged for the whole ship to be re-painted.

This is no exaggeration because almost as soon as Himalaya was berthed the ship was invaded by hordes of Chinese workers with chipping hammers that set to work tapping and scraping away all traces of flaking or rusting white paint.

The noise was incessant and almost unbearable, so any passengers who thought they might pass a few quiet hours relaxing on board rapidly changed their minds and were pretty much obliged to go sight-seeing whether they wanted to or not.

The ship was festooned with ropes over its sides supporting planks on which the painters clambered like monkeys in order to reach every square inch of the hull and superstructure. In a couple of days Himalaya looked as though she had a severe attack of measles as she was dotted all over with splodges of lead oxide primer.

Then came the top coat applied by brush or roller by the same workers who must have numbered a couple of hundred and in the space of five or six days the ship was completely repainted in P&O's signature brilliant dazzling white.

Deep within the ship was a very different scenario. While the painters invaded the outside a quite large but tightly controlled number of local traders were allowed on board and permitted to set out their wares along the length of the working alleyway that ran the length of the crew's quarters.

There was the usual predictably tatty rubbish in the form of cheap souvenirs but there was also a good selection of other items including watches, cameras, radios and Hi-Fi all at remarkably low prices compared to home. You had to be careful of course because a lot of the stuff was counterfeit but with care it was possible to come away with a bargain.

The joke always was that if you bought a Hong Kong watch it would stop as the ship left port and on examining the works you'd discover that the cockroach inside had expired.

Clothes were also quite a good bet and while they weren't exactly top notch they were of acceptable quality and incredibly cheap, and then there was the legendary Hong Kong 24hour suit.

The tailors came aboard with the other traders loaded with pattern books and fabric samples from which the deal was that they would produce a made-to-measure suit in 24 hours. Well at the time the thing everyone wanted was the Italian style with short boxy jacket and slimly tapered trousers so I decided to go for it.

I chose a really nice fabric (at least I thought it was!) – Deep chestnut brown with a sort of shiny finish and the tailor got to work with his tape measure. Full measurements taken and away he went with the promise to return the following morning for a fitting which incredibly he did.

Fourteen hours and counting! It was beginning to look as though it might actually happen. A couple of quick adjustments and he was off again with an invitation for me to come to the shop later that day.

Six o'clock and I collected a fully finished suit with about half an hour to spare. Certainly not the best quality in the world but far from the worst and at a very cheap price that I sadly cannot recall. I was certainly still wearing it three years later.

Just to ensure that I had remembered things correctly I recently checked on the internet. Apparently the HK 24 hour tailors not only still thrive but count the rich and famous among their clients. In reality they now take a bit longer to produce a quality garment but you can be wearing it in 3 - 5 days and still at a very affordable price compared to Europe.

If there were a few rip-off merchants among the Chinese traders that came aboard, the dodgy practice was far from being in one direction. I'm ashamed to say that the crew had a few tricks of their own to balance things up as you might say.

It was simple really. Because competition for pitches along the working alleyway was quite fierce traders would lay out their goods in a virtually continuous display on the floor without any space between their pitches for crew members to get to their cabin doors. This meant that we had to literally step over and among the laid out goods to get in and out.

When one of us saw an item we fancied the MO was to make a show of examining it and then apparently lose interest before putting it back down on the deck within reach of the cabin door before stepping over the goods to enter the cabin.

At this point one of your mates or perhaps I should say 'your accomplice' would engage the trader in discussion and barter over an item well away from the door and engineer that the trader's back was towards the door. At this point the door would be opened for just long enough for the item to disappear into the cabin. With the general level of frenetic dealing going on it was virtually impossible for the traders to keep an eye on everything or to remember what they had sold or not.

Predictably I guess, our last night in Hong Kong was marked by another fairly extreme booze-up that ended around 4 am in the most hilarious fashion.

I had gone out late, having had to serve and clear up after dinner so the group I went ashore with didn't really get started until around 11pm. We'd had a fairly leisurely start but by around 2 or 3in the morning we were all pretty well oiled when we ran into a bunch of 'queens' off the ship who'd clearly had a great evening and were camping it up outrageously.

They weren't exactly in drag but were all heavily made-up, and dressed to the nines. One was wearing a bright yellow vest and the skimpiest pair of fluorescent blue hot pants that left absolutely nothing to the imagination at all. His (or her?) friend had a pair of skin tight white pants and a pink shirt tied up in a knot around the waist. I could go on to describe the three or four others but I imagine you get the picture well enough.

Falling into yet another bar with pounding rock music we all basically danced to near exhaustion for another hour or so before once again tipping out onto the street and began heading vaguely back towards the ship.

When we were about a quarter mile or so from the dockyard entrance we came upon what might best be described as a rickshaw parking lot, at which point our pink shirted friend leapt into one of the rickshaws and started screaming *"Look. I'm Cinderella. Where's my fucking prince?"*

Then it was Hot Pant's turn. *"Here I am Darling"* as he jumps in as well and then starts shouting *"We need coachmen and ponies. Come on you lazy sods. Start pulling."*

So a couple of us (what possessed me I'll never know) grab the shafts and start off with it along the street while another one or two are shoving from behind and the remaining motley crew are trotting along laughing and yelling and the whole thing is a huge joke.

For about twenty seconds, until we hear more shouting but this time in Chinese as a bunch of rickshaw wallahs come charging out of a nearby alley.

At this point for the pullers, pushers and hangers-on the joke ceased and it became almost a race for our lives but for Cinderella and her Prince who hadn't sussed out what was going on the ride was just getting better and better and the clamour of the pursuing Chinese was almost drowned out by their shrieks of excited laughter.

Fortunately the security crew at the gates could see what was happening and had the gates open as we careered up. Grabbing a still screaming Cinderella and Prince Charming we just managed to abandon the rickshaw and dive through the gates to safety as the angry bunch of rickshaw boys arrived. There was a fair amount of unintelligible shouting and arguing in Chinese but the security crew managed to cool the whole thing down and if not exactly mollified our pursuers quite quickly calmed down and went off having had their rickshaw returned undamaged although I reckon that was more by luck than judgment.

Over the years I've listened to various people describing their holiday or business visits to Hong Kong and for the most part kept my mouth shut. Whilst I don't feel especially proud of the daft escapades I've described they were of their time and for me as an immature eighteen year old, far more interesting, exciting and memorable than being conducted from one historic or cultural site to another by an umbrella waving tour guide. That's not to say I wouldn't like to go back as a proper tourist one day. Who knows?

From Hong Kong the ship headed back via Japan towards Vancouver and it was on that leg that we encountered the roughest weather of the whole trip. Fortunately it didn't affect me much; in fact for all of my time at sea I never once suffered any sickness. It seemed I had natural sea-legs.

After one rough night a group of distinctly queasy passengers appeared for breakfast on my colleague's table in the Tourist restaurant and he brightly said *"Good morning. Who's for a lovely kipper?"*, at which six of the eight got up and left. It was certainly one way to get your sitting finished early.

Talking of weather though, reminds me of a couple of really odd experiences. In order to understand you need to imagine the ship ploughing through a rough sea with waves and spray breaking over it and realise that the bow could be rising and falling as much as twenty feet or more each time.

Now you also need to know that as on a see-saw the part rising and falling least is in the centre which is where the passenger accommodation is concentrated whereas the crew's cabins are right up in the bow. Ok. Get the picture?

The first experience I had was one day when the weather was just a bit choppy and I was heading back to my cabin. I was in a hurry and almost running so when I came to some stairs I went to jump the first couple just at the moment the bow began to drop into another wave trough. I actually jumped seven steps. It was really odd and just as I imagine weightlessness might be in space.

The other occasion was in the crew bar which is also located well forward in the bow. I was drinking a pint and took a mouthful of beer just at the moment the ship began to drop which meant that I was going down with the ship at the same rate that the beer was falling down my throat so relative to each other the liquid was stationary. It was only for a moment or two but I almost choked.

It was good to visit San Francisco again especially as this time I somehow managed to get a bit more time ashore and got a close-up look at the magnificent Golden Gate Bridge.

This fabulous Art Deco construction took four years to build between 1933 and 1937 and for many years held an extensive range of records for height, length, weight of steel and so on.

Bizarrely it still holds the record as the world's number one suicide location with an official tally standing at more than 1700 although the true number is thought to be more. (2015 stats)

With a four second drop of 245 feet from the bridge deck very few jumpers survive the fall with most deaths actually being due to trauma arising from the 75 mph impact with the water. Those that do survive the jump usually die from drowning or hypothermia apart that is from one young man who in 1979 survived the jump, swam to shore and drove himself to a hospital. (According to Wikipedia???)

San Francisco's China Town made quite an impact too with its wealth of smells, sights and sounds.

This enclave of more than 100,000 people in an area 1.0 by 1.3 miles continues to retain its own customs, languages, places of worship, social clubs, and identity. There are two hospitals, numerous parks and squares, a post office, and other infrastructure. Wandering through the largest Chinatown outside of Asia visitors can easily become immersed in a microcosmic world, filled with herbal shops, temples, pagoda roofs and dragon parades. Truly another world. I loved it.

Finally and probably my strongest memory of San Francisco was an evening at the legendary Jazz Workshop where I was privileged to hear the great jazz saxophonists John Coltrane and Stan Getz playing together. Dark, smoky and just so chilled it was at once one of the most relaxing and exciting moments of my life.

A few years ago visiting a blues bar in downtown Chicago I was instantly transported back to that night and the wonderfully friendly and laid-back atmosphere in which nothing matters but the music.

At the next stop in Long Beach (for Los Angeles) I said my goodbyes to Winkin, Blinkin and Nod as they left the ship and went back to their cosseted lifestyle in the hills near Hollywood. They were really lovely ladies and extremely generous with their tip as they left me after breakfast on that last day.

I was allocated another couple to my table for the trip back to Sydney. They were an Australian couple who had been on holiday in the States for a while visiting family and combining it with a cruise. Their view was if you have the time why on earth would you fly if you can cruise. - Especially first class.

It was on this last leg of the Pacific cruise that things in the saloon really became quite hilarious because after a while as a table waiter you really got to know your passengers and even in First Class you tended to drop the formality at least to a degree. I guess it was also in the run up to Christmas which put everyone in a good mood. As a result mealtimes became one long laugh mainly due to the camp behaviour of a couple of stewards on nearby tables. These two were known as Bunny and Betty below decks but by their proper names to their passengers.

What I'll call the 'silly season' began one morning when one of the passengers made a casual remark.
"I don't know if it was the fish last night but something's made me quite queer this morning."
At which point Bunny turned around with a pout and a shrug of the shoulder in the camp style of Kenneth Williams and said *"Not as queer as me darling."* and minced off in a much exaggerated way towards the galley.

Well, we all broke down laughing, crew and passengers alike. It was as if what everyone had known was now out into the open and at last we could all admit that half the crew was gay and proud of it, which in those days was quite something.

The Second Steward whose job it was to oversee the First Class saloon told us off for being over-familiar with our passengers but to no real avail. And for those last three weeks the formality of First Class descended to something more akin to Holiday Camp at least in our corner of the restaurant. Every meal sitting was the same with Betty and Bunny bouncing remarks and innuendo off each other whilst flirting gently with the male passengers or sharing conspiratorial jokes with their wives.

There was one very funny but at the same time rather sad episode involving a lady passenger on a table about three away from mine.

She had joined the ship in L.A. and after a while one of the stewards noticed that every time she sat down at the table she would fish about in her handbag for a handkerchief and then with a somewhat furtive look around she would bring the hanky up to her mouth and quickly stuff it back in her bag

At the end of the meal she went through the reverse procedure and after watching this for a while we realised that the poor woman had some problem with her false teeth and was taking them out in order to eat.

I can't really for the life of me understand why she didn't do it before coming to the table but sufficient to say, it wasn't long before not only the stewards but most of the passengers in our corner of the restaurant were watching this performance.

In fact I'd go so far as to say that there were some passengers who might not have bothered with every meal had it not been for the entertainment value of Betty, Bunny and the poor woman we christened The Tooth Fairy.

Anyway the whole thing came to a head one lunch time at the end of the meal with almost everyone in our corner of the room surreptitiously watching from the corner of their eyes, between fingers or via reflections in mirrors.

Tooth Fairy was in the process of getting her denture back to her mouth when it shot out of her hanky and went skidding across the floor to end up under another table. I'm ashamed to say that no-one went to help and left it to her to go and retrieve the denture which she rapidly stuffed back in her bag before almost running from the room.

We didn't see her for a couple of days but then she came back to the table although now without the tooth problem. Whether she had been to see the on-board dentist or simply done what she should have originally and dealt with the problem outside of the restaurant, we'll never know. However, praise where it's due, she came back and carried on as though the incident never happened.

Although Bunny and Betty as well as a number of the other waiters had only 'come out' to the passengers in that last month or so before Christmas they would have had to be pretty blind or naïve not to have worked out that a fair number of the crew were gay even though in those days it was not a subject for 'polite company'.

However below decks, illegal or not, homosexuality was rife with relationships being made and broken, jealousies and arguments between jilted lovers descending on occasions into screaming matches and even fights.

I remember one guy receiving a nasty head wound from the stiletto heel of a shoe wielded by Big Mary after she/he discovered that the 'boyfriend' had been seeing one of the other 'girls'.

Despite the sexual rivalries that existed, most of the effeminate gay stewards managed to arrange to be in the same cabins as each other which meant that there were at least six or seven 'Queen Rooms' as we called them.

Not that I spent much time exploring them but to get a look inside was a revelation. It was remarkable how pretty a square steel box could be made to appear. Elaborate drapes and curtains around the bunks, coloured light bulbs and a pervasive heady mix of perfume combined to create an atmosphere a million miles away from any of the neigbouring cabins occupied by half a dozen sweaty seamen.

Of course it's easy to laugh at things with the benefit of hindsight although at the time incidents can be pretty disastrous if not actually dangerous and that's how I can best describe my working day in the First Class saloon on that Christmas Day 1962.

We had been at sea for several days and were due to arrive in Sydney a couple of days after Christmas so, not surprisingly seasonal booze had been flowing freely below decks pretty much day and night when we weren't actually working.

The sea was a bit choppy around lunch time as the saloon began to fill up for Christmas Day lunch but it hadn't put my lot off their food and before long they were installed and ordering their meals.

First course served and I toddled off to collect the mains from the galley which meant a tray stacked with silver oval servers containing the mains and additional vegetables in divided dishes.

These were all tucked away in my dumb waiter to keep warm until starters were finished when I got the places cleared and began to serve the next course.

Four of my six passengers had opted for roast pork which involved me carrying to each place a dish of the meat with some crackling and juices together with a divided dish of vegetables balanced across my wrist which in normal circumstances was absolutely fine and would have presented no problems.

However, as I've said, today wasn't totally normal in that I was, to say the least, slightly the worse for wear.

So when, just as I began to serve one of my ladies, the ship gave a sudden lurch I almost lost my balance. Although I didn't actually fall in my passenger's lap, the contents of the dishes I was holding did.

Now I don't really know whether it was a good or bad thing that the woman's handbag was open on her lap. It certainly avoided her clothes and perhaps more importantly, her legs being splattered with hot food but it did result in the contents of her bag swimming about in a fairly grotty mixture of roast pork, gravy, crackling and the odd Brussels Sprout.

Looking back on the event, I'm inclined to believe that on balance she might have preferred to take the hit herself so to speak as I'm sure that the contents of her bag probably proved more difficult to recover than her knees and skirt that would have washed out easily enough.

Not of course that I ever had that conversation with her!

"Oh God! I'm so sorry" I spluttered as I endeavored to extract a rather nice slice of pork from her bag where it was lodged in a side pocket with her comb. *"I don't know how I did that. It was so clumsy."*

I couldn't believe how calm she was. Could the storm be about to come? *"Don't worry Brian".* She said. *"It was a total accident. We all saw what happened. Not your fault at all."*

"I know, but look at the mess." I blathered, still trying to retrieve remnants of crackling and the odd sprout. I was beside myself and they were all being so amazingly generous about it. I couldn't believe it.
"Look," she said, *"this will all clean up. The most important thing is can you get me another one. I don't want to miss out on a good meal."*

So, that it seemed was the end of an incident that could have been the abrupt conclusion of my waiting career. In the event we managed to keep things so calm that the Chief Steward never even knew anything had happened. I was so grateful to them all but it would certainly be a Christmas to remember.

In all the time I was working as a steward that was the worst disaster ever, but the day hadn't quite finished with me yet!

Christmas Dinner was the main event of this particular part of the cruise and we spent most of the afternoon decorating the First Class saloon ready for the evening. Special table pieces came out, flowers appeared from the cool rooms, balloons and streamers were draped around the walls to create a real party atmosphere. Glasses and silver were polished as if our lives depended on it so that by the time we'd finished the restaurant looked absolutely stunning.

There had been other party nights on the cruise such as fancy dress events or themed evenings when the passengers were invited to let their hair down and have a good time but Christmas was the big one and as the saloon began to fill up it was clear that they saw it that way too.

They all looked amazing in their formal dinner wear with most of the men in white dinner jackets and the women in the most wonderful variety of evening dress. Some even wore little tiara style headpieces. The whole thing was just so unbelievably opulent. These really were the POSH set.

Port Out Starboard Home is the expression often said to have given rise to the adjective 'posh'. It was supposed to have originated in the heyday of the ocean liners between UK and India when the wealthy would stipulate a change of cabin for the outward and homeward leg of a journey to ensure the cabins were not too hot in the afternoons.

Well I guess it's a plausible explanation but as far as I can make out there is in fact no real evidence for this.

And so the evening got under way. Soups, entrees and main courses were served with all the traditional trimmings. Champagne corks popped all around and crackers cracked. Gentlemen posed and ladies glittered whilst waiters buzzed hither and thither attending to their every need. Perfect – so far!

Naturally, the menu included Christmas Pudding which tradition dictated should be flambéed and carried spectacularly into the restaurant by a procession of waiters.

So with previous courses all cleared away we trooped off into the galley whilst the restaurant lights were lowered, collected our puddings and waited in line for the flambé treatment. However, I'd never done this before and as I mentioned previously we had no training as such so it was not surprising that I was feeling a little apprehensive.

The flambé process is very simple. Warm brandy on a hot pudding produces inflammable alcohol vapour which is lit to produce an attractive and somewhat ethereal blue flame and creates an impressive display when carried in procession through a darkened restaurant.

Now if all this sounds potentially dangerous it actually isn't for a couple of reasons. Firstly, the alcohol vapour does not burn very hot and secondly it burns out very rapidly, both of which are all very fine if you know what you are doing.

The technique is to hold the platter with the flaming pudding high and to one side with the fingers splayed underneath.

This is a bit of a balancing act but quite easily learnt with a little practice and is all very well if you know but as I said no-one told me. Being a bit apprehensive as I waited in line for the lighting process I hadn't actually noticed that as each preceding waiter disappeared through the door they were indeed hoisting their puddings impressively above their shoulders.

My turn arrived and as the brandy was poured and ignited with a soft 'whoof', the chef said *"Off you go then."*

Someone opened the door and as I strode forward with the pudding in front of me a slight draught from the door and my forward motion wafted the flames into my face and a gentle fizz accompanied by a smell of burning hair encouraged me to quickly change my grip on the platter.

I realised I must have singed something but not being actually burnt I carried on to the table to be greeted by appreciative applause as I presented the still flaming pudding.

As I began to serve them the one of my passengers said "I can smell burning." and I laughingly explained what had happened. She looked up at me and gasped *"Oh my God Brian. It's a bit more than that. Your eyebrows have gone and your hair is all burnt."*

Fortunately no serious damage was done but when I checked later in the mirror I was surprised to see that my eyebrows had indeed almost completely gone, my eyelashes were well singed and the quiff I so carefully styled each morning was never going to be the same again.

So that was my Christmas and pretty much the end of our Pacific cruise. We arrived in Sydney a couple of days later passing P&O's latest flagship, the almost brand new SS Oriana on her way out.

More than half as big again as the Himalaya and much faster she looked really impressive at full speed.

We'd shared a lot of laughs over the previous weeks so it was with some sadness that I said goodbye to my once again very generous passengers and was able to relax for a few days before we were due to sail again for the homeward leg of my trip.

"What a Gay Day"

The crew Christmas Dinner was in the afternoon directly after lunch had been served to the passengers

Himalaya takes a brief 'breather' in Sydney between Pacific cruise and the home trip.- 28 December 1962

Chapter 18 – Homeward Bound

We sailed from Sydney a few days later and although there was still quite a long time left before we would be back in the UK, being on the homeward leg of the journey put something of a damper on my mood.

You know how it is as you come towards the end of a holiday and your mind turns to things back home. Things you know have to be done or decisions made that you have avoided by the holiday, return to the surface and start nagging again. So then all you really want to do is get back as soon as possible and make a start. In my case the main issue was what I would do next. I had known all along that joining P&O was escapism pure and simple but what I had not yet faced up to was my next move.

The easy option would have been to stay for the next trip which was going to be the same again and I guess would have given me the chance to see a few different things and save a bit more money. However, I was by now starting to miss home quite a bit and was also finding the somewhat sleazy and boozy atmosphere of life below decks a bit wearing despite the sometimes hilarious aspects of it. Well, typically I decided not to decide, at least not until I had to.

Having made that decision and thinking through the homeward trip in more detail I then began to feel quite lifted again as I mentally listed our scheduled ports of call.

From Sydney we would be heading around the south coast of Australia calling at Melbourne and Adelaide before striking out across the Great Australian Bight, that vast bay between the continent's central desert and the Southern Ocean with a reputation for weather every bit as fearsome as the Bay of Biscay in the North Atlantic. Our final landfall in Australasia would be Freemantle that is the port for the city of Perth in Western Australia in the same way that Long Beach is to Los Angeles.

From here our route would take us halfway across the Indian Ocean to Colombo in Ceylon as it then was – now Sri Lanka of course, and thence up the west coast of India to call at the great port of Bombay (now Mumbai).

It's interesting how many of the countries or cities that were once part of the British Empire (remember all the pink on the world atlas) having regained their independence have also changed their names. Something of a two-finger farewell to British control perhaps.

Next stop would be Aden, and north through the Red Sea to Port Said in Egypt before the Suez Canal and into the Mediterranean. A final stop at Marseilles and then back to Blighty and our terminal port of Tilbury.

Mulling this through I had to admit that even if the next few weeks were dead boring, which I knew they wouldn't be, any young lad my age would have been over the moon to have had the experience. So whatever was to come next I really should be grateful and make the most of what was left. Then I needed to take a positive view about getting back to finding myself a decent career and showing my parents that it hadn't been a complete waste of time and that I really could repay their investment in my education.

However, I didn't have time to give things that much thought because just before we sailed I was taken out of the saloon and appointed Assistant Bedroom Steward (known as ABR) to a bedroom steward on B deck. This was a definite promotion but the way the gradings worked, it meant that the promotion would not be confirmed if and until I signed on again for the next trip. However it did mean a complete change in work type and pattern.

Each bedroom steward was responsible for a group of First Class cabins, probably six or eight, and it was my job to act as assistant to a steward called Terry by the passengers but known as Lulu below decks because he was also gay.

The bedroom steward's role was to be available to attend to passengers' every need and they usually worked a split work pattern in order to be on hand first thing in the morning should they require breakfast in their rooms as well as late in the evenings should the little darlings require a pre-dinner drink. In addition they were responsible for cleanliness and sanitation of cabins; room service as and when required as well as assisting and advising passengers on all aspects of the journey and activities of the day.

Obviously they could not fulfil this role without some assistance which is where the ABR's came in. After breakfast we would spend most of the day up in the far more pleasant areas of the ship occupied by the passengers. Assisting the bedroom stewards usually meant in reality doing the things they didn't have time for or didn't like doing which in Terry's case was the bathrooms.

Whilst a few passengers would take breakfast in their cabins, for the majority breakfast signalled the start of yet another day of fun and frolics. Also it was at breakfast that announcement of the day's activities would be made so most were up and away quite early. This was ideal for us because it meant that we could get in to service the cabins.

Terry and I developed a routine whereby we would do the beds together as it was easier that way, then, while he tidied and cleaned the room as necessary I serviced the bathrooms. Not always the most savoury of activities, brushing out toilets and removing clumps of questionable hair from plug-holes, but it was strange how quickly I developed a commitment to the job and a pride in doing it well.

Ever since then I've taken enormous satisfaction in cleaning things (my wife would say –"Once you actually get around to doing it."), and I applied the same level of care to the bathroom in the small B&B we used to run.

During the afternoons whilst the bedroom stewards were off duty, we assistants were supposed to be available on the section to respond to calls for cabin service. It was on one such day I received a call from the galley to collect a tray of pastries that had been ordered by one of the passengers on my section. Once I'd collected the cake tray I had to put it together with a pot of tea that we prepared in a little kitchenette on the section and deliver it to the cabin.

There was no reply to my knock on the door and as was normal practice after knocking again it was usual to slowly and tactfully enter the cabin. On this occasion as I entered I heard some movement in the bathroom and thinking I could put the tray down quickly and get out, I went to do so.

But, just as I turned to leave, the bathroom door opened and in strode this guy; stark naked, somewhat red-faced and a bit breathless and displaying the most enormous erection that I had ever seen. Actually I'd never seen anyone else's erection apart from the participants in the Hong Kong film show but I must say this guy would have run any of them a close second.

"Oh my God." he says, *"Caught me in all my glory. Sorry about that."* And calm as you like he marches straight ahead and picks up a cake, slumps down naked in a chair and starts eating it.

I had no idea where to look or what to say so stammering my apologies I made a bee line for the door and a quick exit. Mulling it over later I had to smile as I wondered what Lulu would have made of the situation. Probably would have thought it was his lucky day.

Actually the gay crew members usually made excellent cabin stewards because of how they related to both the male and female passengers. They were even asked for advice by the ladies on what to wear or how this or that dress suited them which utilised their 'feminine' side whilst at the same time gently flirting with the husbands.

It was so funny to watch and quite remarkable how relaxed the passengers were with these openly gay guys whilst back home and away from the cruise they would probably have reacted quite differently as homosexuality was still illegal and 'unmentionable' in the UK.

For all my adolescent bravado I was still very naïve and sexually inexperienced when I went to sea.

Although the hostesses in the many bars we visited were almost irresistibly tempting, and in many ways would have been the ideal route for a youngster to 'learn the ropes' so to speak; unlike many of my colleagues I never did take the plunge.

I guess it was a combination of all the Catholic 'sins of the flesh' teaching (and Oh how I wanted to touch some flesh) and some straightforward fear of going home with a 'dose' that kept me on the straight and narrow. In any event I came home with my virginity intact which in retrospect was probably a missed opportunity.

If I knew little about straight sex my knowledge of matters 'gay' was a big zero so when someone said to me before I left, *"Remember, if the Chief Steward drops the soap in the shower, you just kick it about."* I didn't have a clue what he was talking about and it was the same with references to 'golden rivets' and the like. However, once on board and living in the often sexually charged environment below decks I quickly cottoned on.

I thought I was used to most of the antics of my gay crew mates. Coming out of the shower in the washroom one day I was faced with Bunny who was standing in front of the mirror, having spread shaving foam all over his chest and privates and was now fastidiously engaged is shaving off all his chest hair and most from down below as well.

"Oh hello darling." he says in pure Larry Grayson style. *"Girl's got do what a girl's gotta do."* Thinking this was just another gay quirk that I was unfamiliar with I said *"No problem Bunny. Don't mind me."* And off I went.
End of story? Well not exactly.

A few days after leaving Sydney was New Year's Eve so in addition to a very special evening for the passengers there was later on one hell of a party in the crew's bar. On this rare occasion there were even three or four real girls present in the shape of some girls from the Purser's office and even a few of the deck officers had deigned to honour us with their presence.

Not that there was any real resentment but it was clear that some of our 'queens' viewed the female Pursers as competition so when it came to the dancing our 'girls' were really pulling out the stops and strutting their stuff like it was going out of fashion.

Bunny however managed the greatest coup because at one point someone got hold of a microphone and announced *"Ladies and gentlemen will you please welcome, direct from Paris, France, Mademoiselle Mimi."*

At which point Bunny came prancing in decked out in a stunning vivid red and gold Parisian Follies costume, blonde wig and full stage make-up.

As someone put on The Stripper music he started out on the most amazing striptease routine that would have done credit to a real Moulin Rouge or Windmill girl. Bumping and grinding his way around the room he started shedding garments until he was down to nothing but a pair of high heels, tiny pants and a bra and everyone stood holding their breaths to see just how far he would go. As he shimmied his way from one onlooker to the next Bunny teased us by gradually reaching around to undo his bra before finally whisking it away to reveal a pair of water-filled balloons taped to his hairless chest at which point of course things immediately made sense.

Well, to be fair it would have taken a lot to follow that and as it was by then about four in the morning we all drifted off to our peaks to sleep the sleep of the drunk or so we thought. Wrong!

I don't know how long we'd been asleep when the sound of loud shouting and shrieking dragged us back to consciousness.

The noise was coming from one of the 'Queen' cabins almost opposite ours across the alley so we all dived out to see what was going on and I have to say the scene that greeted us was one of the most hilarious I have ever seen. Apparently they had gone to bed and inadvertently left a port hole open and as the weather worsened a wave had caught the ship high enough to deposit gallons of sea water through the porthole.

By the time we arrived the shrieking had subsided and the six occupants dressed in an interesting assortment of nightwear ranging from the briefest of pants to frilly short nighties were busy trying to bale water, wring out clothing and change bedding. Coloured lacy curtains around their bunks were hanging in sodden shreds while the pink bulbs cast a surreal tint over the whole scene.

The funniest thing of all however was the parrot. This lived in a cage that hung right in front of the porthole and I guess must have caught pretty well the full impact of the water.

Fortunately it had survived but the poor bedraggled creature, clearly terrified, was flapping about in its cage squawking madly and looking like something from a Walt Disney cartoon in rather the same way that poor old Road Runner does when blown up or drowned for the umpteenth time.

In the event, the voyage back was indeed relatively uneventful and we had a fairly relaxed time of it. As the ship was not full, apart from not having to 'run ourselves ragged' we on the bedroom sections also had a particular bonus.

Strictly against the rules of course, the bedroom stewards and their assistants (me in this case), took up occupancy of some of the vacant cabins and I can tell you it was as they say, 'just the job'.

My steward Terry moved into the most luxurious cabin on the section that even had its own balcony and magnificent sea view. Mine was almost as good lacking only the balcony and was certainly a million miles from the six berth tin box I should have been sleeping in down in the crew's quarters.

I suppose in a sense this practice was more or less an open secret because it certainly wasn't unnoticed by our mates that we were absent overnight but if any of the senior hands were aware nothing was said.

There was only one little challenge and that was 'Captain's Inspection'. These weekly visit by the Chief Steward, Staff Captain and sometimes the ship's Captain himself were tours of inspection notionally covering the whole ship although clearly this was an impossibility and like so many similar charades was more or less stage managed with target areas briefed in advance to make sure things went without a hitch.

However, it was part of the process for the inspecting officers to check passenger accommodation too and so the bedroom stewards had to be on hand to advise them which were free to be inspected and which were occupied. Fortunately the system did not provide the inspection team with a passenger cabin list so whenever the team looked like checking out one of the cabins we were illicitly using the answer was always *"Sorry Sir. That one's occupied at the moment."*

There was another little flaw in the admin or accounting system that worked in our favour too which meant that there was no direct correlation in the galley between which meals were taken via room service or which were taken in the restaurant. It also appeared that being mainly interested in supplying restaurant food the galley had no records as to which cabins were occupied by which passenger.

As a result if the bedroom stewards or their assistants decided that we fancied a steak sandwich or anything else for that matter we would simply collect it from the galley, then repair to our luxury suite to enjoy it in comfort and simply stick it on the bill of one of the unoccupied cabins. If this was ever picked up I can only assume it was put down to a mistake and passed over.

Once Australia was behind us our next port of call was Colombo on the south-west coast of Sri Lanka. We were not there long but I did fortunately have the opportunity to get ashore and according to those that knew, nearby Mount Lavinia Beach was the place to head for.

Located about 10 kilometres south of Colombo it was easy to reach by the local bus shared with a motley collection of locals and their considerable luggage.

Live chickens squawked in crates and even a goat stood bleating and crapping in the aisle so it was just as well that the bus was deficient in the window and door department or the smell which was noticeable to say the least, would have been unbearable.

However the beach itself made the trip worthwhile. It was the stereotypical tropical beach with palm fringed golden sands lapped by a warm azure sea and at the time I was there it was still pretty much unspoilt. Strange the things that stick in the memory though – my main recollection of Mount Lavinia Beach is the ravens. They seemed to be everywhere. Large, black and incredibly unafraid, they strutted about on the beach and seemed to be mainly concerned with consuming the tiny crabs that were all over the place.

Checking up on-line as I wrote this I was so disappointed to see how commercialised and touristic the place has become. Palms still lean out over the sandy beach and the blue water still laps but now it is against a backdrop of hotels and although the many market stalls I remember are still there it all looks so much more sanitized and presented for visitors than before.

Mount Lavinia Beach, Sri Lanka

Our next stop was the huge Indian port of Bombay. Unfortunately I didn't get much shore leave here and at first I'm inclined to say it was just as well. First impressions were that it was a stinking, heaving, sweltering cauldron of humanity, vehicles and animals all competing for some sort of survival and that was just my view from the ship.

I need to be fair though because once I got away from the immediate port area the frenetic activity did calm down a bit but not a lot and wherever one went the whole place really did seem pretty squalid. But as I said, time was limited and I didn't really have the time to give the place a chance. For all that, I was not sorry to leave the heat and the smell and get out on the water once again.

One interesting thing about Bombay though was that it was also in a sense a terminal port, at least for many of our Asian crew. I couldn't work it out at first but after we sailed I became aware that there seemed to be quite a few new Goanese faces (so, it can't be right that to Europeans all Indians, Africans or whatever foreign races, look the same.)

What had happened in fact was that around 40% of the Goanese crew had changed at Bombay, it being the major international seaport closest to their home area. There were a few that I'd thought I had got to know a little but not one of them had mentioned that they were leaving the ship.

Apart from feeling a little hurt I was also sorry as I realised I would never see them again or hear any more about their wives and kids. It was unusual for the two communities on board to mix very much and I felt that I'd had some small success there and now it had come to nothing. That's life I guess.

Anyway; 'Onwards and upwards' as they say. Literally in this case as we were heading first west for the Gulf of Aden and then north into the Red Sea.

I bought a camera in Aden and was lucky. I remember going ashore with the intention of buying one but also knowing that there was a fair chance of being ripped off in one way or another.

In the event I bought Samoca Japanese 35mm camera. It was pretty much state of the art for its type at the time and, wonder of wonders it was still going strong, not just the next day but probably twenty years later and in its way contributed to a life-long interest in photography.

Rocky Aden

I thought Aden a bleak place being at that time a fairly squalid settlement against a looming mountain with a desert climate. Not in the least appealing visually but it does have the significant advantage of a particularly sheltered natural port that is actually the collapsed crater of a former volcano (hopefully extinct).

The British first became involved there in 1839 when they landed a detachment of military in order to deal with what was described as "a nest of pirates" that was posing a threat to our trade routes to the east.

As sail was replaced by steam power Aden developed under British control into a major water and coal supply station and no doubt handsomely rewarded English entrepreneurial interference in another country to whom we brought our "civilising influence." It does rather raise the question "Who were the pirates?

Aden remained under British control until 1963 when a developing pan-Arab movement began to kick against their presence giving rise to what became known as The Aden Emergency. After some while trying to hang on to influence and power, British troops eventually withdrew in 1967 and the People's Republic of South Yemen was born.

The maritime aspect of Aden was interesting because as well as being a major international port it also served as a kind of marshalling yard for ships heading for the Suez Canal. The Gulf of Aden and the narrow straits at the entrance to the Red Sea are one of the busiest sea routes in the world and give rise to something of a bottle neck.

Given the volume of shipping passing in both directions there is clearly a need for a fair amount of careful management not to mention the opportunity to provide pilots and other remunerative services for the countries involved.

A few days and almost two thousand miles later having cruised the length of the Red Sea we entered the Gulf of Suez and arrived at Port Suez. Here Himalaya was assembled with other ships into a convoy for transit through the canal. Now, rather like Panama, nothing really prepares you for Suez and it was a fascinating experience.

When first built in 1869, the canal was 102 miles long and 26 feet deep. I'm not sure what the dimensions were at the time I passed through but now, after multiple enlargements, the canal is 120 miles long, 79 feet deep and

673 feet wide. It consists of the northern access channel of 14 miles, the canal itself of 100 miles and the southern access channel of 5.6 miles

The canal is single lane with passing places in the "Ballah By-Pass" and the Great Bitter Lake and it is a distinctly odd experience to be in either the main channel or the by-pass channel and look across the sand to see a convoy of ships apparently sailing through the desert.

A significant increase in the canal's capacity was achieved recently by enlargement of the by-pass areas and was dubbed The New Suez Canal. It was officially opened on 6th August 2015 and increased daily traffic from 49 to 97 ships per day.

Quite unlike Panama, there are no locks and seawater flows freely through the canal. In general, the canal north of the Bitter Lakes flows north in winter and south in summer. (I haven't quite worked that out yet) The current south of the lakes changes with the tide at Suez.

Looking north with populated and cultivated Egypt to the left

One striking feature I recall was the dramatic contrast between the Egyptian and the Arabian sides of the canal, especially towards the north where the more intensive cultivation and irrigation on the west bank created a vivid green landscape as far as the eye could see as compared to the arid desert in the east. With the benefit of satellite imagery and Google maps this difference can be clearly seen.

Having transited the canal we entered the Mediterranean at Port Said, turned left (or west for those of you who prefer it that way) and headed diagonally towards the toe of Italy and the Straits of Messina where we were able to see Etna and Stromboli, Europe's two most active volcanos smoking menacingly. No fireworks though unfortunately.

The following day we docked at our last port of the trip, the historic old port of Marseilles where sadly I was unable to go ashore due to some sort of stomach bug.

It definitely was not over indulgence so it was pretty bad luck to have travelled all those months and miles with never a problem in that direction only to be laid out for a couple of days right at the last minute so to speak. It was a shame because it was one of the places that had been on my list to have a look at. It still is. I must get there one day.

With Marseilles behind us within a few days were out through Gibraltar and home, not to Southampton this time but to Tilbury. In Essex on the north side of the Thames estuary it was at the time a major passenger terminal for cruise liners although that came to an end in the mid 1960's.

By now I had made up my mind that I would not be going back on the next trip. It was quite hard, knowing that I was forcing myself to a decision point about what to do next but to be honest I'd had enough of life at sea and was missing my family and friends more than I cared to admit.

Another issue was the homosexual dimension to life below decks. True, the camp performances provided a lot of entertainment which was OK if I didn't think too much about what they were all actually DOING to each other.

The truth was I hated it with all the constant innuendo. Now I am far from being a prude and I like my sex straight and I suspect the thoughts and feelings I now describe would today be seen as positively homophobic.

However it was what a relatively immature Catholic eighteen year old felt in 1963, fully four years before the law came to the aid of the homosexual community and decriminalised their practices with certain exceptions.

What I found particularly hard to understand was how in the space of those last three months the two guys I had joined up with had turned.

Dave the rough-neck Cockney was still the macho one but was heavily involved in a relationship with one of the most outrageous 'queens' on the ship and quiet Tim was last seen at a below deck 'homecoming' party tottering about in high heels and a full length sequined evening dress with pouting red lips and an amazing set of fake emerald jewelry.

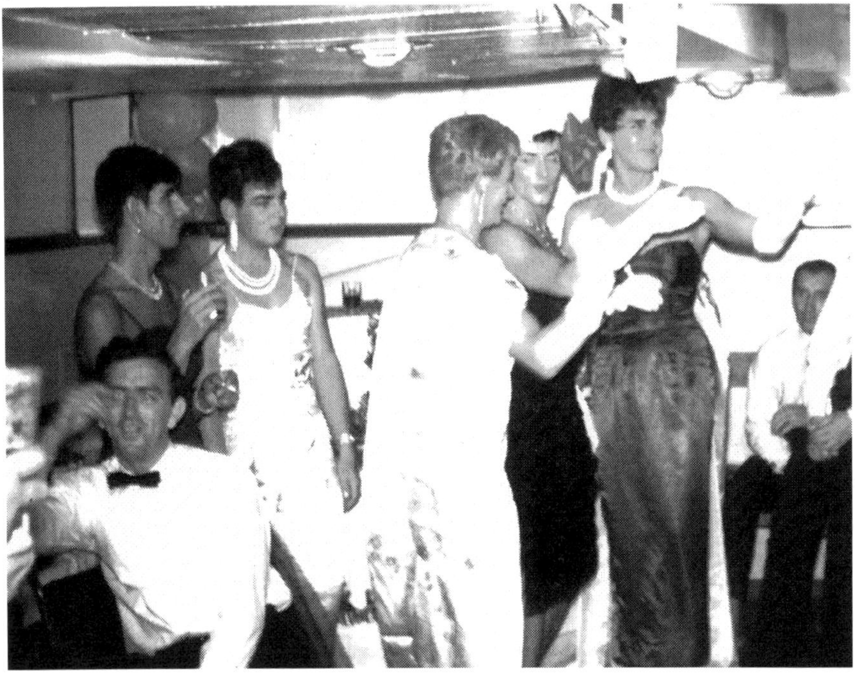

I couldn't even bring myself to say goodbye. However I'd certainly enjoyed my time away if my spend was anything to go by, because when I went to collect my pay packet I finally signed off the ship with £3. It was just as well that Mum and Dad were there to meet me. Oh and of course I had a hundred pounds in the bank. Result!

SS.Himalaya was the last P&O ship to depart from Tilbury arriving in Sydney on 30th October 1974 after which she was sold for breaking in Taiwan.

A sad end to a lovely old lady (And a lot of old queens!)

Thanks for a lot of memories.

Chapter 19 – A New Beginning (The first of several)

Well, what to do next?
Once the euphoria of the homecoming had subsided and my many tales had been told and re-told I had to face the reality of what to do with myself.

An interesting aspect of this situation was that the relationship with my parents seemed subtly different. There was little hint of the previous disapproval and they seemed to have, if not exactly great respect for what I'd done then at least some small recognition that I was now more my own person – own man even.

I was honest with my parents about the realities of studying for higher qualification in the scientific field, particularly with regard to maths. Although disappointed they both seemed to understand that unless I could feel both reasonably happy and hopeful for some kind of future in whatever field I went for it was probably going to be doomed from the start. The question was though "What would I do?" or perhaps more relevantly "What could I do?" Truth was that I didn't have a clue.

One thing was made clear though and that was that I was definitely expected to work and to make my contribution to the housekeeping budget. Whatever *their* idea, my greatest priority was to get mobile and so I started to explore the possibilities with regard to buying the longed-for car. I had the £100 but almost as soon as I started looking it became obvious that even in those days I wasn't going to get too much for my money so I was more or less resigned to that. However, the killer was not so much the cost of buying the car but getting it taxed and insured which would leave me with less for the car itself. Basically I didn't really have enough, because as Mum and Dad said – buying a wreck was sure to result in having to keep throwing good money after bad when things went wrong as they undoubtedly would.

Quite cleverly, I realize now in hindsight, Dad offered to lend me the £80 or so that I would need to get on the road with a half reasonable car but he would only do it once I was working. Crafty old devil! So it seemed finding a job was going to have to be the priority. And you won't be surprised to hear that yet again it was Dad who came to my rescue with the idea that I might very well make a successful career in the retail food industry.

To inspire my interest in the possibility he described the rapidity with which youngsters going into his company's training scheme were finding themselves as departmental managers by their early 20's and some even managing their own stores before their 30th birthdays. *"It's a really dynamic business son."* he said. *"Why don't you give it a go?"*

I have to admit that the idea, especially the possibility of rapid advancement, was certainly attractive although there was a little voice inside saying *"This isn't really you."*

"What the hell!" I needed a job or more honestly I needed the money so I embarked on the application and after an initial interview with a regional manager at Epsom I was called up to be seen by the personnel department at Hainault in Essex and was offered a place on the management training programme. Now I'm not under any illusions about this. I have never been much good at interviews and this was only the third I had ever done so I imagine that my appointment may well have had just the tiniest bit to do with my father's role in the company.

I was given a position at the Walton-on-Thames branch which was an absolute nightmare to get to by public transport and only served to emphasise my need for wheels and now that I was working Mum and Dad came up with the goods in the shape of a £75 loan to be paid off over the following year. So, armed with my 'wedge' I started looking at car adverts and went around to see one wreck after another before Dad said he'd heard of a car for sale at the Blue Star garage in Ashtead where he had bought our Hillman Minx.

Dad knew the manager, 'Paddy' Madigan, from the time he'd worked in the Ashtead shop so felt we would get a fair deal.

The car in question proved to be a shiny black Austin A30 – I can even remember the number – WPJ523 – so its year was 1956, the last year it was made before being superseded by the A35 (the model John used to collect the nuns from the airport)

I was bowled over, not because it was especially cool, fast, smart, flashy or anything like that but because it was clearly in good condition for its seven years of age; it wasn't a rust bucket, but most of all because I could afford it and it was going to get me on the road at last. So that was me, mobile and able to go wherever and whenever I fancied which in the first instance was from home to the shop at Walton every day.

The training programme with Keymarkets involved moving around the store from one department to another where we spent some two to three months learning how the various sections worked.

On the shop floor I stacked shelves till I was sick of the sight of them whilst in theory at least learning some of the science and psychology behind the supermarket 'stack 'em high – sell 'em cheap' philosophy.

I learnt about how piped music could be used to 'change the mood' of customers or to speed them up or slow them down – important at busy times when we needed to get them in and out to make space for the next lot. I learnt about how every square foot of selling space had to return a required level of sales and how by clever merchandising every foot of shelf space could be made to return the maximum possible turnover.
If I'm boring you, then you'll have an idea how I was beginning to feel after a few weeks of this.

'Provisions' - a general term for bacon, cooked meats, cheese and other dairy products - was my favourite department because I had some experience and expertise from the time worked with Dad in the Ashtead shop so here at least I could shine (well, glow) a little.

The rest however, it has to be said, left me pretty cold and by the time it came to moving into greengrocery I'd pretty much lost the plot and had more or less convinced myself that the programme was nothing more than a con to attract cheap labour into the business.

I know I had a pretty jaundiced and perhaps rather immature view of the system but I must say that the main problem with the programme was not the idea itself but the quality of the training or more particularly the individuals concerned.

As I have learnt from personal experience over the years, training is a definite skill that has to be taught and carried out really well if it is to be successful. While one or two of the department heads and deputies were actually very good and motivational trainers, most were not which simply left us trainees frustrated and disillusioned. By the October of 1963 I'd had enough and begun casting around as to what I might do instead. So on one particular day I went sick in order to attend an interview for a job selling insurance at a company in Dorking.

On the way I stopped to ask a policeman the way to the address I was looking for and got involved in a conversation about his job. The copper was a really nice guy and he did such a good job telling me about his life in the force that I never did go to the insurance interview but immediately made an application to join the police. The officer I'd spoken to had asked where I lived and hearing it was Ashtead advised me to try for the Metropolitan force as it was very close to Epsom, one of the Met's outermost stations and according to him the Met was where it all happened, besides, they paid more than the county forces too.

Things moved quite quickly then and within a month or so I'd been interviewed, accepted and allocated a place on a training course in January 1964.

Meanwhile at the Walton shop things went from bad to worse. I behaved like a complete pain and after a row with the manager only narrowly missed being sacked by getting my notice in first before he had a chance to get approval from personnel department to fire me. I walked out without thinking very clearly so there I was without work; housekeeping and loan to pay but no job. What a dope. Why couldn't I have just strung it out a bit longer?

Mum and Dad didn't actually say a lot. Obviously they knew about the police job but that was not for a couple of months so perhaps that's why there was no big drama. However, as Dad pointed out, if I thought I was going to just laze around the place at home until January, I'd best think again, in any event he had an idea.

As an area manager he had some authority for employing casual and temporary staff on his area in the run up to Christmas. He had control of this budget and so long as it wasn't overspent, Personnel didn't want to know.

So from November until Christmas I became a van-man. Not a white van but a rather scruffy dark green one if I recall correctly and I had a fine old time driving between shops on Dad's area transferring stock urgently required from one shop to another.

I got around all over the place, from the company's main distribution centre in Essex on occasions to almost anywhere else in the counties of Surrey, Kent, Hampshire, Sussex and even some London branches.

In the meantime of course I was also getting out and about socially now that I was mobile and not having to rely totally on Ken Thorn and his car. We still went around together but independently too and one of our favourite haunts was The Orchid ballroom at Purley where we rocked or smooched our nights away to the sounds of Ray McVay and his band.

Another band leader we became familiar with there was Brian Fahey who later became Shirley Bassey's musical director. Interestingly I got to know his son Michael a few years later when we found ourselves working for the same company.

Another popular venue of ours at the time was The Locarno Ballroom in Streatham Hill. Opened in 1928, (just a bit before our time!) it was the first purpose built dance hall in the UK. It later became The Cat's Whiskers club and then Caesars Night club in 1994 before finally closing for redevelopment in 2010.

Going two or even three times each week to the Orchid we soon got to know a few people there including a couple of girls called Theresa and Wendy. Theresa became my particular dancing partner and was to become quite a big part of my life although we drifted apart for a while when I first joined the police a few months later.

Other friends included Bob Cloutte from Ashtead who had this fabulous old 1949 red Triumph Roadster, the same as driven by John Nettles in the Bergerac TV series.

My friend Reg James friend also had a car I really coveted. Reg lived on the rather posh Givons Grove estate at Leatherhead and his father who owned an engineering company, had bought him a Ford Lotus-Cortina. This was a seriously fast and interesting motor made famous by the successes it enjoyed racing in the hands of the legendary Jim Clark.

Thinking back around those times they were just so hilarious and mostly quite idiotic really. The law around drinking and driving did not include the breathalyser so we never really thought twice about getting a skinful and then climbing in behind the wheel. Frighteningly irresponsible certainly, but that was just the way it was and thank goodness most of the time we got away with it. The odd bump or shunt but fortunately nothing more serious.

One silly night I remember we had been to the Orchid and for some reason best known to no-one had decided to return by a very indirect route via Reigate and Dorking. There were four of us in Ken's car I think, pretty much the worse for wear and at this time there were major road works at Dorking where a new dual carriageway was going in.

For some daft reason we pinched one of those rubber traffic cones from the works and arriving in Leatherhead decided to put it in the centre of the cross-roads and then went and parked up a short distance away to watch what would happen.

After a few minutes a large lorry arrived at the junction and then proceeded to negotiate the cone very slowly and laboriously toing and froing to avoid touching it when there was no reason in the world not to simply drive over the thing. We were in hysterics in the car when there was suddenly a loud knocking on the car roof and looking out we saw two rows of silver buttons standing there.

The policemen got two of the lads out of the front seats and one of the officers got in. I was in the back with Bob I think. We were swearing 'black was white' that we'd not been anywhere near Dorking despite the fact that the cone had Dorking Council stamped on it and was smothered in the same colour mud that was also caking out shoes and the floor of the car. What we didn't know at first was that the two others outside had owned up to the stunt.

Anyway it all came out eventually and when it came to the point of having our names taken the copper said *"Brian Simmons?*
I was round your house talking to your mother the other day. What would that have been about? "
I said *"It might be something to do with an application to join the Metropolitan Police."*
To which he says *"Well this is a bloody fine start isn't it?"*

Terrified of being arrested, we were all apologising frantically and offering to take the cone back to Dorking but after telling us a few home truths the coppers said *"No don't worry about it. We'll lose it. Just think twice before you do anything like that again."*
I'm sure they were laughing as they walked away but we certainly weren't.

For me those first few months of car ownership were fantastic and I very quickly began to delve into the detail of car maintenance and most Sunday mornings would find me with my head under the bonnet checking that all was well. Those BMC engines were so simple and accessible that it was nothing to have the cylinder head off and back or the brakes dismantled and reassembled before lunch - just for the sake of it. I learnt by doing and with the help of my trusty Haynes Manual developed quite a good level of expertise. Nowadays it seems, you need a degree in motor engineering and a computer to plug into before you can begin to do anything to a car.

The time spent previously with the old Norton was also helpful as it had at least given me a basic understanding of how engines worked.

Influenced by my friend John who had the hotted-up A35 it wasn't long before I was looking at ways to make my new motor go a bit faster or if not then at least sound as though it could. The problem was I didn't have spare money for any really effective tuning aids like twin carbs or a properly tuned exhaust system but thanks to him I was able to create a bit of an illusion.

John had done a bit of circuit racing and also used to compete in timed sprints down at Goodwood so when he bought a new exhaust system as part of his on-going process of modification he passed his old one to me.

The silencer was of the 'straight-through' design but he'd got it second-hand after it had already done a couple of seasons racing on a Lotus Elite. So by the time it came my way there really was no effective 'silencing' going on at all which suited me just fine as to my ear it sounded so loud and powerful I thought I was the bee's knees. Truth was of course it was just noisy or as my dad might have said *"All piss and wind."* He wasn't at all vulgar normally but occasionally and as I'd got older, something would just slip out

By this time I was very accustomed to having my own wheels and was turning into a bit of a wannabee boy racer, really spreading my wings around Surrey, Sussex and as far as Brands Hatch in Kent where I used to go to race meetings then drive home like a 'looney' whilst trying to emulate my current hero. To be honest, that I survived those first few months behind the wheel probably owed more to luck than judgement.

I did have a couple of small 'touches' though but I always felt they were due more to bad luck than my poor driving although lack of experience was undoubtedly a factor.

The first incident really was bad luck. I was in the process of overtaking a slower car when it suddenly swerved and collided with me broadside on. Apparently what had happened was that a dog on board had suddenly jumped over from the back seat and bitten the baby causing the driver to swerve into me as I passed.

Well, you couldn't make that one up could you? Reminds me of Jasper Carrott's Insurance Claim Form Statements:

As I approached an intersection a sign suddenly appeared in a place where no stop sign had ever appeared before.

Look them up on-line, they're brilliant and there is even a video of him reading them.

The second one happened on a dark wet night in Trafalgar Square when a woman stepped off the kerb right in front of me. Fortunately I was hardly moving so no serious harm was done but as things tend to happen in threes I should have been on my guard when I undertook a trip to London a couple of weeks before Christmas.

Piers Connor, an old school friend had moved to a flat in Bayswater and one evening I had taken his younger brother Martin up to London to see him when we came to grief. This one was undoubtedly my fault although the dark and wet conditions were contributory.

One the way home I came around a bend and seeing the street lights stretching ahead accelerated right into a low traffic island on which the illuminated 'Keep Left' sign wasn't - having been demolished in a previous accident earlier the same evening.

The collision ripped the front suspension off the car and sent young Martin through the windscreen as back in those days there were no seat belts. I was uninjured but Martin had a couple of cuts on his chin which bled a lot but fortunately once cleaned up turned out to be just scratches really but it could have been so much worse.

Unfortunately, with money being in short supply my insurance was only third party and I couldn't afford to repair the car myself so at a stroke my new found mobility and independence came to an end. Even worse, I still had the debt to my parents to pay off. I guess they could have written it off but it was their view that car or no car I'd undertaken to repay the loan and that's the way it should be. As far as I was concerned it was a bit like buying hay for a dead horse.

My friends were great as ever, and I simply reverted to the former arrangement of going around with them in their cars but it never was the same. They say 'it's an ill wind' and it was a bit of bad luck for John that got me back in the driving seat at least from time to time.

He'd gone to see a friend in Clapham who owned a little light-weight sports car called a Frisky Sprint, a weird little contraption powered by a 500 cc three cylinder two-stroke motor cycle engine. If that sounds a bit feeble for a car engine it's important to bear in mind that combined with a light fibreglass body the power to weight ratio was quite impressive and these little bombs were good for 90 mph which in those days was pretty fast for a road car.

John couldn't remember how it happened but apparently his friend was driving when they collided with another car, the plastic body had done an eggshell impression and left John in a heap in the road with a couple of broken ankles and a collection of other cuts and bruises.

Frisky Sprint - circa 1958 at a classic car show

Once released from hospital his most urgent need was to get his own car back from Clapham which is how he came to call on me for help as both his legs were in plaster and he obviously couldn't drive.

We got someone to ferry us up to Clapham, shoved John in the passenger seat and I drove back to Ashtead, in the process getting absolutely hooked because the difference between his car and mine was a million miles. I just couldn't believe the power until he explained that the engine was virtually the same as a Formula Junior racing car but obviously the body wasn't as light. Even so it was a real thrill to drive and over the next few weeks I took every opportunity to act as John's chauffeur.

Once or twice a week I'd go round to his place, load him into his car and set off for some pub or other with me in the process getting lessons from him on how to follow the 'racing line' through corners and various tips for getting the most out of his little road rocket.

I remember one evening we got into a bit of a race on the Dorking by-pass with a Bristol 405, a luxury sports car of the period and left a very surprised and pissed-off toff in the distance. The Bristol, which had twice as much engine as John's car could more or less stay with us on the straight but was wallowing like a pig in a rough sea on the corners whilst our little 'teapot' handled like it was on rails.

All huge fun but incredibly foolish of course and quite embarrassing really now when I think back on it especially as I have since become a member of the Institute of Advanced Motorists.

However, I've digressed again haven't I? So here I am approaching the end of 1963, car-less, relying on friends for transport and looking forward, it has to be said, with a certain amount of apprehension to my new job as a copper in London.

Right, let's give it a go!!

Chapter 20 – In and out of The Met

Training at Peel House

Monday 6th January 1964 and I'm on the platform at Epsom station having just been dropped off by Dad. Today is my first day of service with the Met police and I'm en-route to the recruit training centre in London and making my own way as Dad couldn't get the time off to take me all the way.

On the train it occurs to me that this is the day I really am leaving home for a new life, having concluded on reflection, that the few months with P&O didn't really count in the leaving home stakes.

As the realisation dawns, I start to wonder what I'm letting myself in for. Unlike my arrival at Southampton eighteen months before with my two new found friends, this time I really am flying solo.

Mum and Dad have given me a few pounds to keep me going and suggested that I get a cab from Waterloo to the centre which is over the river in Westminster. Not a long way but far enough with the huge case I'm lugging along.

I don't know London and I'm not exactly the 'man about town' yet, so having the confidence to simply wave down a cab like they do on the films isn't second nature, but I do. Amazingly it works, and a few minutes later I'm on the way.

We sweep out of Waterloo, along the Embankment with the Houses of Parliament opposite, over a very mucky looking river and it occurs to me that as a London policeman I might one day have to pull someone out of it. (dead or alive) I hope not.

All too soon my new 'man about town' moment is over and I'm on the pavement in Regency Street looking up at Peel House and suddenly my heart feels as heavy as the case beside me.

The six storey Edwardian edifice looms above me, its once impressive red brick façade now grimy from the polluted air of 1960's London. (It has since been converted into extremely expensive apartments)

Standing there, my accustomed confidence ebbs a little as I behold what is to be my home for the next three months and I contemplate how different this is going to be from the fun and games of life on board ship and to my comfy family life in Ashtead.

Climbing the two or three stone steps, I drag my case through a pair of glazed doors into a hall with a reception window to one side.

I give my name and a moment later a uniformed sergeant appears with a clip board, ticks off my name and ushers me through a door into a large room with a bunch of twenty or so equally apprehensive looking rookies.

What a mixed bunch we are, ranging in age from 'wet behind the ears' 19 year old kids like me who are in the majority to one or two who are clearly nudging the 30 year age limit. There is also a seriously tough looking guy who must be best part of 40 and who it turns out is ex-army so allowed to join later than the rest of us.

Dress is an interesting mix too. Starting a new job I imagined that most people would turn up in a suit and I would have worn my new Burton's made-to-measure if I hadn't ripped the pocket out of it in Long Beach last year. My only other suit is the Hong Kong Special which Dad hates.

He reckons the short jacket and shiny fabric make me look 'queer' and he doesn't want me turning up to join the Police looking like a poof. So I'm in this dog's tooth check sports jacket and a pair of smart slacks which I reckon looks OK. Certainly compared to a few of the others who have turned up in everything from jeans and jumpers to what look like gardening clothes, I feel quite superior.

Apart from a list of required kit to be brought along, including two pairs of black boots, civilian clothes for off-duty time and outside visits, sports kit, swimming gear and personal toiletries; the joining instructions were quite explicit about hair being cut short and tidy. However, looking around, some of the others are clearly hoping to hang on to their longer styles.

I guess we're all quite apprehensive and perhaps a bit shy too so there's not a lot of conversation apart from among three lads who have clearly arrived together. Meanwhile the rest of us carefully avoid eye contact while we contemplate what's likely to happen next.

We don't wait long before 'clipboard sergeant' reappears, runs through a roll call of our names and all being apparently present says,

"Today gentleman your new life begins. It is not going to be easy, especially for those of you who haven't been used to any sort of discipline. In here you will jump, sit, stand, march, speak and maybe even shit when told but if you approach it in the right spirit you will enjoy it. And that's an order" he adds.

I detect the hint of a smile just visible and it occurs to me that he is probably not quite as severe as he sounds. Also that perhaps the marching and saluting we did in the scouts all those years back and the strictness of the Captain's inspections on the ship might have had their uses after all.

"Right." he says, *"On your feet and let's show you around a bit. Bring your bags and we'll get rid of those first."*

And so it began. Like a file of ducklings we dutifully followed him out of another door and down steps into a large internal quadrangle which was pretty dingy anyway on a bleak January day but was robbed of direct light by the high surrounding walls.

This, we were told was the parade square where we would shortly be learning to drill like soldiers. Although, as he pointed out, it also had painted road markings, street signs, a pedestrian crossing and traffic lights which the sergeant explained was where we would also be learning traffic direction, the application of traffic law and how to deal with incidents ranging from road accidents to fighting drunks.

I think that even by this early stage one or two of us were in some doubt about the wisdom of signing up for this particular course. I for one didn't like the sound of the fighting drunks.

Diagonally across the square, stone steps with black painted handrails led up to the ground floor and into a lobby with stairs rising to the four floors above. A notice board had signs showing fire procedures, exit routes and timetables for what looked like three courses running in the school.

There was also a small cartoon of a large mushroom cloud above what was intended to be a crater with a little pin-figure of a policeman stood on the edge and a speech bubble from his mouth with the words,
"*What has happened here Sir please?*" I eventually found out what that was about. Very funny – I'll explain later.

The sergeant said "*This is the main classroom level. The canteen is also on this floor. Downstairs you've got the gym and changing rooms. Ok keep up.*" And he headed for the stairs.

My room was on the third floor. Well, I say room. It was actually a cubicle in a dormitory containing a dozen such spaces.

It was effectively an open plan arrangement with dividing partitions rather than walls. These were about eight feet high with a gap of a few inches at floor level – presumably to facilitate cleaning and whilst high enough for visual privacy that was about the limit. Of course there were no mobile phones at the time or I imagine life would have been impossible with the constant intrusion of other people's conversations.

(Have you noticed that no-one seems able to talk quietly on a mobile? I wonder why that is.) Radios were banned although a couple of chaps had them, albeit with headphones.

Toilets and bathrooms were apart (not much good for me now in my prostatically challenged state), but each cubicle had a hand-basin and mirror sufficient for basic ablutions, chest of drawers, a curtained hanging alcove, bedside cabinet with reading light and a small desk. So for most purposes I guess that if not exactly four star, it was adequate.

The privacy was however a bit of an illusion because of the way sound and vibration carries. So if someone, thinking his mates were all asleep, should give in to what the priests at school delicately referred to as the temptation of self-abuse or, not that uncommonly, the tears of homesickness they were likely to be treated to a round of applause or hoots of derision.

Whilst most of the cubicles had a window there was one on the inside of the building whose window also served as the access point to the fire escape leading down to the yard which I guess was fine in the event of a fire because the occupant could be the first out. Unfortunately for the same occupant, he was left in no doubt that he must never shut the window because it also served as the illicit way back into the building for anyone who stayed out past locking up time.

On such occasion the trick was to hop over the rear gates, scoot through the shadows around the parade square and simply nip up the fire escape to your floor. So if the occupant, either inadvertently or out of sheer cussedness were to lock the window and refuse to wake up, late arrivals were left with no choice but to surrender to the night porter and take the consequences.

Once we had dropped our bags off we had to gather for an address by the Commandant, a Chief Superintendent who welcomed us to the school, introduced our instructors that included a couple of Inspectors and several sergeants. It was a bit like being back at school again with our own dedicated Inspector as Course Director, a class Sergeant who seemed to teach general studies and other sergeants who taught various more specialist subjects.

The only other one and the only name I can actually remember was Sergeant Castle who was to be our drill, PE and self-defence instructor. Known as 'Punchy' due to his broken nose and boxing background Herbert Castle was a man we would come to fear and respect in equal measure.

His former army service and a good few years policing in the East End had prepared him perfectly for the job of knocking raw recruits into shape and helping to build the confidence needed to carry some authority on the streets.

That afternoon we were issued with a number of books the most important of which was Moriarty's Police Law which was to become our bible, and a book of definitions which was to become our bête-noir as they would all have to be learnt by heart and tested daily. The last one was The Metropolitan Police Instruction Book. Known at the IB it was more in the nature of procedural guidelines or as one of the instructors described it, "*A catalogue of a million cock-ups.*" As he explained it, whenever a copper had done something wrong over the years, someone then wrote a procedure in an attempt to ensure it didn't happen again.

Surprisingly after the book issue we were sent off the 'settle in', find our way around the place and were not required again until the following morning when we were assured *"We'll really get started."* I couldn't wait!!

From the following morning the course was in earnest and absolutely full-on. The first things were haircuts and uniform issue. A barber arrived who was clearly briefed to accept no entreaties and so in a few short minutes the few who had hoped to retain their slicked 60's hair styles were reduced to short back and sides all round and almost to tears in a couple of cases. Even my own recently trimmed locks didn't escape although my experience was less traumatic.

Following the haircuts we were bussed over to Lambeth where the Met's Central Stores were located and we lined up to be measured first and then progressed through to receive our uniform issue.

Apart from two or three sets (I can't quite remember) of tunic and trousers in the typical dark blue serge we were also issued with one ceremonial set which comprised an old-fashioned high-collar tunic and trousers in a really heavy fabric that was almost twice the weight of the daily wear. I dreaded the day I might have to wear it.

Half a dozen blue cotton shirts came as part pf the issue but also in those days, loose collars to go with them which had to be separately starched and carefully pressed if they were to ever look any good. There was also a heavy greatcoat, raincoat and even a cape.

So much for the clothing but then of course came the famous helmet that so identifies the British 'Bobby' world-wide. These are much lighter than they look, being fashioned from cork segments and inside there is a light string and leather web that sits on the head and is adjustable for fit.

There is nothing I hate more than the badly fitted coppers' helmets that are invariable present on TV programmes depicting the police, and sometimes sadly on real ones.

They either look too big like some sort of comic inverted flowerpot or they perch like a pea on a drum and look equally silly. In either case they have the effect of making the wearer look totally gormless and with about as much authority as PC Plod of the Christmas pantomime.

From top to toe and the question of boots. Boots were not issued as each recruit had been required to bring two pairs. It was explained that one pair was for daily wear whilst the other was to be highly polished and retained for parades, inspections and other special occasions. Police Regulations specified that officers were paid a 'boot allowance' for this purpose. It was however also explained that whilst the regulation pattern boots were fine for normal use some officers also chose to buy some soft-soled black footwear that would enable them to move more quietly around the streets at night. For this purpose the most popular style was the unhappily named thick – soled, black suede 'brothel creepers' favoured by the Teddy Boys of the time. No good at all in the wet but perfect for nights and very comfortable. It was left to us and I did get some later.

Along with the uniform came what were known as appointments. These were your ancillary items and included pocket notebook and holder, another wallet for the small catalogue of forms we had to carry, and a set of handcuffs. The issue also included the truncheon, a stout weapon about an inch and a half in diameter by fifteen or sixteen inches in length and fashioned out of a tropical hardwood known as 'lignum vitae'.

The truncheon was turned on a lathe to be slightly thicker at the business end with a ribbed grip at the other. We were told that some of them were made by prisoners learning woodworking skills in Dartmoor, an irony that was obviously intended to appeal to our developing policemen's mentality but I've no idea if it was true or not.

The uniform trousers were cleverly designed to incorporate a long truncheon pocket located down the outside and slightly behind the right thigh. It was not in the least uncomfortable and completely invisible but the position on the **outside** of the leg did give the lie to the jokey line "Is that your truncheon or are you just pleased to see me?" The line was apparently coined by street walkers to wind up their local beat officer although adopted by any number of comedians ever since.

Another appointment was the whistle that was attached by a chain to the top tunic button. It really is quite laughable in this modern world of efficient radio communication to realise that such a short time ago the only communication system available to the beat officer in an emergency was the whistle and I can quote from the instruction book (IB) that I was issued with at the time:

"*To raise the alarm or call another officer to your assistance, blow three loud blasts on your whistle. At night, or to call for assistance without raising the alarm an officer should signal with his lantern in the direction that another officer is likely to be.* "Not exactly high tech but that really was all we had and I can only marvel at the comparison with the sagging belts of today's beat officers laden with handcuff pouches, radios and Tazers, not to mention the stab vest and so on.

The only other items issued were two keys. One for the handcuffs and the other for the police boxes. Yes that's right, the TARDIS of Doctor Who was still very much a part of the police communication system as I shall describe in more detail later.

Once the uniform was issued it was made very clear that we were responsible for getting it pressed and into tip-top form for our first drill session and inspection in a couple of days' time. By the crestfallen looks on some of the faces it was clear that most didn't have a clue where to start but here in common with the ex-service chap I had some advantage.

Dad had always had a thing about appearance and not only encouraged but insisted that whenever I went out, certainly anywhere that mattered, I should be properly turned out, which as far as he was concerned meant pressed clothes and shiny shoes and to that end he had passed on a trick or two from his own service experience.

He had, for example, shown me how to press a pair of trousers using a damp cloth to avoid making them shiny and also how running a bar of soap down the inside could make a 'knife-edge' crease that would last longer. Having had to prepare uniform in both the scouts and as a waiter on the ship I was no stranger to using a hot iron whereas some of the lads scarcely knew where to begin.

Between us, the former squaddy (who's name I sadly cannot recall so I'm going to call him Dave) and I instructed the whole class in the practices of pressing and brushing.

He in particular was able to coach all of us in the fine art of 'bulling boots' or creating a mirror like polish on the toe caps of our best boots and a well above average finish on our regular ones. It really was done with spit and polish and only Kiwi 'Parade Gloss' would do. I still use it today but not quite so conscientiously.

The result was that when the first drill parade arrived Punchy Castle had very little to complain about, at least as far as the uniform was concerned. However, as far as our bearing and how we carried the uniform was concerned, it was a very different matter.

There are those, especially today, who would say that drill and military style discipline like saluting and so on has no place in the modern police service and to the extent that the service is not and should not ever appear militaristic, they would be right.

However, the police always used to be and I think should have remained a disciplined service to the extent that there is a clear rank structure and people should expect to do what they are told and when. Because in difficult situations it is only by having an organised and functioning command structure that things get done correctly. Time enough for questions at the de-brief.

Unfortunately in recent years modern democratic and participative management systems have encouraged a more laisser-faire attitude to the rank structure, and it seems to me that to a significant extent the discipline of the service has suffered. I include here self-discipline and pride in appearance because by and large modern police officers are nowhere near as smart as their predecessors. Many are overweight and clearly unfit with scruffy ill-turned out uniform and they have nowhere near the bearing and presence required to command either authority or respect on the streets.

Sorry about that little rant and back to the story!

Punchy may have been happy with our uniform but as he explained it was his task to get us looking the part and that was about more than wearing the outfit. So the first thing he said was about how to stand, -your bearing.

"Think tall." He said *"And you'll become tall. Think strong and you'll be strong. Wear this uniform with pride and you'll carry it all the better and if you can do that there are not many who'll want to argue with you. And that after all is the object of the exercise. You represent authority and the law but you also represent safety and fairness. Carry your uniform well and you'll be able to do it all. Now brace up and let's see some straight backs."*

It may not be word perfect but I will never forget that little speech by Herbert Castle. It was to inform my attitude to the rest of my police career in both the short and long term.

I got to like drill and soon got into the swing of it and it really did make me feel good. By virtue of his previous experience, Dave was made our drill leader and was really helpful to those who had trouble with marching. It's fascinating; we all walk naturally and swing our arms in the right arm – left leg rhythm but ask some people to march and they immediately want to do the same arm – same leg.

Others seemed to have no idea of left from right but eventually we all got the hang of it and could put on quite a passable show.

Another thing 'Herbie' Castle was responsible for was teaching us self-defence which in those days was based largely around the Japanese unarmed combat system known as Aikido. In this technique an attacker's movement and momentum is used to deflect, throw and immobilise the person or at least that's the theory. But to be good at it requires a great deal of time in practice which unfortunately we didn't have.

As a result the best we could really hope for was to be able to get an arm lock on an attacker and this was only realistic with a person of relatively slight build who was not putting up too much of a fight.

I can recount from bitter experience that twisting (or even getting a hold of) the arm of a fifteen stone fighting drunk labourer is actually not a possibility and a much better result was usually achieved by the combined weight of six or seven colleagues assuming they happened to be on hand. In my limited experience in a one to one confrontation like that, talking the situation down almost always worked for me apart from on a couple of occasions when a sharp tap with my truncheon or even its appearance worked wonders.

Herbie did cover use of the truncheon which can be used to great effect as a last resort. The instructions were very clear that they were only to be used in extremis and that "*officers should aim at the parts of the body least likely to suffer severe or permanent injury*" which is all very well if you actually have time to think about it.

I must say that initially it struck me that a sharp tap on the nut was likely to get the best immediate result but as Herbie told us "*Do that and you'll be writing for weeks.*"

His advice about the use of the stick was "*Go for the bits that are going for you.*" By which he meant that if a person was reaching out a hand to grab or otherwise attack you, it's the easiest bit to hit. And in his experience a sharp crack on the hand, wrist, ankle or knee caused a lot of pain and usually enough to give an attacker pause for thought, drop a weapon and enough of a pause for you to either escape or get some sort of hold on depending on circumstances.

Back in the classroom we studied the history of policing. We learnt how in 1829 the Metropolitan Police Act authorised the establishment of the force and how Sir Richard Mayne, joint first Commissioner (never did quite understand that) of the force enunciated 'The Primary Objects'. These were a couple of paragraphs that I suppose today would be called a mission statement and which we had to learn by heart – the first of many such statements and definitions.

A major part of the law we had to take on board was under The Larceny Act of 1916. This well-drafted piece of legislation with just a few amendments had over the years managed to deal pretty successfully with just about all offences against property until it would be replaced more than 50 years later by the Theft Act 1968.

Other pieces of law were the Offences against the Person Act of 1861 which covered assault both minor and serious and even dealt with such bizarre crimes as infanticide, concealment of birth and child destruction. Not exactly the sort of thing you'd meet every day on London streets but 'hey-ho', it's all knowledge and as they say knowledge is power (and confidence). I must say that by the end of the course we were pretty well walking law books and could recite far more law than a newly qualified solicitor. Whether we fully understood it was of course a different matter.

Then there was also the (now infamous) Vagrancy Act of 1824 that dealt with begging and similar street offences, which included simply being on the street in suspicious circumstances, and became known far more recently as the hated "sus" law.

There was a bit more to it than that, but not a lot and it was undoubtedly appropriate for the time of its introduction in the 19th century for dealing with 'sturdy beggars and vagabonds' that were roaming the country after the Napoleonic wars. However, to my certain knowledge the act was much misused back in the 60's when I joined up and well before we had the ethnic minority groups who in later years would allege their victimisation under its 'stop and search' powers.

For all their faults when viewed through 20th and 21st century eyes, these old acts had a lot going for them to the extent that they were meticulously drafted and took a long time to enact.

This meant they had fewer loopholes than more modern legislation that often seems to have been drafted 'on the hoof' or as a knee-jerk response to circumstances with far too little thought.

My personal view stated here but one I have heard expressed more than a few times by people who should know.

Sudden death is something that sooner or later every police officer will have to deal with whether as a result of a road accident, 'murder most foul' or simply sudden and unexpected death at home or in the street. The law places a responsibility on police officers becoming aware of such a death to report the matter to a Coroner unless a doctor can certify the cause with reasonable certainty.

And we should all be grateful for this because it is a measure that exists for our protection and helps to ensure that we don't go around bumping off our neighbours willy-nilly.

Given the young age of most recruits, the majority of us had never seen a dead body close to and fewer still would have been exposed to the sometimes horrific appearance of murder or accident victims. Part of our training therefore was a visit to the mortuary at St Thomas' Hospital just across the river in Lambeth and to actually observe a post-mortem although this latter was not obligatory.

For the instructors this was a heaven sent opportunity to really wind up the more sensitive recruits by ensuring that they were in the front and closest to the action so to speak. I think they had somehow involved the mortician, a grizzled white haired and somewhat stooped old gent who revelled in the name of Grinstead. I don't know why but somehow the name just seemed incredibly apt. "Grizzly Grinstead".

It was bad enough that he was eating a sandwich when we were all shown into the mortuary. However, I couldn't believe it when in order point out where he would be making incisions on the cadaver laid out in front of us, needing both hands free he calmly put his sandwich into the palm of the dead hand saying *"Hold that a minute mate."*.

I always assumed it was done for effect but maybe that was something he did every day. Whatever, it was a moment I'll never forget for its casual insensitivity. However, as I was to discover over time police officers and other professions that have to deal with emotionally difficult situations frequently develop a kind of black humour as a form of barrier to protect their own sensitivities.

Road traffic law also had quite a high priority as did the Motor Vehicle Construction and Use Regulations that dealt with everything from noisy exhausts through defective tyres and lights to parking and driving under the influence.

However in those pre-breathalyser days 'under the influence' had to be proved by the testament of an officer that the alleged offender, "smelled of alcohol, had glazed eyes and was unsteady on his / her feet". Such facts were usually tested by requiring the suspect to walk along the white line in the road or stand on one leg, either of which carried out beside or along a road carried its own risks.

It was still common practice at the time for police officers to be allocated to 'traffic points' during peak hours, the theory being that by controlling traffic manually, they could ease congestion or perhaps at least deter some of the bad driving induced by frustration.

If the truth be told, except as a last resort, it was a practice best avoided as interference by a police officer almost always caused more congestion than it solved especially if the officer concerned was not very skilled or lacking in confidence.

It takes some personal courage to walk out into the centre of a busy road junction and effectively take control of four or more lanes of traffic. Which is why in the back yard of Peel House we were often to be found shuffling around in little 'crocodile' processions as we pretended to be vehicles on the marked out road junctions whilst one of our number attempted to establish a bit of order.

As you might imagine this could easily get out of hand once we started playing about a bit with the intention of deliberately confusing the luckless officer on the point. You always got your own back though, because on another day it was going to be someone else's turn on the point.

Road traffic accidents were regarded as very much part of the beat officer's daily life and knowing how to deal with them was an important skill to master. (Always assuming your own poor traffic control was not the primary cause!!) This included placating the often irate drivers, to the point on occasion, of threatening arrest for Breach of the Peace (extreme, but always worked well), as well as working out who was at fault, identifying witnesses, recording details and reporting the offending driver(s) as appropriate.

Sounds easy enough but quite difficult remembering everything especially the first few times, hence the importance of practicing in the yard at Peel House before we were unleashed on the unsuspecting public.

We were taught a more or less standard form of approach to any incident we might encounter on our beats which was, (and there was obviously room for individual variation) that one should the approach the scene in an unhurried manner and in a calm but authoritative voice say -
"What has happened here Sir, please?" or something similar. (So long as it was not *"What the F**k is going on here?")*

I know it sounds awfully Dixon of Dock Green and in fairness it was around the same time, but at least they didn't tell us to say *"Hello Hello."* or *"Evening All."*

As new recruits one of the main things the training tried to instil was a sense of personal confidence, part of which was not to be afraid to take control of situations and not to be afraid of the sound of your own voice. At its simplest this might be at the scene of an incident when seeking witnesses to say loudly to all around *"Did anyone see what happened?"*
This may not sound significant but it puts you in charge and often encourages the shy witness to come forward.

Back in those days and it is still to some extent true today, the basic unit of police protection was the constable patrolling his beat which is the area for which he/she is responsible whilst on duty. Therefore, part of our training also concerned what was known as 'beat craft'. It certainly was not rocket science but did include a few tips that one might not immediately think about.

Firstly we were advised to remember that a principal role was to help the public and to deter offenders so to that end we were instructed to walk on the outside of the pavement in order to enhance our visibility.

That was all very fine back then, when 5' 10" was the minimum height requirements for male officers. But I reckon quite a few of the current crop could easily be lost in a crowd even with their helmets on which sadly today seems often to have become an optional extra. Also, working a beat in a random fashion and avoiding a fixed pattern of patrol was advised so that potential offenders would not know where or when you might appear next.

Conversely at night, we were advised to walk on the inside of pavements and seek areas of shadow in order to observe without being seen and hopefully to surprise miscreants with a loud *"Gotcha!"*

If this sounds a bit light-hearted it is intended to be but it is also true that the British public are as much in love today with the George Dixon image of the 'Bobby on the beat' as they ever were. So the challenge of modern policing is to give the public what it wants in terms of that visible presence despite the fact that it is an almost total waste of time and manpower!

Bold statement? - Maybe, but look up the records if they exist for the number of offenders captured by beat officers just 'happening' on a crime in progress and the number will be extremely small.

It is hard however to evaluate the deterrent effect of the patrolling officer and the public 'comfort factor' is so important that forces are obliged to maintain a level of beat patrolling despite the huge cost.

Back in 1964 it would be true to say that the east - west cold war was still very much an issue and the police were responsible for what used to be called Civil Defence but by that time had become Home Defence. Apart from the name I don't think a lot else had changed. It was still pretty much a Dad's Army sort of arrangement with local wardens and tin hats.

The primary police role, at least at a local level was the Warning and Monitoring system. Every police station had this sort of squawk box or loudspeaker on a shelf somewhere near the front office and a red telephone which, if the nuclear balloon ever went up and normal communications were down, was supposed to provide the back up.

This would pass messages of impending fall-out and in response some local officer would have to go and sound the alarm which had moved on from the wailing siren of the last war to the firing of maroons (exploding rockets) to warn the populace to take cover. Sounds awfully hit and miss doesn't it and the truth of the matter, certainly viewed from today's perspective and more advanced knowledge, is that it was.

So, to return to Peel House and the training in Home Defence; among other things, we had to learn some basic firefighting skills. So given the assumption that come the big day, all power would be down and fire brigades would be stretched to the limit fighting big fires, the idea was that it would be down to wardens, police and whoever else working together as 'Stirrup Pump Teams' to deal with local fires.

Now for those that don't know a Stirrup pump is a vertical double-action hand pump intended for pumping water out of a bucket that has a bracket going down outside the bucket to the ground which the user stands on in order to steady the thing. Hence – 'stirrup'. A hose comes off the body of the pump which can then be used to direct a jet of water wherever it is required. To get an idea of this thing in action look it up on-line. Amazingly they can still be bought today, albeit somewhat upgraded

The team comprised four people identified unsurprisingly as No 1. No 2. No 3. No 4. Number One's role in fighting a fire was to run forward towards the fire, getting as close as safely possible and dragging with him the nozzle end of the hose attached to the Stirrup Pump. This would ideally be kept back and away from the fire and preferably around a protective corner to shield No 2, who was the pumper from the heat. It was also suggested that No 1 might use an upturned chair or similar item as a heat shield for himself. (Naïve or what !!)

No 2's role as 'pumper' required him to pump like mad whilst no's 3 and 4 were the runners whose task it was to refill the bucket by running a chain of buckets from the supply and pouring them into No 2's bucket. If this is beginning to sound a bit Laurel and Hardy, you're right but it gets better yet!

So the team in action went something like this:

No 1 runs towards the fire and casts himself before it and No 2 shouts *"Alright No 1?"* to which No 1 responds *"Alright No 2."*

No 2 then shouts the question *"Water on No 1?"* to which the response is supposed to be *"Water on. No 2."* However a more predictable reply might be *"Just pump the f***ing water No 2."*

At this point No 2 begins pumping like a mad thing whilst No's 3 and 4 begin their supply chain which is OK if the source is not far away. However, if its more than a few yards the system soon starts to falter as buckets arrive half empty because No's 3 and 4 keep slipping on the water they are spilling on the way. It is of course also the job of No's 3 and 4 to take over from No 2 when he is all pumped out.

The photo is included to show the stirrup pump being used by just two people – presumable just for demonstration because it does not show team member 1 who should be prostrate in front of the fire, nor number 4 who would also be fetching the water to refill the bucket.

Now I wouldn't want to paint too ludicrous a picture for you because many a home was saved from fire during the last war by the practised use of the Stirrup pump and there are some excellent on-line references and even a video of a team in action. However, back to Peel House.

Prior to my arrival in January 1964 the fire-fighting element of the Home Defence training involved students in donning much faded and mostly oversized boiler suits, wellies and tin hats and being bussed a short distance to a nearby derelict site where there were the remains of an old (appropriately) bombed building.

A couple of hay bales were tossed in, soaked in paraffin and set ablaze. Students then had to take it in turns to form stirrup pump teams and using the above procedure set about extinguishing the fire whilst the Inspector in charge, notionally to add a touch of realism but actually for his own amusement, wandered around tossing Thunderflashes into the building and scaring everyone witless in the process.

In fact, as an exercise in team-building and an illustration of the intensity a fire can display it worked very well, even if the likelihood of them ever having to actually do it was minimal.

Unfortunately for my own and subsequent intakes, at the end of 1963 as part of the efforts to reduce London's infamous pollution, this area of London was made a smokeless zone so prohibiting at a stroke the lighting of bonfires etc. including the Met's Home Defence training at Peel House.

So by the time it was my turn for training we had to go through the same procedure, running round like demented creatures in a shack on an old bomb site, yelling inane expressions and squirting water all over a non-existent fire. Really, Laurel and Hardy had nothing on us.

On a more serious note, other elements of Home defence instruction included information on the levels of devastation and loss of life that even a small nuclear strike on London would cause. We learnt about fall-out and how long it might last, radiation effects and how to measure it and some realistic assessments of what it would mean for the country if the nuclear button ever was pushed and we became the target of even a few strikes.

Whilst the story for public consumption was that government had it all in hand with this great Home Defence strategy in place we were left in no doubt by our Inspector (probably breaking all the rules) when he said *"It's all complete bollocks."*

It was apparently someone on the previous course to ours who, seeing the whole thing for the charade that it was, drew the cartoon that I'd seen on the notice board of the policeman standing beside a nuclear crater saying *"What has happened here Sir please?"*

I felt tempted to add another speech bubble with the supplementary question *"Did anyone see what happened?"* Not much chance of an answer there.

Another trip out during the course was to visit a local magistrate's court and the London Quarter Sessions in Southwark which is what the Crown Court used to be called.

Quite a lot of our training involved learning to give evidence as credible and unflappable witnesses. So it was very useful for us to go along and sit for a few hours in the back of the courts to generally get a feel for the procedures and the rather awe-inspiring atmosphere especially in the higher courts full of the lawyers in their wigs and gowns etc.

Towards the end of the course we all returned to the local Magistrate in order to be sworn in as Constables, promising to "uphold the law, keep the peace and prosecute offenders without favour or affection, malice or ill will." or words pretty much to the same effect. Quite a moving moment really.

Part of the police conditions of service included a number of restrictions on the private life of a constable, one of which was that you have no other employment; nor could a constable live in licensed premises and no close member of an officer's family could be a licence holder.

There were various other conditions too which whilst appearing a bit draconian at first were quite logical really as they were intended to ensure officers were able to carry out their enforcement duties without being affected by conflicts of interest arising from family connections and so on.

The Police Discipline Code was hammered home relentlessly during the course and there appeared to be a million ways where by stepping out of line just a fraction you could find yourself in trouble.

A major one of these however seemed to be around the issue of drinking on duty and entering licensed premises without due cause. This became easier to understand when some years later I was able to browse through some historic discipline records. From the number of officers who found themselves in breach of this particular rule you might be forgiven for thinking the country was policed by a bunch of drunks which in the early years of the police service was not far from the truth.

With all this emphasis on the 'evils of the demon drink' it was not surprising that whatever little transgressions we might have imagined ourselves committing, those relating to drink would be the last. How wrong can you be? I would find out within weeks. And so, in no time at all it seemed the course was over, we were sworn in, had our little passing out parade, lined up in the yard for the course photo and were packing our bags ready to move out to our respective postings, which in my case was M Division and Kennington Road Police Station.

As a single officer my new home was to be Gilmour Section House in the company of about 300 other coppers. I can't say I relished the idea. We were granted a few days leave prior to taking up our postings which, having dumped my uniform and other kit in the section house, I made use of to go home and see parents and friends before returning once again to 'the smoke' to begin life as a London policeman for real.

Gilmour Police Section House near the Elephant and Castle

Out there for real

Kennington Road Police Station - 'The Nick'

As a probationary constable the first thing that happened on arrival at a new station was to be allocated a 'parent constable' who was supposed to become a 'friend', mentor, advisor and tutor and basically show one the ropes which included learning the geography of the area and the beats or patrols into which the patch was divided.

My 'parent' was an Irish chap whose name I can't recall so I'll call him Patrick. He was probably in his late thirties, tall, good looking in an Irish sort of way if you get my meaning although to be honest I'm not even sure what I mean by it. It's just a look.

Pat had been about a bit and had been at Kennington Road – the 'nick' as I quickly came to call it in common with everyone else, for about six years so he certainly know his way around. He was friendly enough when it came to showing me the ropes although there were times when I had the distinct feeling that I was cramping his style and this was particularly so when it came to chatting up women.

I'd heard talk about the Blarney of the Irish; well Pat had it in spades and I hardly remember a day when he didn't go off duty with at least one or two phone numbers in his pocket. Mind you, I can give it some too if I've a mind to but at that time and feeling such a newbie that was about the last thing I was thinking about.

I recall one terribly embarrassing day when we were setting out from the nick along Kennington Road towards Waterloo. I saw this figure in a clerical black suit and dog collar coming towards us and even from some distance immediately recognised him as Father Maxwell our parish priest in Ashtead.

I knew instinctively what would happen but before I could explain to Pat or cross the road it became clear he had recognised me (which was surprising given the uniform and all) and was making an enthusiastic beeline towards us beaming broadly.

"Brian my dear boy". He gushes, pumping my hand madly. *"So here you are and me the first of the village to see you on duty."*

Of course with Mum's church friends and the neighbours it seemed that half of Ashtead knew more about me joining the force than I did myself. *"And I see you've made a friend already."* he enthused, grasping Pat's hand too.

"Actually he is my parent constable, a kind of tutor." I gabbled trying to cover my embarrassment to Pat's huge amusement.

"Well don't let me stop the parenting. Anyway I mustn't keep the bishop waiting." he said and then gave me a huge hug and was gone while I stood in a kind of blur with Pat beside me laughing his socks off.

Watching him disappear I remember thinking
"Well that certainly wasn't what I imagined my first encounter with a member of the public would be like but probably better that than some major crime or one of the fighting drunks we'd been warned about in Peel House"

Our shifts took a bit of getting used to, as apart from my brief spell of split hours working on board the ship, I had never done shifts and certainly not experienced night working. The standard pattern at the time for our station was six weeks of alternate early and late shifts between 6am and 2 pm and then 2 pm until 10 at night. This was followed by three weeks of night working between 10pm and 6 am. It was a bit of a killer at first but it actually worked quite well for me because my body took almost a week to get used to night working so by the second week of nights I began to feel almost normal.

Each shift began with everyone on duty 'parading', well just lining up in the parade room where we were inspected to see that we were smart and had all our appointments which we had to hold out in front of us to be seen.

There was one day when I somehow managed to forget my truncheon but thanks to the guy next to me who held his out in his left hand instead of his right while I just held out an empty fist, I managed somehow to get away with it as the sergeant glanced cursorily along the line. First thing after parade, I then had to beetle back to the section house to collect it. From then on I left it in my locker at the nick.

After this inspection we were allocated our beats or patrols together with our points or ringing-in times. This was all well before the time of personal radios so in order to keep a measure of albeit distant supervision over patrolling constables we were required to be at certain places known as points at a particular time during the shift. Usually these points would be at or near public telephone boxes so that the station could get in touch if they needed to pass out information. Other points that included a ringing-in requirement would be at one of the three or four Police Boxes on the division.

Yes the good old TARDIS was very much in evidence then and was indeed a very welcome bolt-hole at any time in bad weather or especially in the early hours of a winter morning.

Only about 3-4 feet square they had a shelf at about waist height that served as a writing surface, a stool and a telephone that could also be reached from the outside by opening a panel and was intended for the public to call for police assistance. Believe me it is surprising how quickly one could drop off to sleep even in such an uncomfortable space.

Those who can remember police boxes before they had a second incarnation as Doctor Who's time machine may recall a light on the top. This could be made to flash when the station wanted to contact the bobby on that particular area so that, although the phone had a low volume ring tone, a policeman passing some distance away might also spot it and come to take the call.

I mentioned beats and patrols just now and whilst they were both a constable's area of responsibility they were slightly different. A beat could be quite a large area the size of which basically reflected its nature. For example a rural area beat could be extremely large on the basis that the population and property density were low whereas in more densely populated urban areas beats were smaller.

Patrols were in general even smaller than a beat and were usually arranged to provide fairly intensive police cover for an area that might be seen as vulnerable.

For example, Lambeth Walk was a single street comprising mostly lock-up shops, some with flats above and it was located in what used to be regarded as a relatively high risk area. Favourite targets were the cigarette shop and off-licence. At the time few of these had sophisticated alarm systems, if any, and so were quite often victims of burglary. For this reason, just that single street justified its own bobby and this was designated as a patrol and was actually surrounded by a larger separate beat area.

Looking around us today it is hard to believe that there ever was a time when local commanders had the luxury of deploying so many officers on a shift.

Not that long after this it all started to change of course with the introduction of 'Panda' cars which certainly did provide officers with much needed mobility and a better response capability. However, human nature being what it is, they also provided a comfy cocooned environment in which to withdraw especially if the weather were bad. And so, in my opinion, began the great separation between the police and communities that has been a feature in so much urban unrest over the years since.

Just going briefly back to Lambeth Walk as an example; community relations there in the 60's were such that if I wanted to it was possible to spend a full eight hour shift just walking down one side and up the other and the street was only a couple of hundred yards long.

On the way you spoke to almost every shopkeeper, had an ice cream in Luigi's and a couple of cups of tea. The locals actually valued their beat officers and wanted to talk to them, in the course of which it was possible for the attentive copper to pick up all manner of useful information.

There were two other things that Pat taught me during my parenting period that certainly were not on the official curriculum.

You'll recall my comments about the discipline code and it being against all the rules to enter licensed premises whilst on duty (except of course, in the pursuance of that duty) so as I said, doing so in contravention of this was absolutely the last place you were going to find me. Right? - WRONG!

On this particular day we were on an early shift and due to finish at two o'clock and we were wandering casually (sorry – patrolling) along, just nattering about this and that and I swear to this day that I never saw it happen. One moment we were on Bowling Green Street just near The Oval cricket ground and the next or so it seemed, I was standing in the back kitchen of a pub with a half-drunk pint in my hand.

Clearly this was pretty run of the mill as far as Pat was concerned judging by the casual and relaxed manner of his conversation with the landlord but it suddenly hit me like a bolt from the blue. *"Shit! What the hell are we doing?"* I thought, and as the reality dawned I was hit by such a panic attack that I remember I started to shake and I can recall as clear as day my knee-caps jigging about with a life of their own.

Obviously I tried not to show it but I can tell you I was never so pleased to get out of anywhere as I was on that day. I had these visions of us being discovered by the sergeant and my career going up the ''Swannee' almost before it had started. Just goes to show, you need to watch where you're walking!

There was another thing which, whilst equally against the rules, was very useful and I, along with many others got into it on a routine basis.

There really is nothing worse, especially at the beginning of a week of night duty, than that awful overpowering tiredness that spreads over one like a veil in those small hours between 3 and 5 in the morning and one's natural biorhythms are screaming to go to sleep. Well, as Pat showed me, there was an answer.

One of the police boxes where we had to 'ring-in' from was located close to Vauxhall Bridge on the embankment where coincidentally M division (mine) and L division bordered each other.

There was also an all-night garage very close by that was built into the railway arches below the lines coming out of Waterloo station and the garage offered long term parking under these arches.

Pat explained that over time a practice had arisen whereby night duty officers on the nearby beats were allowed by the garage attendant to bunk down in the cars for a couple of hours or so. So we'd give a note of our ringing-in times to the garage man and he would come and give us a shake a few minutes before we were due to make the call.

You could, I guess, say that no great harm was done and no-one was any the wiser although I doubt if the last bit was true because knowledge of the practice seemed pretty wide spread and it would have been surprising if the 'guvnors' weren't aware.

In no time at all it seemed my two weeks 'parenting' with Pat came to an end and I was flying solo. Not exactly full of confidence but truthfully not feeling too bad either, and little by little the confidence grew, especially if you didn't push the boundaries too hard.

On duty time was better than off duty for me because having no transport and all my friends being down in Ashtead and around I felt quite lonely a lot of the time, or at least I did until I got in touch with Theresa again.

We had not lost touch completely as I was still managing to get down to home from time to time and thanks to good friends and their transport we were still making it to the various dance venues including The Orchid Ballroom at Purley where Terri and I had first met.

She was working in London although still living in Mitcham at this time but we started dating regularly and doing the bars and discos of the West End which were really quite exciting and places like Tiffany's in Shaftesbury Avenue, The Empire and the Blue Boar Inn in Leicester Square became our regular haunts.

There was another little (unlawful) bonus that came with membership of the Met and that was the fact that you could get into almost any London club, cinema or dance hall, bus or underground train by simply flashing the warrant card. Not right of course but just another one of those things that had become established over time.

Clearly, as a police officer you should always be asking "*Why?*" when someone offers little perks like free entry (or sleeping on duty for that matter)

Well as far as club owners were concerned, the way it was explained to me was that if there was ever any trouble, the management were always happy to think they had a few members of the force on hand to help out.

I could see that but never could work out what the petrol attendant had to gain. Keeping on the right side I guess – Just in case.

Bottom line however was that it was, in the words of the discipline code, an 'improper and corrupt practice' and when a few years later Robert Mark became the Commissioner and set about cleaning up this and many far worse practices, this was one of our little 'perks' that came to an end and quite right too I guess.

I remember my dad saying *"There's no such thing as a free lunch. Just be ready when pay day comes."*

We had so many laughs at the nick and although I never made any close or lasting friendships there was a tremendous sense of camaraderie and you could always rely on your mates looking out for you, and especially for us younger ones.

There was one young Scots lad by the name of Eric who joined with me and was also posted to Kennington Road. He was quite immature and if I was a bit of a fish out of water at first he was even more so. As one older bobby said *"He's about as green as the Scottish valley he came from."* And not surprisingly Eric took the brunt of quite a few pranks which most of us would have seen coming but he didn't. The kind of guy that in another profession would be the one sent to buy a tin of elbow grease.

One night shift, Eric was allocated the beat that included Lambeth Churchyard where Captain Bligh of The Bounty is buried. At parade the sergeant announced that there had been some incidents of vandalism and asked Eric if after his meal break (about 2 –3 am) he would make a point of going and having a look around the cemetery.

Well, for the pranksters this was too good a chance to miss and they got there ahead of him. Eric was always whistling; whether on this occasion it was a bit of a self-confidence boost I don't know but around three in the morning whistling Eric comes wandering into the cemetery, parks himself on a grave stone and starts to roll a cigarette at which point the 'haunting' begins.

Three of the lads from the nick draped in bed-sheets with torches underneath and rattling chains or suchlike emerged from behind some tombs and Eric was off like a long-dog up the Lambeth Road. He came bursting in the door of the nick with this tale of being haunted by ghosts in the cemetery shortly followed by the three convulsed with laughter and carrying rolls of sheets and other 'haunting' kit under their arms.

Captain Bligh's tomb in Lambeth Churchyard

On another occasion Eric was on duty as night telephonist at one of those old switchboards where you had to plug leads into sockets until they criss-crossed like some sort of crazy cat's cradle.

When a call came in a little flap on that particular line would drop down to alert the operator and on this board, apart from the incoming public lines (you could actually phone a local police station in those days!!), there were all the ring-in lines from police boxes around the division and various internal extensions.

Just by way of a little prank all the rest of us synchronised our watches and on the dot of the agreed time we all picked up a phone or dialled a number so that at the other end poor Eric was faced with a mini-avalanche of these falling tabs which he frantically tried to answer all at once. Childish I guess but just the sort of thing that happens in work groups, raises a smile and helps the time pass. There was another very funny (in retrospect) incident and against me this time.

This was also on a night shift but in the early morning as it was just getting light. I was on patrol in Kennington Road when I smelled burning and quite strongly too. Looking up in the half-light I suddenly say this huge cloud of smoke coming from a building a couple of streets away and was convinced I'd stumbled on a major fire.

Fortunately there was a call box nearby so I sprinted up to it and called the fire brigade and then started to run back towards the fire although locating the actual building was difficult as it seemed to be in the centre of a block.

After a couple of minutes I heard the sound of fire engines heading towards me and at about the same moment found an alley that appeared to head for exactly where I imagined the seat of the fire would be. Running up the alley I started beating on the only door there was which after a few of moments was opened by a guy in a white overall.

"I think you're on fire I gasped." and was not amused when a broad smile began to spread across his face. *"Don't just stand there I shouted. Get everyone out. The Fire brigade will be here in a moment".*
The expression on his face changed slightly but he was still apparently amused

"Oh you haven't have you. It's a smokery. Didn't you know? Don't worry. You're not alone. It's happened before but not for a couple of years now"

I was speechless with embarrassment especially as two burly firemen who had clearly already sussed out the situation, came up the alley grinning broadly too.

We had walked past this place on several occasions over the last couple of weeks. If only Pat had told me. Apparently it is a daily occurrence. After the required smoking period large vents in the roof are opened to let the smoke escape and the contents to cool. I never even knew what a smokery was. – I certainly do now!

There was another occasion too when I nearly came to grief due to my lack of knowledge and experience. Close by Waterloo station there is a Road called Mepham Street that runs alongside the railways arches carrying the lines out towards Charring Cross. At number 5 and actually built into the railway arch there was a pub called The Hole in the Wall, widely reputed at the time to be not only the dirtiest pub in London but also the haunt of criminals.

Indeed the whole area was terribly run down and awash with vagrants and prostitutes. A very far cry from today when after the extensive rehabilitation of the whole of the South Bank area the Hole in the Wall still exists but today is a bistro style gastro-bar or whatever the term is. Talk about a great survivor.

Well on the night in question I'd noticed what to me appeared to be three highly suspicious looking men parked up in the shadows close to Mepham Street in a fairly scruffy old Humber Hawk car. By virtue of the fact they were doing nothing but loitering I observed them for a while and having decided they were up to no good decided to investigate.

They could not have been less cooperative, initially declining even to open the windows. They point blank refused to give an account of themselves and whilst they were not in any way aggressive, I had begun to wonder, as my confidence evaporated, quite what my next move would be if I decided that they might be arrestable under the vagrancy Act. There were after all three of them to my one!

In the event I was saved by circumstances when from the interior of the car there came the sound of a radio transmission and it dawned on me that I had come close to arresting a trio of undercover coppers. They then came clean, showed me their cards and told me in no uncertain terms to go away before I ruined their observation.

I discovered later talking to colleagues back at the nick that the 'The Sweeny' as the Flying Squad are called were notorious for giving young coppers a hard time and have even allowed themselves to be arrested before admitting their true identity. Quite hilarious I guess from their point of view but I'd have died of embarrassment if my little adventure had gone that far.

The traffic control practice we'd done in Peel House certainly stood me in good stead at Kennington Road because we manned several traffic points in the area on a regular basis.

One was on the Embankment at Lambeth Bridge where the roundabout invariably became blocked. To be honest it was really better left alone but sometimes just by stepping into a more prominent and visible position the appearance of the uniform was enough to bring a little more patience and courtesy out in the drivers, which is all it needs really for things to sort themselves out.

The other point which always did need to be controlled was up by Waterloo station at the junction with Westminster Bridge Road and Lower Marsh and almost under the wide bridge over which all the lines came out of the station. There really should have been traffic light control but for whatever reason there wasn't and so it fell to us to man the junction during peak periods.

It was very daunting at first due to the sheer volume and proximity of the traffic and not without its risks. One colleague actually lost the back out of a boot to a passing bus which was certainly a bit close for comfort

Nevertheless after a while I came to love that traffic point and felt really confident whirling around and waving my arms and with all this traffic mine to command. I remembered seeing films of the traffic police in Rome and tried to emulate them. I was pretty good at the control bit but nowhere near as stylish as they are.

The only down-side to this traffic duty was the pollution which was aggravated by the confined area being almost beneath the bridge. I dread to think what it did to my lungs but I could certainly brush clouds of exhaust soot out of my uniform at the end of a session there.

Numerous pigeons used to nest or roost up in the girders of the bridge and immediately below were several bus stops where queues would form at peak times. A favourite trick of the police area car drivers was to turn off their ignition and coast for a few yards as they passed below the bridge and then turn on the ignition which caused the cars to back-fire and startled the pigeons into crapping on the bus queues below. Extremely infantile certainly, but to us quite hilarious.

Actually this silly nonsense caught up with me some years later when I tried the same trick, left the ignition off for a bit too long and blew my exhaust system off completely at some considerable cost! Karma in action I guess.

Drink and its consequences have always featured large in police work and drunkenness in its various forms took up quite a lot of my time on late and night shifts. Apart from the spin-offs such as serious assaults, domestic violence and drunken driving that tended to occur away from where the drink was consumed, our main concerns were 'drunk and disorderly' and 'drunk and incapable' the full title of which is 'incapable of taking care of his/her self.'

If anything this last was the one that created the most demand because what tended to happen was that on a Friday night (pay day for many), large numbers of working men, and it was almost invariably men, would hit the pubs and drink until they were chucked out either for being drunk or at closing time.

So around 11pm in the area between Waterloo Station and The Elephant and Castle there were usually dozens of drunks many of whom were literally incapable of taking care of themselves, spewing up all over the place, falling in heaps along the pavements or tottering out in to the traffic.

Often with a drunk who hasn't got to quite that state it is possible to jolly them along to find their way home and a little bit of banter can go a long way to calm things down and let everyone move on happily.

At the very least, getting them off our patch and onto the neighbouring division before they finally became incapable was a common objective. (Unless of course one needed the arrest as I shall explain shortly)

Unfortunately, and this was often the case in this area, many were too far gone to respond and had to be arrested for their own safety and over time quite an efficient process for mopping them up had been established.

At one time called the 'Black Maria', the dark blue Morris 30cwt van was the favoured vehicle for prisoner transport in the Met and the practice would be for half a dozen of us to go out with the van and almost literally 'hoover' up the drunks from the road and pavements.

On arrival at the 'nick' each was presented to the station sergeant to be charged with being drunk and incapable and locked in the cells overnight to sober up and appear before magistrates in the morning.

Evidence was never a problem because the evidence was pretty much the same in each case – "*slurred speech, reeking of alcohol, and unable to stand. He's drunk Sergeant.*"

There have over the years been a number of cases where police have assumed drunkenness only to come seriously unstuck when their 'drunk' has died in custody. So while the 'sausage machine' approach was appropriate 99 percent of the time there was a heavy responsibility on the station sergeant when accepting the charge to be sure he was looking at a drunk and not some other situation. However from my own experience there were times when the volume and throughput was so high that getting the job done became the priority. Fortunately it never backfired on us in my time there.

One problem was that at very busy times, it was difficult to keep track of which officer had arrested which prisoner. In practice it made little difference anyway as the prisoner wouldn't remember and the charges and supporting evidence were the same in each case.

The simple approach on such occasions was to just allocate a bobby to each prisoner (or even two or three prisoners) and put his name down as the arresting officer.

At the end of the day it didn't really matter, although what the Police and Criminal Evidence Act would have to say about that today, I dread to imagine.

We did have a very funny incident one day, Easter Bank Holiday I believe. We had once again 'hoovered' up all these drunks that turned out to be more than we could accommodate in the cells at Kennington so a decision was made to ferry a few down to Nine Elms nick in the blue van.

This was certainly going to solve the problem until the van broke down on the one way system down by Vauxhall Bridge. We finished up getting the three or four escorting coppers and as many of the prisoners that could actually stand to push the van in what was quite busy traffic until the driver managed to 'bump start' it and we all got back on to finish the journey. I don't actually recall anyone doing a recount of the prisoners we were supposed to have but fortunately they were all there, probably because they were too inebriated to even think of doing a runner.

They say 'It's an ill wind etc.' and such was the case with a drunk or any other arrest you made on a night shift.

Finishing a night shift at six o'clock you could walk back to Gilmour House and be in bed by half six or quarter to seven. However, if you'd made an arrest this meant getting up again in time to get to court for ten. So living in the section house was very useful as it was immediately over the road from Lambeth Magistrate's Court.

Normal practice was that we'd stick our uniforms on again and slip over the road to the court where if we timed it right our case would quickly be called. This was another 'sausage machine process' and the stipendiary magistrates had it down to a fine art. Once your case was called your prisoner was invariably in the dock and entered a Guilty plea before you could even get round to the witness box. The clerk would say *"Any trouble officer?"* you'd say *"No trouble your worship."* Next the magistrate would ask the offender if he had anything to say to which the response was usually *"Sorry Sir"* or quite often *"I'd like to thank the officer for looking after me."*

Your man would be fined £5 or one day and as he'd already been in custody overnight he would then be released to shamble off to do the same thing again tonight or next pay day. One even asked me if I wanted to go and have a drink with him!

Overall the whole process could take less than three quarters of an hour and you could be back in bed with four hours time-off on your card. Oh I forgot to mention that didn't I!

Police regulations stated that if you had to return to duty within eight hours of finishing a shift we were entitled to four hours overtime. This was not paid but accrued as time-off so if you had some important social function coming up and no annual leave due it was quite an easy matter to ensure that in a week of nights you had a few arrests and consequently enough accrued overtime to be able to book the time off when you needed it.

This is not of course to say that people were arrested that shouldn't have been but it did mean that one could choose to be more or less assiduous according to your needs.

We certainly saw many different sides of life as a coppers in that area and one aspect that always touched my heart was the number of homeless and rough sleepers.

I'm ashamed to say that many of my erstwhile colleagues were less than sympathetic to people's situation and would just move them on. Sometimes just 'on to somewhere else – so long as it's not on my beat', without any consideration at all it seemed to me. There were a couple of hostels in the area but to be honest judging from what I saw, you'd be more comfortable and safer on a park bench.

I was quite often on the beat down by the river. It used to be called The Festival Site as it was that part of the embankment where the Festival Hall now stands but where The Festival of Britain was held in 1950.

These days, The South Bank as it is now known, is quite an attractive and arty area with lots going on but back then it was little more than a large car park and a bit of a walkway with a few benches beside the river. It was popular with the rough sleepers and I saw no reason to move them on and quite often would have a chat and even got to know one or two a bit.

One of the 'down and outs' as they were often called was a woman who was probably in her forties. I was intrigued as to what had brought her to that situation but unlike some of the others she was very private and would never say much about herself.

She put me very much in mind of the song 'Streets of London' by Ralph Mctell when he sings about the homeless woman carrying her world in two carrier bags. Every word of that song is so accurate and I saw it all in the area around Waterloo as a young and quite naïve policeman.

South Bank and Festival Hall in the 60's

One aspect of the job I didn't enjoy was the ongoing probationer training. Apart from private study (ideally on a daily basis, but rarely so in my case) we also had to attend a weekly half day session at Southwark nick were our classes were held and where it quite rapidly became clear that I was not really keeping up with the required work.

At twenty years of age my thoughts were understandably often elsewhere, namely, when was my next date with Terri or when was I next going to be able to get back down to Surrey and see my friends.

I still had no car at this point which was fine, even a positive benefit when living in London but for keeping in touch with the Surrey 'scene' I had to rely on public transport or the kindness of my mates for ferrying me around. The net result was that despite the undoubted interest of the new job I was becoming progressively disenchanted with the negative aspects and I began to cast around in my mind for an alternative occupation.

After unsuccessfully exploring a couple of sales rep positions which interested me mainly because a major perk was the company car, I suddenly thought about the possibility of trying to get into the motor trade on the sales side.

While I was thus preoccupied in the late summer of 1964, life was dramatically disrupted by Mum being taken ill and whisked into hospital for a hysterectomy.

The precise detail was never spelled out to me and I sometimes wonder whether the full import of her condition was explained to Dad. I rather suspect that the phrase 'woman's problem' might have been all he knew. (Or perhaps that was all he felt Angela and I needed to know). The truth as I discovered later was that she had cervical cancer for which the treatment at the time was the complete hysterectomy but there was no follow-up radio or chemotherapy as there would be today.

For me this was the final straw in deciding me to leave the Met and return home. My search for a job intensified and fortunately quite quickly bore fruit in the shape of a junior car sales position in Ewell which was quite near home.

It was probably in the August or September that I went for the interview at Ewell Downs Motor Company which was a main dealer for the Rootes Group range of vehicles that included Hillman, Humber, Sunbeam and Singer cars.

I was initially interviewed by Geoffrey Welton the Managing Director, and all seemed to go quite well. He then called in the Sales Manager Jack Moxley who I immediately took to and it seemed that the feeling was mutual because after a few minutes chat and a private moment between them I was offered the job.

It was my plan to go home to Ashtead after the interview, especially as I had some positive news to convey and was about to set out when Jack explained that he lived in Leatherhead and could drop me off en route.

His name had seemed vaguely familiar when we were first introduced but when he explained where he lived the penny dropped with quite a clang. I realised he was the father of a certain young lady I'd taken out a few times before writing my car off and had invested numerous hours and many gin and tonics in my attempts to make her my number one in the seduction stakes.

I prayed she had never mentioned my name indoors and it appeared that she hadn't because on several subsequent occasions when Jack took me home for a drink we both played out the charade of not knowing each other until then.

So, that's how it turned out that in the October of 1964 I left the Metropolitan Police, returned to live at home and took up a new career in the motor trade.

If my life until then had been somewhat cosseted in my comfortable family surrounding plus a certain amount of fairly safe adventure, the next few years were to prove very different.

…..oooOooo…..

What Next

I mentioned at the beginning of this little wander down my personal memory lane that some thanks were owed to Jane Baker, tutor of the Guildford WEA writing group.

When, clutching my pages of notes, I presented myself to the group and explained that I had in mind to write an autobiography, one of the first things Jane asked was what sort of time period I planned to cover. Well I hadn't thought of that one!

She pointed out that it might be wise to divide the years of my life thus far into several significant periods and write about each in turn as a complete memoir covering just those years. (Or, I guess, risk still be writing on my death bed!!)

So that is the plan. The foregoing pages have meandered through the first twenty years of a not very distinguished but hopefully interesting and often amusing life.

I cannot say that at the age of twenty I was terribly mature but then I doubt that many can and having some fun is probably the thing to do during those years prior to taking on the heavier responsibilities of life.

However, as I set out on the compilation of my next offering I am aware that it is going to be a very different experience.

It is going to look at the following thirty years of my life during which time I experienced several bereavements, two marriages; two children; one divorce; major career change; a significant inheritance, a range of successes and failures and a major breakdown.

I'm alright now though and would be delighted if you'd care to join me.

As of now (January 2017) it is half written. So if you are interested to see where the next thirty years takes me just let me know on brianseye@outlook.com and I will let you know when it is available. Your comments on this effort would also be much appreciated.

86568551R00152

Made in the USA
Columbia, SC
16 January 2018